12/06 B.T 24⁰⁰

# PRISONER OF TREBEKISTAN

# PRISONER OF TREBEKISTAN

## A DECADE IN *JEOPARDY!*

## BOB HARRIS

**CROWN PUBLISHERS**
NEW YORK

*For my family*
*And for Jane*

Library of Congress Cataloging-in-Publication Data

Harris, Bob, 1963–
Prisoner of Trebekistan: a decade in Jeopardy! / Bob Harris.—1st ed. Includes index.
1. Jeopardy! (Television program) I. Title.
PN1992.77.J363H37 2006
791.45'72—dc22                                                      2006006267

ISBN-13: 978-0-307-33956-0
ISBN-10: 0-307-33956-4

Printed in the United States of America

Design by Ruth Lee-Mui

10 9 8 7 6 5 4 3 2 1

First Edition

**AUTHOR'S NOTE**

A few names from my personal life have been changed. Otherwise, all *Jeopardy!* games are on videotape, which can be examined down to the thirtieth of a second, and I have fact-checked until I can't fact-check no more. Still, I'm sure there must be a few errors I've missed, and that these will become obvious five seconds after publication. These will be entirely my fault, and I will be waiting expectantly. In addition, a few moments in the story are inevitably based merely on my own perception and memory, which are admittedly fallible, as I have demonstrated on national television with some frequency.

# CONTENTS

Chapter 1    **Why Alex May Not Have a Physical Body**    1
Also, Choosing the Correct Millisecond

Chapter 2    **A Complete Inability to Learn from Failure**    5
Also, Incompetence, Ignorance, and Clumsiness

Chapter 3    **The Thing That Came from Merv's Dining Room**    11
Also, A Hiawatha Much Bigger Than Yours

Chapter 4    **Close Your Eyes, Breathe Deeply, and Scream**    19
Also, I Discover More in My Head Than Just Knowledge

Chapter 5    **Halloween Comes Suddenly**    31
Also, Scandalous Thoughts About Ned Flanders's Wife

Chapter 6    **Thinking Ahead While Not Thinking at All**    42
Also, Safety Instructions for Your Jeopardy Weapon

Chapter 7    **How Everything Is Connected**    54
Also, Twenty-One Interesting Uses for Rubber

Chapter 8    **Evening Falls**    78
Also, A Fifty-Foot Wall in My Head

Chapter 9    **Fun with Howards End**    88
Also, I Kick William Shakespeare's Ass

Chapter 10    **The Longest Day**    105
Also, I Am Attacked by Ravenous Badgers

Chapter 11    **The War Comes Home**    130
Also, Detaching My Althing from My Knesset

Chapter 12    **Jeopardy Fever**    144
Also, I Am Ambushed by the Bishop of Hippo

Chapter 13    **Facing the Think Music**    155
Also, Strangers Seize Me by the Udder and Yank

Chapter 14    **We're Malaysia-Bound**    161
Also, Why People Are Looking at Me Funny in This Coffee Shop

Chapter 15    **A Hail Mary for Anthony Hopkins**    177
Also, Fishing Up the Urethra

Chapter 16    **Things to Do on *Jeopardy!* When You're Dead**    194
Also, Private Moments with Mrs. Butterworth

Chapter 17    **A Pep Talk from President Garfield**    204
Also, What I Bought from the J. H. Gilbert Co. of Willoughby, Ohio

Chapter 18    **Greed, a Quick Smush, and a Shameful Little Booby**    214
Also, I Help with Another Howard's End

Chapter 19    **Jane**    223
Also, Jane

Chapter 20    **The Importance of Memory in Recovery**    232
Also, A Brief Look at Estonian Revolutionary Movements

Chapter 21 **My Life as a Rockette** 243
Also, Why I Have an Ancient Civilization in My Pants

Chapter 22 **Attack of the Pudu** 251
Also, I Get Lost in Africa

Chapter 23 **Love, Kindness, and an Old Chicken Sandwich** 274
Also, Why Penguins Throw Up Down Under

Chapter 24 **The Ultimate Tournament** 286
Also, I Swear Off the Weapon

Chapter 25 **Not Quite Letting Go of Outcome** 306
Also, A Massive Explosion Caught Live on Videotape

Chapter 26 **Where All Knowledge Is Kept** 324
Also, Eleven More Sentences That Are Actually True

*Acknowledgments* 329
*Recommended Reading* 331
*Index* 335

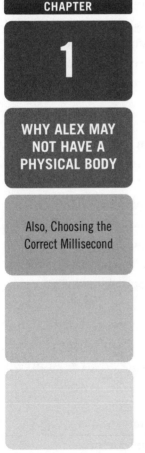

I'm standing at the centermost of the three contestant podiums, which are wider and deeper than they look on TV. My feet are teetering on a wooden box, creating the illusion of height for the camera. To a viewer at home, the game board is as near as the screen. But here, it's a faraway wall, the opposite side of a river-blue stage.

Though glowing with color from remote-controlled spotlights, the room is remarkably quiet and still. The black plastic buzzer feels cold in my hand.

I can't see my opponents while we're playing the game, but I can feel their movements, the bodily cues of who's winning and losing: the small changes in posture, the shuffling of feet, the tensing of shoulders. With every response, our voices betray our excitement or calm, confusion or certainty, eagerness or dread. Choices of category and clue reveal personal strengths and confidence. Sometimes, I can even sense someone's breath being held very slightly when they realize—faster than me, far too often—that they know the next response.

As Alex reads a clue, I now sense such a breath being held on my left. A full second passes. And another. Our buzzers are powerless, disconnected until Alex has finished. Instants tick by. On my right, barely glimpsed, a thumb readies. But we wait.

I can't see Alex, either. I hear him, of course. His voice fills the room, reciting each clue with the perfect insistence of the timeline itself, a new clue every twelve seconds (on average) for more than twenty years. He is standing, as always, at his podium, just ten feet away, and almost in front of my eyes. But I cannot see Alex. In this moment, to my knowledge, he may not have physical form.

I am target-locked on the vast, distant game board: scanning the categories, thinking ahead, searching each clue for that one telling hint, considering dollar amounts and Daily Doubles and doing small silent bursts of math. And five times a minute, I am focusing on the last letter of the last word at the end of each clue, anticipating Alex's last syllable, preparing my signal, tweaking my rhythm, adjusting my perception of time.

Millions may watch. Friends, family, lovers, all those I've cared about, or ever will, might be silently present in spirit. If the TVs in Heaven have decent reception, even my dad may be watching right now. But while actually playing, I am deep in my head. Surrounded by cameras, I can see no one. In this moment, I'm completely alone.

Even Alex is simply a voice from within, a Freudian ego with perfect inflection, pushing your memory, probing your defenses, testing your tiniest grasp of reality. Move your eyes for an instant, break the trance for one moment, and the game will be finished too soon. As will you.

So every twelve seconds, every twelve seconds, every twelve seconds, *finally*: plastic cacophony, *cliklikikkitylikkityclikit*, fingers and thumbs, fingers and thumbs, frantically seeking correct milliseconds, white buttons crashing down hard on black buzzers, *cliklikikkitylikkityclikit*, an urgent loud triple attack.

I drive an old car named Max.

I am wearing shoes I bought for a funeral almost ten years ago.

I am competing in a tournament with a $2 million prize.

In the spaces between instants, entire futures float by.
This . . . is . . . *JEOPARDY!*

Eventually, mercifully: one player's light will come on.

It will very likely not be mine. Every contestant is always outnumbered.

To my right stands a five-time champion. He is taller and older and better educated than me. I have learned, in this very minute, that he knows words I've never heard. To my left stands a man who won an International Tournament of Champions. More than just a five-time champ, he was arguably once the best player on earth. He seems to know everything I've ever learned, at a minimum, and he's better on the buzzer than I am.

Surrounding the game board is a series of lights that will flash when it's time to respond. Since more than one player knows almost every response, precision of rhythm can sometimes trump brilliance. Winning and losing often turn not on memory, but on mastery of these electronic milliseconds.

I am not winning.

For almost an entire game, I have been choosing the wrong millisecond. And twelve seconds later, I have chosen the wrong millisecond again. So far, twenty-five clues into this Double Jeopardy round, I have won on the buzzer and then responded correctly exactly four times.

I am wondering, amid a hundred other racing thoughts, how I ever got here.

Whoever leads at the end of the Double Jeopardy round is usually the victor. But I am thousands of dollars behind. To have any real chance, I need to start winning quite suddenly, every twelve seconds. I will most likely need to beat both of these players on the buzzer and answer correctly at least four more times.

One problem: there are only five clues remaining.

The next clue begins. As Alex's voice echoes softly inside my head, my eyes race through the words on the game board, hoping to gain perhaps one extra second. In a moment, I know the response. There is no sense of relief.

I take a breath, focus only on pacing and rhythm, and start sorting small fractions of time.

To my right, I feel a breath slightly held. To my left, a barely glimpsed thumb again readies.

A second passes. And then another. Alex approaches the end of the clue.

The right millisecond approaches.

I just have to find it.

If you're interested in what a player might try in that position, that's part of what this book is about.

If you're curious how anybody remembers the capital of Bhutan, great composers of Finland, or the Seven Wonders of the Ancient World, that's another big chunk of what follows.

You might also wonder how winning and losing and studying so hard might affect a player's life, or if friendships evolve, or what Alex is like, or how having a bunch of new stuff in your head might feel. There's a lot of all that in here, too.

We will bounce between all these categories, sometimes quite suddenly. But just keep playing. We'll get the whole board cleared off by the end.

And if part of you doubts that you'd ever belong in a game like this, I understand.

That, in fact, is what everything else in the book is about.

## A COMPLETE INABILITY TO LEARN FROM FAILURE

Also, Incompetence, Ignorance, and Clumsiness

I don't remember what year it was the first time I failed the *Jeopardy!* test.

That might tell you a lot right there.

I also don't remember how many times I failed it. I'm pretty sure it was five, over the course of several years, beginning well over a decade ago. It might have only been four. Maybe six. I actually lost count.

I didn't go to Harvard or Berkeley or any school you'd probably recognize. I've read a good bit on my own about history and politics, but I have no advanced education in literature, the visual arts, or a hundred other subjects. For much of my life, the most sophisticated works I've been able to appreciate have been narrated by Morgan Freeman. I've never done anything distinguished enough to merit the sound of his voice.

I did once get a degree in electrical engineering, but *Jeopardy!* is about playing the giant game board, not giving it service under warranty.

In a pinch, my college years might have been handy if you could rig your buzzer for "stun," replace the light pens with Tasers, or reboot Alex every time you start losing. Unfortunately, none of the wiring is all that accessible. Alex barely comes within reach.

I was never even much of an engineer. What formal training I did receive was made useless by time itself. The "advanced" computer language I studied as a sophomore was obsolete by the time I was a senior. Soon after my graduation, technology had accelerated so much that I might as well have studied Plowing With Oxen, Posing Naked On Ceremonial Pottery, or Things To Do With An Armored Codpiece. My academic relevance ended with Pong.

What I *do* have going for me is a diverse and stimulating range of failures.

The following is true, I swear: I once bought the book *Speed Reading Made Easy*. And I never finished it.

Let that sink in.

However, one afternoon when I was hanging pictures and couldn't find a hammer, I actually used the book's spine to drive a nail in the wall.

So at least it wasn't a complete waste.

I took the *Jeopardy!* test, all five or four or possibly six times, in the audience bleachers of the actual *Jeopardy!* studio. A hundred hopefuls would assemble at the Sony parking garage, chatter nervously about nothing, and follow an escort past an array of Sony-owned props, potted plants, and glamorous showbiz detritus.

At last, we would reach the hallowed *Jeopardy!* hall. This was pretty cool in itself, at least the first few times. The distant, darkened stage would seem ready to shimmer at any moment, honored ground where only a few might tread.

The contestant podiums, right across the room, were still mainly in our imaginations. But perhaps, we all hoped, not for long. Perhaps someday we would stand beside legends like Michael Daunt (at the time, the International Tournament champion) or Frank Spangenberg (the highest-scoring five-time champ in history) or Chuck Forrest (inventor of the "Forrest Bounce" board strategy, about which you will soon read more) or Ken Jennings and Brad Rutter (neither of whom would pick up a buzzer for another ten years, but since we were dreaming impossible things, they belong just as well as the others).

Perhaps someday we, too, would stand in brilliant light and recall unbelievably small details from the database of everything that happened to anyone, anywhere, ever. So we hundred hopefuls would lean forward, earnest and focused, read the clues off the monitors, and pencil our way through a Johnny Gilbert–narrated SAT.

The test itself was simple yet tough: fifty clues, each obscure enough to appear in the difficult bottom rows of the game board, announced with relentless rhythm in a total of perhaps fifteen minutes.

If that seems fast, the total time of an actual sixty-clue Jeopardy game (leaving aside the thirty-second fever dream of—*p-TING!*—Final Jeopardy): just under thirteen minutes. Sixty twelve-second cycles slowed only slightly by three Daily Doubles. As the game flies along, your total time-to-think period, as Alex reads each clue aloud: usually between two and seven seconds, followed by the wait-wait-*now* spasm of thumby buzzer-whacking. Twelve seconds, again. Twelve seconds, *again*.

Fast as the *Jeopardy!* test seemed, we were actually going much more slowly than in a real game.

Pencils down. A hundred exhales. Quiet. Then: nervous chatter. *Did-you-get-its* and *aaagh-I-should-have-known-thats* shared between competitive strangers made friendly by stress.

Most of the clues, predictably, were from the wide variety of categories completely outside my experience. For me, things like British Literature, Ancient History, and Norse Mythology might as well have been titled Books You've Never Heard Of, Answers You Can't Pronounce, and More Proof You Don't Belong Here, Bob.

I couldn't have gotten more than half of the responses right.

At the end of each of my five (or four or possibly six) lame flails, one of the contestant handlers would thank everyone for coming and reassure us that we shouldn't feel bad if we didn't pass. After all, they would always insist, it's *impossible* to study for *Jeopardy!*

Then someone would read the list of the names of people who had passed the test, one by one. And then stop. Sooner than I'd hoped.

I would rise, put on either my sunglasses or a warm jacket, depending on the season, shuffle back to where Max was parked in the Sony garage, climb in, drive home, and sit through the show's six-month total-failure-quarantine period. And then I'd try again. Eventually, I gave up.

I didn't even succeed at *that*.

The final time I drove down for the *Jeopardy!* test, I realized I was wasting my time.

The show had never (and has never, I believe) specified how many correct responses were necessary to pass—to this day I'm not certain if it's even a fixed number—but by my last trip, the widely rumored threshold was precisely thirty-five. I heard this very gossip, in fact, in the Sony parking garage, chatting with other hopefuls while waiting for the escorted march.

Sure enough, for the fifth (±one) time, I was certain of only about twenty-five of the fifty responses. Beyond those, a handful of my guesses looked pretty decent. But I would still need perhaps a half-dozen Hail Mary lobs to land. The chances seemed remote. They still do.

As I turned in my paper and No. 2 pencil, it dawned on me that there were stalkers who gave up more easily.

I wondered why I kept trying.

The money was a nice incentive, of course. *Jeopardy!* hands out huge crunchy bales of cash to people whose brains unspool on command. Plus, the Pavlovian reward loop—respond correctly, get a jolt of pride—was already rewarding.

Maybe it was sheer stubbornness, or trying to feel worthy of educational chances I hadn't made the most of, or a lifetime of using my brain as a kind of preemptive self-defense. Maybe I was still trying to prove something to my parents, but one of them was dead, and the other would give me a warm buttered pretzel if I had just knocked over a hardware store.

Perhaps it was animal instinct. In any band of primates, males compete to display their alpha-ness for the females in the troop. Maybe this was all some elaborate reproductive ruse. If so, though, it was certainly among the least efficient in history.

I realized, finally: I didn't even know why I was there.

As the names of the non-failures were read aloud, I knew I was going home for good. So this was the end of my *Jeopardy!* career.

And then the contestant coordinator, Susanne Thurber, a woman of firm countenance around nervous strangers but (I would learn) sweet and funny and eager to dish about Broadway shows when sitting backstage in the green room of Radio City Music Hall, took one more breath, nearing the end of her list . . . and called my name.

My journey into Trebekistan had begun.

In almost a decade since, I've been on *Jeopardy!* thirteen times.

I've won over $150,000 in cash and prizes and defeated two Tournament of Champions winners. The show has put me up in fancy hotels on both coasts, flown me across the country twice—once for a million-dollar "Masters" tournament—given me two sports cars, and even invited me to the ceremony where Alex got his star on the Hollywood Walk of Fame.

Given how things started, I barely find this plausible myself sometimes.

Along the way, thanks to doing my *Jeopardy!* homework, I've also picked up over $200,000 on other quiz shows and even helped a friend pay off his house by answering his $250,000 question on *Who Wants to Be a Millionaire*.

Then again, I've also *not* won on *Jeopardy!* with a certain inescapable rhythm—perhaps as frequently as anyone who has ever played. Nobody I can find keeps exact data on incompetence, but I'd be one of the first names in the grid.

This is fine by me. Since tournament contestants often bond like plane-crashed rugby players in the Andes, a loose fraternity of unbelievably smart and curious people has gradually developed. Win or lose, being a small part of this group is easily as great a prize as anything the show hands out.

Besides, as a lifelong Cleveland sports fan, I've learned to appreciate sudden, utter doom. Failure and defeat are, after all, the largest part of human endeavor. We might as well do it with gusto. Fumbling away the ball on the last play is painful; fumbling it away *as you're crossing the goal line* will one day become funny as hell.

Someday Ken Jennings's record of seventy-four straight victories will fall. Brad Rutter has already passed him as the all-time money winner. Somebody else will break Brad's record next. Possibly someone who reads this book.

It could even be you.

You will almost certainly *not*, however, screw up more frequently than I have. That's one achievement, at least, that you and Ken and Brad will probably never touch.

In the coming pages, you'll see me lose (and occasionally win) against some of the best players in the show's twenty-year history. I lose in Los Angeles. I lose in New York. I lose by massive amounts. I lose by one dollar. I lose in ways I see coming. I lose in ways I never imagined.

I win sometimes, too, just to keep you guessing. (And thank goodness. This book would be a real drag otherwise.) Winning is just as much fun as you'd think. So I hope you'll feel like you're sharing in the wins when they happen, even if our losses might often be so much more memorable.

But even this leads to a key point about memory itself, one we'll not only revisit often, but transform into a key tool that I use during the story, and which you can use happily ever after: we all tend to remember intense, visceral, even traumatic experiences more easily than anything else. It's hard-wired, just a part of how human brains operate. We don't wind up with the memories we'd choose; we wind up with the memories our *brains* choose. These are not at all the same thing. Understanding the difference, and taking control of it, is vital to improving your memory.

It might seem strange to think of your brain as not always wanting what you do. But then, if it were easy to choose our memories, a game like *Jeopardy!* wouldn't exist.

So this is a memory book, in every sense: my memories of the show, what memories I used to win on the show, how memories work in general, what you need to remember in order to remember stuff you need to remember, and someone please shoot this sentence before it devours the rest of the book.

I hope you'll be willing to free-associate and think silly things and zigzag off the path sometimes while we're at it. After all, daydreaming and making ourselves laugh with silly ideas is how we figure out which memories we want in the first place.

It's also how *Jeopardy!* itself was invented.

CHAPTER

3

THE THING THAT
CAME FROM
MERV'S DINING
ROOM

Also, A Hiawatha Much
Bigger Than Yours

In 1963, the year of my birth, entertainer Merv Griffin and his then-wife Julann were flying home to their New York City apartment from a small Michigan village called Ironwood.

What the Griffins were doing in Ironwood, I don't really know, although what I can learn about the place reminds me a little of the small wintry suburb where I grew up. Other than "lake effect" snow (about which you will soon learn more) in excess of sixteen feet per year, Ironwood's most notable attraction seems to be the world's largest statue of Hiawatha, five stories tall and made from eight tons of solid fiberglass. (The town brags about it, in fact: their Hiawatha is not only bigger than yours, it can withstand 140 mph winds. I guess you take pride in whatever you've got.) So whether or not the Griffins were actually visiting a fifty-foot typhoon-reinforced Hiawatha buried keister-deep in a snow drift, I prefer this to all other theories.

At the time, Merv already had an impressive career. As an actor he had appeared on Broadway and in Hollywood films, and as a singer he'd scored a number one hit with "I've Got a Lovely Bunch of Coconuts," which sold over three million copies at a time when the U.S. population was about half what it is now. Per capita, Merv's coconuts were more pervasive in their day than almost any record since, the "Whoomp! (There It Is)" of their era.

Merv had also become a frequent guest on TV talk and game shows. After he became the regular substitute host of *The Tonight Show*, his NBC contract also enabled him to create his own game shows, a format Merv had grown to love. And it's at that point the Griffins were approaching New York from the air.

Quiz shows back then had a bad reputation, thanks to the producers' nasty habit of giving the players the answers in advance, the players' custom of admitting the scam, and everyone's penchant for going to jail. This had happened on *Dotto* and *Twenty-One* at least, and producers elsewhere had already admitted other forms of tampering. Isolation booths across America were at risk of being converted into solitary confinement cells.

However, instead of letting controversy kill their ideas, Julann and Merv let it inspire them. "What about a quiz show in reverse?" Julann suggested. As a former comedienne, she was unafraid to brainstorm and play. "Why not just give them the answers to start with?"

Once Merv got over his fear of prison, he was hooked.

As Merv has told the story in several interviews, the following was the very first clue in the yet-unnamed show's history, created by Julann on the plane:

> ### FIVE THOUSAND, TWO HUNDRED EIGHTY

"*How many feet in a mile?*" Merv responded. If this were a movie, the camera would now hold on Merv's face for an extra moment. The idea would twinkle in Merv's eyes. The music would then crescendo, leading into a busy making-it-happen montage with plucky-sounding woodwinds in the background. The fifty-foot Hiawatha would smile knowingly in the distance.

Months of run-throughs followed, mostly at Merv's dining room table, as he worked out the details of game play using friends as contestants. Not everything worked right away; Merv's original game board was reportedly a ten-category by ten-clue monster, too large to work on TV (although the right size for fiberglass giants).

Still, Merv kept working, and the plucky woodwind music soon gave way to a trumpet fanfare. The first run-through for NBC was held in a small theater in Radio City Music Hall. The original working title: *What's the Question?*

NBC's response was mixed: Merv's pet project needed—and this is really what they said—"more jeopardies," meaning greater consequences for incorrect answers. Merv, however, heard what they were saying a little more creatively.

You can pretty much see how *that* worked out.

The program's original host was Art Fleming, an actor with no experience hosting game shows. (He was told by his agent simply to *act* like a game show host, a part he grew into for ten happy years.) The announcer was NBC's legendary Don Pardo, whose voice has adorned almost every human activity in Rockefeller Center since nine days after the Normandy invasion, including news programs, *Saturday Night Live* episodes, and probably even the fire drills.

NBC's market research had determined that the show was too difficult, and needed to be dumbed-down to the level of the average junior high school student. Fortunately, Merv ignored them completely, and *Jeopardy!* was an instant success. The show debuted in March of 1964, as did the Final Jeopardy "Think Music," a brief lullaby Merv had originally written for his son. This was to become the most lucrative lullaby in human history.

The original game's dollar amounts now seem microscopic: $10 through $50 in the Jeopardy round and $20 through $100 in Double Jeopardy. However, considering inflation, $10 in 1964 would be worth over $60 today. So the money hasn't really gone up by a factor of twenty; it has in fact only tripled.

The game differed from the modern version in several additional ways. Players were seated in comfy chairs instead of standing. The game board had cardboard pull-cards instead of fancy TVs. Second- and third-place contestants kept their winnings. And players could ring in as soon as the clue was revealed, which allowed a few fast readers with sufficient knowledge to dominate their games utterly. The best example was a young navy sonar operator named Burns Cameron, who won the equivalent of over $200,000 in current dollars. Burns's record stood throughout the show's original run.

The people of Ironwood and thousands of other snowy small Midwestern towns loved the show, which aired at lunchtime during most of my childhood. Unfortunately, NBC made an ill-advised time-slot change, the ratings wilted, and the show finally departed in January of 1975.

Fans cheered up, however, when Art Fleming returned in a new syndicated edition in 1978. In this version, the competition ended after Double Jeopardy, and instead of Final Jeopardy, the winner was given the chance to play a five-by-five board in a Bingo-like attempt to complete a five-clue line.

Baffling? You bet. But this was the height of the disco era. Lots of things were confusing. Back in Ohio, I was reaching the age when it was time to figure out how to attract girls, precisely as ludicrous dancing in tight polyester became the height of fashion. It was a difficult period for all concerned.

This awkward, eager-to-fit-in version of *Jeopardy!*, which tried so hard to please everyone but only made people turn away no matter how much it smiled, retreated from the public after only about a year.

Finally, in 1984, Merv Griffin and King World Productions snapped *Jeopardy!* back to life for one last attempt. Market research was negative (measuring its own uselessness quite accurately yet again), but two recent developments made the show seem worth a shot: (a) Merv's *Wheel of Fortune* had become a major syndicated hit, and (b) the board game Trivial Pursuit had turned into a national mania.

The show's new announcer would be Johnny Gilbert, a courtly Virginian with an easy smile who could charm a coma ward into applauding on cue. (Coincidentally, Johnny had also replaced Don Pardo on *The Price Is Right*, another popular game show. One wonders if Don Pardo will leave his seat in a movie theater without looking over his shoulder for Johnny.)

And Alex Trebek, a broadcasting veteran born forty-four years earlier in Sudbury, a snowy blue-collar town at exactly the same latitude as Ironwood, was brought on as host, producer, and soon-to-be icon.

During the show's formative years, Alex personally signed off on many key elements, including the writing staff and even the clues themselves.

The format itself was updated—the cash values of the clues were increased dramatically, the winner-takes-all format created more challenging wagering, and the set was glammed out with cutting-edge mid-eighties electronics that went whoosh and *p-TING!* (actually two F notes an octave apart, the lower one played a split-second before the higher)—and finally, on August 14, 1984, Alex read the very first clue in modern *Jeopardy!* history, in the category ANIMALS for $100:

THESE RODENTS FIRST GOT
TO AMERICA BY STOWING
AWAY ON SHIPS

OK, so *"What are rats?"* was not the most glamorous start. But the show wasn't getting the glitziest time slots, either. Many local program directors, showing a familiar disdain for their viewers, still thought *Jeopardy!* was too difficult for a mainstream audience. In New York, the most important syndication market in the country, it was originally broadcast at two in the morning.

Yet twenty-plus years and over 5,000 episodes later, the show has won more than twenty-five daytime Emmy awards, including a record eleven statues for Outstanding Game Show and four more for Alex as Outstanding Host. At this writing, the show has been the highest-rated program in the genre for over 1,000 weeks, a longer-running success than over 99 percent—literally—of the shows that have debuted since.

Meanwhile, not *one* of the programmers who considered the show too demanding for their viewers has played himself on *The X-Files*, guest-announced for *Wrestlemania*, or been impersonated by Will Farrell. So much for market research.

The success of the *Jeopardy!* mothership has spawned numerous spin-off products, including at least fifty—*fifty*—various home games. In addition, loyal fans have created online simulations, *Jeopardy!*-themed websites, and at least one ongoing attempt to chronicle every clue and response in the show's history. (There have been, incidentally, over 300,000 clues. And counting. I hope these folks occasionally get out of the house. Then again, as you'll see, I'm hardly in a position to talk.)

Over the years, the producers have added variety with frequent special tournaments, many of them recurring events. The Tournament of Champions became an annual dogfight of returning champs, snarling and growling and reciting Shakespeare over a six-figure prize. Similar tournaments for Teen and College contestants showcase each year's crop of intimidatingly precocious young people. The producers have also freshened the show by adding video and audio clues, many of which are read by the Clue Crew, a team of bright and engaging Alex-in-waitings who, I like to believe, all live together in a van and tour the country fighting crime.

Like any burgeoning empire, *Jeopardy!* has also swept across distant lands, with local versions in Canada, England, Germany, Sweden, Russia, Denmark, Israel, and Australia. This led eventually to the International Tournament of 1997, which was won by Michael Daunt, a mild-mannered accountant from Canada with a kindly demeanor and a killer instinct that emerges about once every twelve seconds. A second International Tournament in 2001 was won by Robin Carroll, a homemaker from Georgia with a sweet smile, a warm laugh, and the ability to bring grown men to their knees with her thumb.

These were soon followed by a Masters Tournament in 2002 and eventually the Ultimate Tournament of Champions in 2005. These both included (a) seven-figure prizes; (b) yours truly, still wearing shoes bought for a funeral; and (c) a young man named Brad Rutter, who is able to swallow other contestants whole without even needing to chew.

As you probably know, the show has recently received more attention than ever. In the fall of 2003, the producers decided to eliminate the mandatory retirement of five-time champions. Before long, a soft-spoken Salt Lake City software engineer named Ken Jennings (aka the Stormin' Mormon, the Utah Computah, or the Splatter-Day Saint) became a celebrity by winning seventy-four games in a row, frequently causing opponents' heads to explode in eye-catching flames. The show's ratings skyrocketed as America was gripped nightly by the sight of Ken's opponents keeling over with fear, weeping balefully, and/or pleading with the producers for mercy. After which they would ask Ken for his autograph.

Today, *Jeopardy!* has rightly assumed its place as a national touchstone, Alex Trebek has better name recognition than most U.S. senators, and Merv's lullaby "Think Music" is played at everything from baseball stadiums to weddings. If the show were any more popular, Alex and Merv would be worshipped as gods on small tropical islands, their temples consisting of three thatch podiums and a lovely bunch of coconuts.

Incidentally, Merv has made over $70 million in royalties from the "Think Music" alone. I probably have to send him a dollar now, just for mentioning it. His production company eventually sold for about a quarter of a billion dollars.

That might seem a bit, um, huge, but give the guy his due: forty years ago, Merv recognized the value of a loopy idea and backed it with hard work, even when quiz shows were a nearly impossible sell. He spent months experimenting and daydreaming. He kept himself open to feedback—the show's title itself came from listening to criticism—and, most of all, insisted on respecting his audience's intelligence, even when well-paid bosses insisted otherwise.

Is it all that surprising that Merv now zips around on a yacht the size of three fiberglass Hiawathas laid end-to-end and holds an ownership stake in (roughly speaking) one-third of the earth's crust? It would be a lot more surprising if he had *dis*respected his audience and wound up with all that.

If there's one lesson here, I think it's this: never underestimate the power of playfulness combined with hard work.

If there's another: always write your own damn theme music.

We are lucky indeed for Merv and Julann and their vision of a game in which "questions" and "answers" are switched. The English language, unfortunately, has not quite caught up.

How much confusion can the reversal of two words possibly cause? I actually typed the following, I swear, the first time I tried to e-mail an overseas friend an explanation of the game:

> *In each question, by which I mean each clue, there is in fact a clue to the answer, by which I mean the question, which is the answer to the clue.*

Even *I* can't quite tell what that means. It's like one of those optical-illusion forks with two and a half prongs. And I know what I meant. So for the sake of clarity, this book follows the show's own convention of scrupulously referring to all question-like objects coming out of Alex's mouth as "clues," and all answer-like objects coming out of the contestants' mouths as "responses."

Keep in mind, however, that *within* each clue there is often a key piece of information that can lead to an educated guess. This will *not* be called a "clue," since this might cause you to notice the faint sizzle of burning neurons, followed by the distant voice of a loved one calling 911, and then a nice quiet darkness. For your safety, any such clue-like object will be called a "hint."

Later on, if you become confused at the meaning of the word "clue," lose consciousness, and eventually awaken to three paramedics extracting you from the book with the Jaws of Life, I renounce all responsibility.

You have been warned.

Another thing that happened in 1963, right about the time Merv was taking the game through its first run-through at Radio City Music Hall: I was born, in a snowy small Midwestern town much like Ironwood. We didn't have a five-story Indian built to withstand atomic-blast winds. But we had quilt shows, lots of ducks and frogs, and mosquitoes the size of lawn darts. Somehow we managed.

Granted, a lot of other stuff happened in 1963, too. Placing these two events side by side is completely arbitrary. There's no reason to imagine they might be connected.

But eventually, as you know, they were. My own life would cross paths with Merv's quiz show juggernaut, and I would be in over my head from the start. My only salvation would be the same playful stick-to-itude Merv had once had, back at his dining room table.

Merv, however, probably wasn't so freaked out by the stress that he accidentally got something painful shoved way up his nose, an event that became the source for my first great insight into how to play *Jeopardy!*

Like I said: you take pride in whatever you've got.

CHAPTER

4

CLOSE YOUR EYES,
BREATHE DEEPLY,
AND SCREAM

Also, I Discover More
in My Head Than
Just Knowledge

Game day.

Before each five-match afternoon begins, long before the audience enters, *Jeopardy!* trots the contestants onstage for a morning rehearsal game. This gives the players a brief chance to warm up and become familiar with the set, so we're less likely to lose gross motor skills once the tape starts rolling. I presume it also gives the show's own director and crew a chance to prepare as well, a pre-game ritual as much a part of their day as infield drills are to a baseball team.

One practice game is split among all fifteen contestants, who are rapidly rotated. You play just a handful of clues. My own first rehearsal was a flood-lit bright-colored blur: *I stand here and look there? And push this? Hey, neat pen! Who was Lincoln?* and it was over.

I had a buzzer strategy in mind, prepared long in advance, but I was rotated out before I could really try it. As I stepped off the stage, the podiums felt almost as distant as ever. I was worried I'd never ring in.

■ ■ ■

Speaking of which, let's clarify "ringing in," the act of moving your thumb or index finger against a small white button on a black plastic cylinder, hoping that Alex will call your name and useful noises will spill out of your mouth.

The term "ringing in" is a vestige of a long-ago period when hitting your button made an electronic noise—*boong*, to be exact. It's not called "buzzing in" because nothing in the game goes "buzz."

If you've already noticed that nothing goes *ring* or *boong* anymore either, then you are a troublemaker, and I will have to keep my eye on you. Unfortunately, there's no verb that fits much better. Clicking, tapping, punching, zapping—nothing quite works. There's just no common verb that sufficiently describes competitive red-hot thumb-on-button action. Clearly, the English language is a wuss.

There isn't even a thrilling name for the cylinder-button-whackity-thingy itself. Most players call it a buzzer, although the preferred, official term seems to be (*anticlimax alert!*) the "Signaling Device."

But "Signaling Device" isn't a name. It's a placeholder for where a name should go. *Anything* can be a "Signaling Device": road flares, pheromones, a discharge of ignited fuel from a shuttlecraft, even the body of a dead guy. (This was in a *Die Hard* movie.) "Signaling Device" is so ambiguous you could rewrite a 1930s melodrama around the phrase, with complete accuracy:

> Woman: Say . . . This (signaling device) on your collar isn't my shade . . .
> Man: Um, sure it is, honey. Stand where the (signaling device) is better—
> Woman: Liar! You've taken up with that cheap (signaling device) again!
> Man: Wait! What are you doing with that (signaling device)?
> —BANG—

You might have noticed your own active—perhaps even lurid—imagination just now. We'll soon put it to use. Harnessed properly, it's the single fastest way to hot-rivet new info into your skull, not to mention a lot of fun. Just realize that I had little to do with whatever your filthy little mind came up with just now. You sick (signaling device).

Hoping to improve on "Signaling Device," I once sought the opinion of an expert in product-naming. We spent a whole afternoon kidding about it, in fact, while drinking champagne in bed and watching tapes of the show.

Jane, who will become a major character later, and in whose apartment all of my personal belongings now sit silently in boxes and bags (and have sat long enough that they are now covered in dust), received an M.A. in linguistics from Berkeley and once made her living inventing evocative trade names.

Many of the products Jane helped name are now quite famous, although there were confidentiality agreements involved, so I am forbidden to divulge details. Even now. So let's just say this: if you've ever heard of a lightly carbonated alcoholic beverage whose name rhymes with "Squeema" . . . wink wink, nudge nudge.

This was our list of alternative names for the Signaling Device:

ClueZapper
Palm Hoopty
Thumbilical Cord
Thought Bopper
ThunderFist, now with realistic Kung Fu Grip
QuizBang
Mr. Smartyhands
Blurt-O-Matic Jr.
The Mervulator
Toyota Corolla

And the one we decided on, since it's closest to the actual user experience:

The Jeopardy Weapon

Jane and I laughed a lot making that list. Sometimes even in the instant you're doing something, you're aware it's a moment you'll want to hang on to forever.

Moving on. I'm calling it a buzzer. Everybody does anyway.

■ ■ ■

Back in the green room, hours after rehearsal and shortly before my first game, I was having trouble breathing.

I was sitting in a makeup chair, near a live set, on a soundstage inside the Sony lot, about to go on national TV. I was just trying to control my nerves and stay focused. I had spent much of the day secretly expecting to do something idiotic, possibly dishonoring my family before millions of people.

And now, only moments before I would play, my head was on fire. For an instant, I wondered if I would stop breathing completely.

That was almost ten years ago now. I'm sitting here writing this in the same exact coffee shop you have in your neighborhood, drinking the same oversweet brownish goo, listening to the same music drowned out by high-speed blenders, and breathing the same aerosol fog of mocha, cleaning products, and sweat. (I do almost all of my writing here, so I don't have to look at the boxes and garbage bags in the apartment.) Close your eyes, and you can imagine precisely the sensory input I'm experiencing right this second. But even here in this coffee shop, if I close *my* eyes, I can still feel one particular dab of makeup going up my left nostril almost a decade ago.

A few feet to my left stood the returning champion. His name was Matt, although with his glasses, perfect hair, and square jaw, he looked a great deal like Clark Kent. Matt appeared smart and confident, as people from high-gravity planets often do. At that moment he was memorizing a set of tiny laser discs that had been placed in his crib when he was jettisoned from a dying world.

It was late afternoon. I had already spent almost an entire day in the green room. As mentioned, *Jeopardy!* shoots five games at each taping, and you don't know when you'll play until your name is read aloud. I had already felt my adrenaline spike four times, as the players for the first four games were called out. Four times I had leaned forward in my chair, full-body clenching with nerves. Four times I had slumped down with both disappointment and relief, sinking back to watch another hour tick by.

By the time Susanne Thurber began to call the last names for the day, I was already exhausted. And I still didn't know if I'd play. An alter-

nate player is kept on hand, usually a local like myself, just in case someone passes out, takes ill, or (this is not hard to imagine now) simply runs
away. So my blood pressure surged once again.

". . . Bob Harris!" she said.

Now there was no turning back. In seconds I was thrust into the
makeup chair for a last-minute touch-up to freshen my flesh tone. I paid
no attention. I was too busy trying hard not to do anything stupid.

So, while a trained professional braved the sheen of my Irish skin
(my entire family bears a strong resemblance to polished chrome), I
silently recited a half-memorized list of 19th Century U.S. Presidents.
I was trying to sort out, again, whether Pierce came before Buchanan.

I have this habit of overthinking during stress, and I had convinced
myself that I couldn't possibly survive the upcoming game without getting this key point resolved: *They always ask about presidents. I know the first
and last bunches, but there's this big hole in the middle with just Lincoln's head sticking
up. Buchanan had to be early, but not very early, and Pierce was, too. But who went when? And
what about Millard goddam Fillmore . . .*

To my left, meanwhile, Matt had quietly moved on to reciting the
entire *K* section of the *Oxford English Dictionary* (second edition) while
crushing a lump of coal into a diamond with one fist. I tried not to notice. *Jeopardy!* requires every neuron you can spare, and I only had one
shot at this. The nineteenth century needed my urgent attention.

Gradually, however, I became aware that my skin stylist had gotten a teeny blob of flesh-colored goo on the inside of my nose. This
was itchy, and I didn't need the distraction. Especially since the issue
was not yet sorted out: Was it Buchanan, then Pierce? Or Pierce, then
Buchanan?

That's when the makeup lady accidentally gooped my nozzle a second time. This dab clung to the edge of my nostril, dangling precari-
ously, attracting a large crowd of curious nerve endings. Three U.S.
presidents were being upstaged. This had to stop.

Being a Midwestern boy of squarish head, the only makeup I'd ever
had on my face had rubbed off someone else's. I wasn't sure quite what
to do. I didn't notice any Kleenex for a quick wipe, so I did the next logical thing.

I sniffed.

*This*, it turned out, was the idiotic mistake I'd been expecting.

I had now snorted the entire glob up into my nose, deep into my sinuses, and possibly six inches along my spinal column. Since I assume you've never passed around a bottle of Jergen's and a straw at an all-night cosmetology rave, imagine brain-freeze from a too-fast cold milkshake, spritzed across the linings of your nasal passages.

*Ow.*

A rubbing-alcohol tingle rolled through my skull, obliterating 19th Century Presidents and everyone they held dear. Civil War Generals started to fade, and Europe began losing its capitals. Asia and Africa would soon fall away. My entire earthly awareness was focusing on the spreading twinge of Maybelline Shiny Man #7.

*Ow ow ow ow owwww.*

Past and future collapsed. Continents drifted. Nine civilizations flourished at Troy. In five minutes, I was about to be quizzed on national TV, and the only fact I could recall: *My brain is filling with painful goo.*

This was bad. While *Jeopardy!* has several recurring categories, Alex rarely trots out Things Rammed Up Your Nose.

So this was the end of my *Jeopardy!* career.

Fortunately, after some interval of between three seconds and six weeks, I realized there was a massive box of facial tissue—identifiable by the words "facial tissue," in fact, near the brand name—directly in front of my face. Always had been. Possibly since the founding of Los Angeles.

I spent the next few minutes making funhouse faces and honking. *Gwoooonngggk!* Six passing geese were greeted in dialect. *Glorngk, glorrrrngk!* A tow truck thought it heard "Hello, sailor."

Finally, *ahhhhh*. And just in time.

But now I would never figure out whether Buchanan or Pierce came first. And don't even talk to me about Millard goddam Fillmore.

Clearly, I was going to lose.


Few great philosophical insights have come from things crammed into someone's nose. It's not clear that many philosophers even looked thoroughly.

But let's take a moment and notice that this whole tingly episode wouldn't have happened if I'd simply managed to notice the giant

Kleenex box *directly in front of my face* when I first sat down. Thus, before the first game even begins, we embark on what I humbly call the Eightfold Path to Enlightened Jeopardy:

### 1. Obvious things may be worth noticing.

Most things aren't nearly as difficult as we make them. This is true of *Jeopardy!*, which gives you hints in almost every clue, as much as anything I've ever been around.

Before long, we'll hit a bunch of other simple ideas that seem handy, in pretty much the order I learned them myself. Many are exceedingly obvious; all are much easier said than done.

Buddhists, of course, follow an Eightfold Path in their own tradition. Enlightened Jeopardy is similar, except instead of a release from suffering and ego, you get lots and lots of money. Sometimes even cars and stuff.

Granted, these objectives may be mutually exclusive.

I never said I had every detail worked out.

Our second step on the Eightfold Path is even more important than the first. In fact, it's essential to everything that follows, including amassing your own series of *Jeopardy!* wins.

To begin, close the book for a while. Seriously. Don't make trouble. I have my eye on you, remember. In just a few pages, we'll march into the studio, meet Alex, and start stumbling through an actual *Jeopardy!* game. But for right now, go away for five full minutes.

And while the book is closed, see how thoroughly you remember your own private mental image of me bouncing around the *Jeopardy!* green room with a half-gallon of Cover Girl horked up my blowhole.

Go ahead. Close the book, enjoy the mental movie, and come back in a few. You'll have fun at my expense, and eventually it'll help lead to a better memory.

Come back when you've got a big dopey grin on your face. I'll wait.

Welcome back from the river of Avon.

Fun? Easy? I bet you have a terrific imagination. You can probably remember complex mental pictures in remarkable detail, almost effortlessly. Yes? Good.

Now, forget all that. And without looking, see if you can reel off all three of the presidents I mentioned, the ones I was trying to put in correct order.

Take a minute. They're in your skull somewhere. For extra credit, recite all three in the order they were first mentioned.

For most people, it's suddenly not quite so simple. But shouldn't the presidents be the easy part? These are, after all, just simple names, not physical sensations and events you've never even experienced. If your brain were a disk drive, three little names would occupy a teeny fraction as much space as your mental video of me caroming around the Sony lot with Estée Lauder's legs dangling from my nose.

Even now, there's a decent chance you still may not remember all three names, even though right this second you now have yet another cartoon image of me in your head.

This is not a flaw of memory. You almost certainly *do* have a remarkable memory, not to mention a playful imagination, as we've just demonstrated. However, your brain's structure has a different set of priorities than you do.

To the chagrin of anyone trying to memorize anything, our heads are much less interested in what we particularly *want*, which tends to be momentary, than in keeping us from becoming dead, which is rather more permanent. And given that many of our natural predators are big foul-smelling things that roar and leap, the rapid creation of memory— one of the keys to our species' survival, in fact—is necessarily a profoundly physical, emotional, and sensory task.

In contrast, the forty-three U.S. presidents (counting Grover Cleveland twice), the forty-six vice presidents (counting twice-serving George Clinton and John C. Calhoun only once each), and the forty British monarchs (excluding the Saxons and Danes, the Cromwells, and Lady Jane Grey) seldom attack you in the night with claws flashing, teeth digging for your throat, and their venomous drool overwhelming your senses. Hardly ever, in fact.

Books themselves are less memorable still. Square little things. Slow on their feet. Trade paperbacks barely so much as spit. Even hardbacks, which at least have an exoskeleton, rarely attack. (Although I'd be leery around page 193 of this book if I were you. Nasty little page. John Quincy Adams is involved, so be alert. He'll creep up on you.) So, like it or not, you'll always have a hard time simply transferring book data to brain with a minimum of blood loss. Instead, it's the physical, emotional, or intensely sensory stuff that stays.

In short, human beings are wired to sweat the *big* stuff: sex, food, combat, sex, birth, death, and sex. Like it or not, your own hippocampus (the brain chunk that decides how much priority to assign to a given memory) has roughly the same tastes and interests as Homer Simpson, drunk, at a bullfight.

Viewed through this lens, my backstage attempt to snort up a majority control of Revlon is loaded with a gazillion little memory grabbers: it's set in a high-pressure situation, there's physical pain causing goofy commotion, and the resolution of the problem is made more urgent by the presence of a ticking clock. Throw in tasty music and Uma Thurman, and Quentin Tarantino could probably make it look kinda cool.

Compare the last time you were in a traffic accident (or similar moment of sudden terror), even if it was months or years ago, to a recent, routine drive to the store (or other mundane experience similar to the sudden terror).

Which do you remember better? If you're human, it's probably the distant car wreck.

Here's how that's possible: Right this second, your brain is quietly, continuously associating the experience of running your eyes across this very page with where you are, the time of day, what you're wearing, what you've eaten, the mood you're in, the sounds and smells around you, how much sleep you've gotten, the brightness of the light, and how your butt feels right this second in that chair. (Did you just suddenly notice your butt just now? Good. You're paying close attention.)

Most of this usually vanishes quickly, replaced by an endless stream of other mundane detail. However, during life-threatening, sexy, or otherwise visceral experiences, the constant flood of information is suddenly considered significant by the little Homer-Simpson-yelling-olé part of your brain. Sex? Violence? Survival issue!?!? *Record everything! NOW!* And since your brain is all about self-preservation and has no time to sort the data, a large chunk of *everything* going on will be retained.

Two months from now, you probably won't remember exactly what you're wearing right this minute. But if, in the next five seconds, eight naked space aliens on an interstellar roller coaster suddenly careen out of the sky and crash ten feet to your left, *boom*, you will.

In fact, every time you put on those same clothes again, they'll be the Naked-Aliens-on-a-Roller-Coaster-Almost-Hit-Me clothes. You'll be flooded with memories, just by glimpsing a shirt, and for the most gratuitous reasons imaginable.

This is only human. And it's an incredibly powerful memory tool.

Thus, another step on the Eightfold Path:

1. Obvious things may be worth noticing.
2. Remember the basics: the basics are what you remember.

The trick, then, will be simple: just make any new information brain-sticky by creating connections with visceral images and sensations. I prefer big, silly ideas, but even then my mental images are usually rooted in sex, death, food, or (if a big tournament is coming up) all of the above.

Later on, we'll use a famous singer's sex habits to study Native American history, examine the novels of E. M. Forster through the lens of a thirty-foot set of buttocks, and visualize a hail of burning arrows to help finally sort out those three 19th Century Presidents.

If only our textbooks would treat learning this seriously.

If you did come up with all three presidents, good for you. Not everyone does.

I bet "Millard goddam Fillmore" popped into your head first, even though the others were mentioned more than twice as often. This is partly because MillFill (as his friends called him), mentioned last, is more likely to be in your short-term memory, but mostly because he was used as a teeny punchline with a mild curse inserted, creating—yes—the slightest emotional response.

See how this works? Your brain tends to assign space to information *not* according to usefulness or importance or even, sad to say, truth (this loophole is responsible for much of modern advertising and politics), but in response to big emotions and sexy drunken bullfight sensations.

Granted, this isn't a pleasant thought for some folks. Good thing they'll forget it soon enough.

And so, to this day, my strongest first memory of the *Jeopardy!* green room consists mostly of wanting to hose out my skull.

It would not be the last time I felt this way.

And so there I was, Dead Man Walking, about to march onto the *Jeopardy!* stage, hopelessly unable to differentiate between Franklin Pierce, James Buchanan, and Millard goddam Fillmore. At the time, contestants walked one by one to the podiums. I can still replay every step of that endless fifteen-foot march in my head.

As I write this, sitting here in a coffee shop, I'm also still standing in darkness, ten feet from the stage. I still hear the surprising loud whirr of electronical doojobbies. I feel the cool dry blast of recirculated air fighting klieg-light heat on my face.

I can hear the studio audience, a dark and faceless but thrumming fourth wall, still hubbubbing about the previous game.

The floor director, John Lauderdale, has the imposing calm of a Marine colonel. His job requires him to control hundreds of total strangers, five times a day, creating the lush empty stillness necessary for the players and Alex to concentrate.

John silences the room without even raising his voice.

"Quiet please," he says, in a soft, commanding tone that would settle a house fire.

"Quiet . . . please."

The crowd becomes still. The electric doojobbies all lower their voices.

There is a lurch in the timeline here. *A brain under stress goes into hyper-record.*

I turn to face the stage, seeing only the back of the champion in front of me. We are preparing to march on command.

As his name is called, Matt strides toward his podium, entering the fantasy world of brilliant color and flooded light into which I have never stepped.

He turns to face the camera. I notice a small bright spot just above his collar. Something is reflecting and dispersing the overhead glare.

That exact moment is flash-fried into my brain pan. Every time I'm reminded of *Jeopardy!*, part of me is still and forever standing on that spot and in that moment. Always beginning, always terrified, frozen on the edge of light, a Hiroshima shadow of fabulous cash and prizes.

My eyes focus. On the champion's neck, a tiny bead of sweat has formed.

For the very first time, I imagine I might have a chance.

CHAPTER

5

HALLOWEEN
COMES SUDDENLY

Also, Scandalous
Thoughts About Ned
Flanders's Wife

"...HARRIS!"

Johnny Gilbert, the voice of God in a satin jacket, suddenly booms my name. Like the subject of a stage hypnotist, I wobble involuntarily into the light and take my place at the center podium.

Thousands of miles away, and several weeks later but felt in this moment, in a small white house not far from a wintry marsh on the shore of Lake Erie, my mother and late father are watching.

Alex Trebek strides to his mark on the floor in the center of the river-blue stage.

*Just like on TV,* I notice. Duh.

Alex is taller than I'd imagined. That is interesting.

Also, he is wearing what looks like a toga. This is unexpected.

It takes a second to realize he is dressed as the Statue of Liberty. It's a slapped-together costume, an impromptu bit of backstage whimsy to surprise us all live on camera, its cheery half-assedness much of its charm. Alex has draped his finely honed suit with a dusty green quilted pad, the kind used by stagehands when moving heavy equipment, and there is a spiky foam souvenir crown on his head. In his right hand is a miniature flashlight, the size you might find attached to a gas station men's room key.

Alex holds this aloft like the torch of freedom.

And so I salute.

We players have been instructed to applaud, of course. It's traditional, it's courteous, it's good TV. Newborn babies instinctively applaud the host of a game show.

But that's not why I'm saluting and applauding. Alex was once a highly respected newsman in Canada, with a degree in philosophy. He is now wildly well-paid and a national icon. It would be very easy for Alex to take himself too seriously. And yet here he is, goofing around like a kindly uncle chosen to baby-sit, eager to be silly if it might amuse the kids at the end of another long five-show day.

I like him immediately. And so I play along, giving Alex and his quilted-pad costume and his men's-room-key-flashlight a full and proper salute.

Alex seems glad to have someone join the charade. We even joke a bit back and forth before the game begins. I don't remember now what we said. It's on a videotape somewhere, but this is the important part: *I don't remember.*

The laughter has inadvertently gotten my body to start calming down. I am coming out of auto-record brainlock, simply because I have embraced a strange moment.

This will be a good habit from now on.

We were taping in mid-September. The game was scheduled for broadcast, however, on October 31. Halloween. *That's* why Alex was Liberty. Aha. And sure enough, the categories for our first round were all linked to Halloween as well:

I made a mental note: Always learn the broadcast date as soon as possible, the better to anticipate seasonal clues. For a game played on the Fourth of July, for example, you might want to brush up on FORT MCHENRY, BETSY ROSS, and THINGS THAT LOOK COOL BLOWING UP.

Then I noticed: This game hadn't even started, and already I was looking forward to others.

How odd. This was a bizarre shift in attitude, certainly not the behavior of someone expecting to lose. *Reel it in*, I thought to myself. *This isn't quite Cleveland of you.* But for reasons we'll soon explore, I was becoming comfortable before the game even started.

This is the very first clue I ever saw on *Jeopardy!*, for $100 in the category FICTIONAL GHOSTS:

> **HE PIONEERED THE NOVEL WITH "ROBINSON CRUSOE" AND THE GHOST STORY WITH "THE APPARITION OF ONE MRS. VEAL"**

The word "novel" jumped off the screen. *Literature*, I thought. *Oh, crap.*

But as soon as I got to the word "Crusoe," I started to feel better. Not because I'd ever read the novel—remember, in college I was a Pong Studies major—but because when I was in third grade, the grocery store where Mom shopped started giving away hardcover versions of classic books.

Our untouched-by-human-hands-since collection of these sat on a shelf near the TV, and thus near my eyeline throughout childhood for at least twenty-eight hours a day. One of these books had these words on its spine:

*Robinson Crusoe—Daniel Defoe*

So I would know at least one response. *Yes!* Just in case I might forget in the next three seconds, I repeated the response in my head, over and over, waiting for the moment to ring in:

*Daniel Defoe Daniel Defoe Daniel Defoe Daniel Defoe . . .*

To this day, I've still never read *Robinson Crusoe*. Or anything by Defoe.

I *should*, I know. Eventually. Someday I will also read *Moby Dick*, *War and Peace*, *Crime and Punishment*, and possibly the rest of *Speed Reading Made Easy*, although at this point I should probably just wait for the movie version.

Meanwhile, here's absolutely everything else I knew about *Robinson Crusoe:*

- A shipwreck was involved
- Some guy named Friday
- Oh, yeah: an island
- Defoe also wrote something called *Moll Flanders*

*Moll Flanders* had stuck in my head because when I first stumbled across that fact (I have no idea where), I made a little joke to myself, imagining Ned Flanders's prudish wife from *The Simpsons* stranded with Crusoe on a desert island, gradually embracing a shameless life of wanton abandon. One taw-diddly-awdry mental image later, *Moll Flanders* was instantly fastened to *Robinson Crusoe*, and thus Daniel Defoe, for good.

I had inadvertently stumbled across several steps of the Eightfold Path at once, although it would take years before I understood how.

Later, I realized that those four facts are also almost half of everything *Jeopardy!* can probably ask about Defoe's entire novel.

The writers can ask about virtually any topic, of course, but they're limited by the brevity of the clues and responses. Using the typeface *Jeopardy!* prefers on its monitors, in fact, a clue can only contain just over 100 characters. Into that, they have to squeeze enough data to limit all possible responses to one, usually include a clear hint of some kind, and if possible even cram in a small dollop of humor.

So far, they have done this almost a third of a million times. I, for one, am impressed.

*Robinson Crusoe* is a classic of English literature, spawning a whole subgenre of castaway works. But little of that fits into a twelve-second rhythm. In fact, here's all of the remaining Crusoe-related material that (in my opinion) is concise enough to prove useful even in one of *Jeopardy!*'s advanced tournaments:

- Crusoe was from York
- The book was published around 1720

- It was partly based on a real guy named Alexander Selkirk
- He was on a Portuguese slave ship headed for Brazil
- The only book he had was the Bible
- Defoe wrote a sequel, *The Further Adventures of Robinson Crusoe*

That's it. The end of the map. Beyond, there be dragons.

Of course, they can ask about anything *else* Defoe wrote, dig into his biography, combine titles in Before & Afters (as "Jackie Robinson Crusoe" perhaps), and riff on the endless derivative works ranging from *Lost* to *Lost in Space* to *Robinson Crusoe on Mars*, a cheesy old sci-fi movie featuring Adam West from *Batman*. (Think of it: I've never read the actual book. But the Batman-crash-lands-on-Mars version, oh, *that* I know really well.)

But now we're no longer talking about Crusoe. Just related stuff.

You *can* study for *Jeopardy!* You just need to think like one of their writers.

You also have to be unhinged enough to try to boil down the entire canon of human knowledge into these convenient bite-size bits, gluing them in with (as you'll see) a headful of explosions and nakedness.

Obviously.

Time slowed down at the podium.

*Daniel Defoe Daniel Defoe Daniel Defoe Daniel Defoe . . .*

As described earlier, you can't simply ring in at will. You have to wait until Alex has finished the entire clue, at which point someone offstage flips a switch, activating all three buzzers at once.

At the same instant the buzzers become active, a series of tiny, nameless lights near the game board flash, telling the players it's safe to ring in. Jump the gun, and your buzzer is disabled for what I'd guess is about a half a second. This is an eternity in *Jeopardy!* time. Someone else will probably ring in before your buzzer works again.

Incidentally, these lights seem to have no official name. They are simply spoken of as "The Lights," sometimes in the same hushed, mystified fashion used by UFO abductees. For clarity's sake, I'll invent the simple term "Go Lights" and use it from here on. (I also forfeit all right to poke gentle fun at "Signaling Device" ever again.)

The basic routine, then, usually becomes:

- Read the question,
- Figure out the answer,
- Wait for the Go Lights,
- Then thumb-thump like crazy.

But I knew going in that my knowledge would be no better than anyone else's, and probably worse than most, since I just barely squeaked through the test. My reflexes are good, but not great. And given that the returning champ would already be more experienced, I would begin at a clear disadvantage.

I would have to try something else entirely to have any chance of winning.

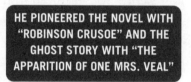

HE PIONEERED THE NOVEL WITH "ROBINSON CRUSOE" AND THE GHOST STORY WITH "THE APPARITION OF ONE MRS. VEAL"

My eyes focus on the final "L."
*Daniel Defoe Daniel Defoe Daniel Defoe Daniel Defoe . . .*
". . . Veal," Alex says.
A half-beat of total silence. Instants pass. I fight myself slightly, keeping my eyes off the Go Lights.
I am hoping my finger will simply move on its own.

Back in Ohio, watching *Jeopardy!* in a small white house with Mom and Dad during a period when my adult life didn't quite, um, *take*, I had gotten into the habit of tapping my index finger in synch with the contestants hitting their buzzers.

It was just something to do, part of playing along. Even if I was completely lost in a category—which was often—I could still flatter myself by hoping I might have gotten the timing right.

I left before long, stumbling out into the world in search of my own actual life, and I didn't see the show much for a long time. Usually I was working nights as a B-minus-list comedian, making a decent living by roving constantly between cheesy nightclubs and small Midwestern colleges. My day for most of the early 1990s consisted of a six-hour drive to a motel in some small Midwestern college town, followed by a performance, food from a gas station, and a little sleep before repeating the process the next day.

Occasionally I'd get to drive back to New York or D.C. or Chicago or wherever my latest One-True-Eternal-Soulmate™ happened to share an apartment with my stuff. This would also be where a landlord and credit-card companies happily collected my money. After a few days of visiting my life, I'd climb back into Max and rumble out to another string of small Midwestern colleges.

Still, every time I'd happen across *Jeopardy!*, the little finger-tapping habit never stopped.

When *Jeopardy!* suddenly called, I had exactly two weeks to prepare. So instead of trying to cram a whole bunch of information into my head, I decided first to go online and read as much as possible about how memory worked.

Since the Internet was still in its Bronze Age—I had a dial-up connection, browsed with Netscape, and wore a helmet made from the tusk of a wild boar—this took time. But when I first stumbled into a description of a phenomenon called "state-dependent retrieval"—basically, the power of things like sights and smells and even our body chemistry to trigger memories—it made instant sense. (Many experts split some of what follows into "context-dependent retrieval," a separate category. Conceptually, it's all pretty darn similar, though.)

Have you ever returned to a city you haven't visited in years, a place you couldn't possibly still be able to navigate, only to find that once there, you instantly knew your way around again? Bingo.

The scatteredness of my own life and the constant travel had taught me the power of individual places to bring back unique memories and powerful emotions. I had wondered how and why this always happened.

The mind-altering effect of specific places is so powerful that we instinctively take it for granted. We even create special places where certain emotions, and *only* those, are to be felt. Cemeteries, for example, are places of death and sadness, despite the fact that they're filled with living creatures and expressions of love. Almost nobody actually dies *in* a cemetery, although it would be pretty convenient.

Carnival rides, on the other hand, reliably send thousands of giggling people across America straight to hospital emergency rooms, year after year. But these remain places of joy and excitement, filled with happy families, all zooming and giddy.

So where do we cry, and where do we go *Wheee?*

Again: human memory is built not on logic, but on intense experience. We *have* grieved in cemeteries, so they literally give us grief. We *have* squealed in carnival rides, so they give us new joy, no matter how many sudden experiments in human flight may occur.

Since our neurons are so interconnected, just one stimulus can trigger a memory—a *response*, in *Jeopardy!* terms—which leads to another, and another, as synapses fire automatically, a long line of falling mental dominoes.

In short: the context stimulates the neurons that create the memories and feelings that create the behavior.

This is a fact of life in sports. Have you ever wondered why there's a home-field advantage in every type of game, even the ones without crowds or referees? State-dependent retrieval. Players whose muscle memories are preconsciously invoked by the nearby sights, smells, and sounds are at an enormous advantage.

State-dependent retrieval is strong stuff. Fortunately, it's also simple to use.

Feeling too blah to exercise? Put on the workout clothes anyway. Pretty soon you'll probably feel like working out, as if the clothes created the feeling. Which they did.

Want to ace that next test? Don't study in your kitchen or dorm room; study in a room as much as possible like the place where the test will be given, at the same time of day. Wear the same clothes you'll wear. Sit in the same seat. (Have you ever picked a random seat in a classroom, and before long discovered that it was inexplicably the place you were most comfortable? *Ta-daa.*) All else being equal, you'll probably feel more comfortable, remember more, and perform better on the day.

And this is our next step on the Eightfold Path to Enlightened Jeopardy:

1. Obvious things may be worth noticing.
2. Remember the basics: the basics are what you remember.
3. Put your head where you can use it later.

So how should you train a split-second muscle response for a nationally televised game show?

*While being flooded with the imagery of the game itself.*

Fortunately, that's exactly what I'd already done with my index finger, thousands and thousands of times.

As I did this research, my current One-True-Eternal-Soulmate™ was named Annika. She and my stuff lived peacefully in a small apartment they shared in West Hollywood. I usually got to visit for a couple of weeks each month.

Annika was (and is, wherever she might be now) spectacularly well educated, good-hearted, and soft-spoken. We had been together for almost two years, during which nothing much happened.

This was, I remember thinking, *fantastic.*

My previous relationships had had a habit of exploding in interesting ways, including flights to Ecuador, undisclosed pre-existing boyfriends, sudden elopements with wealthy horse breeders, and other spontaneous romantic combustions.

This was entirely my own fault, of course. Anyone can singe themselves by accident once or twice. Eight or ten good scorchings, you begin to realize they actually enjoy quality time around open flames. It's one thing to ignore red flags; it's quite another to write sappy love songs to the Triangle Shirtwaist Fire, and then wonder why things never quite work out. But that's all for another book. (Working title, top of my head: *Kissing the Hindenburg.*)

I once visited a gorgeous blonde's apartment and received a guided tour of her many framed self-portraits as Anne Boleyn. There were perhaps a dozen on the walls, and more in her closets. And I thought to myself: OK. This is *manageable.*

Maybe I was just insecure enough that I needed to feel needed, and was willing to pay any price.

Of course, I wasn't such a great catch myself, with my own moments as magnesium flash powder. And my habit of overthinking during stress, seeking solutions not by listening but by retreating into my head, didn't exactly help. This had worked exceptionally well on math tests when I was younger, but proved ineffective during intimate arguments. Too many discussions went like this:

"Bob, I really need you to listen more closely."

*Listen closely? I am listening closely. I bet you're just upset because I hid all your guns, won't give you my PIN number, and can't see the resemblance to Anne Boleyn. Besides which, Anne Boleyn had six fingers on one hand, but it keeps going back and forth between left and right in the paintings. I'd think you'd know where to stick the extra pinky. Say . . . with six digits, where do you put a wedding ring? And is it still possible to extend the middle finger? Or would you use the middle two?*

But with Annika, at last, there was a placidity I adored. Her intelligence and education were attractive, yes, but it was more her sedate reserve that I found attractive. It was soothing to be her boyfriend. We didn't fight. We didn't debate. Looking back, I'm not certain we even spoke. Plus, she had a calming physical presence, the sort of stillness one usually finds in someone trying to break the world record for being covered in the most bees.

This was, at last, a kind of serenity. I certainly wasn't worried about Annika cheating on me. That would involve moving at least a half-dozen major muscle groups. We spent most weekends when I was home sitting in the living room, catching up on our reading, and quite noticeably not burning in a hydrogen fireball down to our bare metal superstructure in just over thirty-seven seconds.

It was on just such a day, shortly after *Jeopardy!* called, that I stumbled across the notion of intentionally not using the Go Lights, instead simply trusting my instincts like a wannabe Jedi, letting my finger react on its own.

Delighted with the sheer lunacy of the idea, I immediately told Annika. But the more I tried to explain the plan, the less rational it must have sounded. I think this was the very first time she thought I was gradually losing my mind.

It would not be the last.

*Daniel Defoe Daniel Defoe Daniel Defoe Daniel Defoe . . .*

There are two small white lights on the contestant's side of the podium that illuminate when you've won on the buzzer. The one closest to my right hand is in my peripheral vision. Sometimes the entire game is only about making this one hidden light come on.

My finger moves slowly amid hard plastic chaos. I only hope that it knows what it's doing.

*Cliklikikkitylikkityclikit.*

CHAPTER

6

THINKING AHEAD
WHILE NOT
THINKING AT ALL

Also, Safety
Instructions for Your
Jeopardy Weapon

About a thirtieth of a second after the buzzer-frenzy began—exactly one frame on the videotape—my finger moved of its own accord.

I glanced down at my podium, afraid even to hope.

*And my light came on.*

Lucky shot? Maybe. I would know for sure in about twelve more seconds. The second clue, under FICTIONAL GHOSTS for $200:

HE WROTE THE GHOST TALE
"THE TURN OF THE SCREW"
WHILE HIS BROTHER WILLIAM
STUDIED SPIRITUALISM

I'd never read this book, either. Luckily, however, as a teenager I'd once briefly worked in a bookstore, where I restocked a paperback edition of *The Turn of the Screw* combined with *Daisy Miller* in one volume. The unfortunate placement of the large word *Screw* on the cover, looming over the innocent-sounding "Daisy Miller," made me wonder if the publisher even *liked* Henry James. The author's name had stuck in my head ever since.

My finger moved of its own free will.

*My light came on again.*

■ ■ ■

*What's the eye?*

*What is, um, water?*

*What's the patella?*

*What are cells?*

*Who is Henry VIII?*

*Who is Houdini?*

The light on my podium *kept coming on*. I just tried to stay calm and let myself believe it was happening.

Three minutes later, one quarter of the game was gone. I had almost twice as much money as the other two players combined.

The returning champion, Matt, had beaten me on the buzzer exactly *once*.

These weren't particularly difficult clues yet, mind you. Consider this, the third clue I ever responded to on *Jeopardy!*:

> **CAVITIES IN THE SKULL**
> **CALLED ORBITS**
> **HOUSE THESE ORGANS**

This doesn't take a neurologist to figure out. Let's assume you have a head, and that your skull has the standard number of holes in it. We're looking for "organs," plural, so you need at least two of them. And the word "orbits" implies a round shape. So: they were asking for a pair of round organs in holes in your skull. If you can find your own eyeballs, you're as strong a player as I was.

Many seemingly difficult clues are actually that simple, once you learn to decode them. Sometimes the only real task is figuring out what they're asking.

The last clue before the commercial was this:

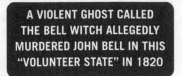

> **A VIOLENT GHOST CALLED THE BELL WITCH ALLEGEDLY MURDERED JOHN BELL IN THIS "VOLUNTEER STATE" IN 1820**

Almost 90 percent of the clue is irrelevant. What they were asking was simple, found simply by scanning for whatever comes after the word "this":

> **BLAH BLAH BLAH BLAH BLAH BLAH BLAH BLAH BLAH BLAH BLAH BLAH THIS "VOLUNTEER STATE" BLAH**

To this day, I know nothing about John Bell, the Bell Witch, how crime scene investigations were pursued in 1820, or what happened to the neato ghost-finding technology they must have had. But most of us probably know Tennessee's nickname.

All three of us playing the actual game certainly did.

But my light just kept coming on.

The first commercial break arrived.

During any stoppage in play, contestant wranglers and makeup people swarm out and slather the contestants with water, encouragement, and (in my case) a fresh layer of chrome de-polisher. But the first break always has an extra degree of breath-catching and realizing where the heck you actually are. The adrenaline can run so high that if *Jeopardy!* were one day to replace the buzzers with switchblades, I doubt many players would notice until this first break.

So I inhaled and exhaled and mumbled shy pleasantries, but mostly I tried to stay focused and think ahead, free-associating from the categories and this day's Halloween theme, getting my mental flash cards prepared for the next burst of play:

> *Halloween. Monsters. Ghosts. Specters. Hauntings. Séances. Goblins. Jack-o'-lanterns. Pumpkins. Candy corn. Costumes. Frank-*

*enstein. Mary—Wait, who wrote that? Right—Mary Shelley.*
*Bram Stoker. Boris Karloff. Lon Chaney Jr. Vincent Price . . .*

And so on.

This paid off almost immediately. One of the clues after the break required exactly the response I had just spent an extra second bringing to mind. It was a video clue in which a guy dressed as Frankenstein came out and grunted while these words appeared on the screen:

> IN A 1935 FILM, ELSA LANCHESTER
> PLAYED MY BRIDE, AND IN THE
> PROLOGUE, THIS AUTHOR

*Who is Mary Shelley?*

I made a mental note never to waste a spare second during a *Jeopardy!* game again. Instead, I would think ahead like this during the first commercial, any technical stoppages, and even during other players' Daily Doubles.

As a result, I probably owe the contestant-herders an apology.

The main Jep-shepherds that day were two bright, easygoing guys named Glenn Kagan and Grant Loud, who could easily have allowed their feather-smoothing-of-strangers gig to devolve into pat box-store-greeter jawboning. Instead, they cultivated playful, even thoughtful conversations with every contestant.

This was odd. A gentle workplace is rare anywhere, much less in show business, where the enormity of wealth can magnify every human flaw. (On a functional level, some offices that entertain America less resemble a dream factory than a Hollywood Kremlin.) But the folks at *Jeopardy!* seemed to honestly like their jobs, each other, and the contestants.

This could mean only one of two things.

Either (a) the bosses at *Jeopardy!* are actually cool, creating an environment where nice people function authentically; or (b) they have blackmail Polaroids of every employee in compromising positions with citrus fruit, a Ukrainian stewardess, and what looks like aluminum ductwork, with orders to never stop smiling.

I believe it is the former.

So, an apology, Glenn, Grant, Susanne, Maggie, and every other commercial-break chaperon over the years. I've usually been giving you my full attention, too. Except with a giant wall of TV screens promising tens of thousands of dollars looming over my entire field of view.

This can be distracting.

So while you were engaging me in sincere conversation, I was often just trying to grunt and mumble enough to camouflage the fact that I was still playing the game. I didn't want the other players to pick up on it and do the same.

I hope you'll forgive me, since this habit has led to thousands of extra dollars, the margins of several Final Jeopardy leads, and eventually a gigantic mistake that arguably even led to the circumstances of a good friend's marriage.

Alex himself even signed the wedding certificate.

We'll loop through that part of the timeline soon enough.

My good fortune continued through the whole first *Jeopardy!* round.

The category BOBBING was entirely about people named Bob. *My own first name.* Another clue was practically written for a guy from Ohio who had spent much of his adult life doing comedy:

> IN HIS BOOK *WITHOUT FEATHERS*, A GHOST REPORTS THAT THE NEXT WORLD RESEMBLES CLEVELAND

In my hometown, this is one of Woody Allen's better-known remarks.

Pure coincidence, of course, and my luck couldn't last. After all, boardfuls of clues are created long in advance and chosen at random with no knowledge of players. There was no way good fortune like this could hold out. But all you need to know about the Double Jeopardy round is that it included this entire category:

SMALL MIDWESTERN COLLEGES

Suddenly all those years of cheap motels and gas-station food were paying off. This hardly seemed fair. My finger kept moving—I was barely even paying attention to it anymore—and my light just *kept coming on.*

At the end of Double Jeopardy, I had more than twice as much money than either of the other players. Thus, I had a "lock game," in which Final Jeopardy is rendered entirely moot. I had won in a runaway.

This lacked suspense, of course, and was less-than-perfect TV. It's a situation I'm sure the producers do everything they can to avoid. However, after a long day of intense concentration, undulating blood pressure, and things going in and out of my nose, it was also an enormous relief.

I found myself wondering how good this Matt fellow, this Clark Kent look-alike of a returning champion, had been in the previous game. For all I knew at the time, maybe luck with categories was a large part of the game. Maybe Matt's first game had included categories like

It was possible. So I'd have to work harder before the next taping. It was the only way I could imagine controlling the outcome.

Years later—tonight, actually, shortly before writing this very sentence—I tracked down Matt by phone. I've always wondered about the guy who spooked me so much.

We chatted for over an hour. Great guy. Manages a winery up near Santa Barbara. The movie *Sideways* was filmed in his neighborhood. Happy, good marriage, enjoying life. Proud of his Pinot Noirs. Next time I'm up his way, I hope to crack a bottle with him.

Matt's proudest moment on *Jeopardy!*? In the game before ours, he did extremely well in a category called SHEEPISH COUNTRIES:

"So, of course, this was all about countries that have lots of sheep," he explained. "You immediately think of New Zealand, maybe Scotland. But I've always been a geography buff. I didn't quite run the category, but for $1,000, the clue asked for a country in the Commonwealth of Independent States which has twice the number of sheep as people . . ."

Matt paused on the phone line, as if he half-expected me to blurt out the answer. This might have been a very long pause indeed.

"... and I said, 'What is Kazakhstan?'"

Here's a humbling thought: Matt was confidently blurting out "What is Kazakhstan?" just five minutes before I began my L'Oréal-induced conniption in the green room.

Looking back at the buzzer-play in my first game, we find another key bit of *Jeopardy!* strategy, a bit of Zen that even the best players struggle to achieve: do not, under any circumstances, allow yourself to ring in. Ever.

Do not. Touch. The. Buzzer.

Unless you are very sure of the correct response.

Here's why: if you and I and your best friend are playing each other on a $1000 clue, and you get it wrong, you've just given us *both* a $1000 advantage. This is already twice as bad as simply letting one of us respond correctly. Worse, there's now an excellent chance that one of us will now do exactly that, especially since we have a few extra seconds to think, and you've eliminated one of the possible responses.

In this case, guessing wrong will put you $1000 behind one opponent, and $2000 behind the other. Total loss: $3000.

On the other hand, if your brain turns to grape jelly and oozes out of your skull entirely, bounces with a loud "plop!" off your podium, and finally makes a large purple stain on the studio floor, the worst possible loss is only $1000.

No big deal. You just scoop your brain back up and play the next clue. And meanwhile, *you* get the extra few seconds to think, so if an opponent screws up, you can pick up the rebound.

It's easier said than done. Way easier. Players whack themselves with their own buzzers all the time. But you win *Jeopardy!* the same way you win a game of Russian roulette: keep your finger off the damn trigger unless you know exactly what's in the chamber. There's a reason Jane and I decided it's properly called the Jeopardy Weapon.

And this leads us to the next step in the Eightfold Path:

1. Obvious things may be worth noticing.
2. Remember the basics: the basics are what you remember.

3. Put your head where you can use it later.
4. Doing nothing is better than doing something really stupid.

On a set of *Jeopardy!* boards, there are sixty potential clues to be revealed. Three will be Daily Doubles, so the maximum number of buzzer chances, ever, is fifty-seven. Because of time limits, however, players sometimes don't complete the entire board. In my first game, there were two clues left on the board in each round. Therefore, there were fifty-three opportunities to ring in.

I just checked the tape. Of those fifty-three chances, I only attempted to ring in thirty-five times. I allowed the other eighteen clues—more than one-third of the game, including most of the high-dollar clues, whose answers of course I did not know—to simply float on by.

And I won in a runaway. Final Jeopardy didn't even matter.

I was not being modest when I told you that I didn't know that much.

You don't win by knowing everything. Often, you won't know squat. All you can do is admit it and make yourself comfortable with ignorance until you have a chance to change your situation.

*Jeopardy!* is often not so much a test of knowledge as it is a test of self-knowledge.

Thus, the next step on the Eightfold Path:

1. Obvious things may be worth noticing.
2. Remember the basics: the basics are what you remember.
3. Put your head where you can use it later.
4. Doing nothing is better than doing something really stupid.
5. Admit you don't know squat as often as possible.

However, when I *did* attempt to answer, my light came on. Almost always, in fact: twenty-eight times, by my count.

Eighty percent of the thirty-five times my finger moved, my light came on. The other 20 percent of those clues were split about evenly between the other two players. Another way to look at it: when my body decided to tell my index finger to move, I won on the buzzer *eight times more often* than either opponent, both of whom were often looking directly at a Go Light telling them exactly when to ring in.

State-dependent retrieval, properly harnessed, can sometimes help you achieve unlikely goals.

Carried too far, on the other hand, it can also drive people around you completely nuts.

If practicing in an image-rich environment might help, what about filling the apartment with bright stage lights? What about moving the furniture to look more like the *Jeopardy!* set while studying? What about wearing the same clothes every single day? Einstein had a famously limited wardrobe, after all, and for exactly the same reason. Why not?

I'm getting ahead of the story again. But not by much now.

The Final Jeopardy category—*p-TING!*—was hardly a huge surprise:

**HALLOWEEN**

All righty, then. The mental note about broadcast dates is hereby underlined.

We wrote down our wagers during the commercial. While other breaks are timed to the advertising segments, the break before Final Jeopardy is allowed to stretch out for a few extra minutes. The players have some calculations to do, and the producers don't want anyone to lose because of a math error. Knowing this, I dawdled a bit over the arithmetic, buying time to let my neurons cool while considering an unusual option. I share this in a confessional tone.

I had $500 more than twice the second-place player's score. So all I had to do was bet less than $500, and the game was won. Instead, I bet $500 exactly. I was actually playing for a worst-case tie. In non-tournament tie games, both winners return, so in the worst case, my next game would include only one new opponent, in addition to one I could definitely beat on the buzzer.

In a full five-game run, I would normally have eight future opponents. But any one of them could be an Ivy League Serial Killer, an inhuman knowledge machine with a degree from Harvard, someone my Jedi buzzer tricks couldn't possibly overwhelm. Why not cut that number down to seven, while I could? For all I knew, the monster was lurking in the very next green room.

I mention this strategy for two reasons. First, it is a move I have never heard anyone else suggest, much less try. Perhaps it was brilliant. More likely, it was both cocky and somehow stunningly stupid. I don't know which. You decide. Second, notice that the first game wasn't even over, and I was already becoming focused, quite clearly, on going *undefeated*.

Kind of a leap, isn't it? You may begin to wonder if the gentle narrator you have come to trust may, intoxicated with his good fortune, start to show occasional flashes of a man becoming slightly unhinged.

Do not discount this possibility.

The Final clue was fairly simple, even in the unlikely event you've never seen the show to which it referred:

MYTHICAL HALLOWEEN BEING
IN THE TITLE OF THE OFT-REPEATED
ANIMATED TV SPECIAL THAT
DEBUTED OCTOBER 27, 1966

I knew the correct response because when I was a child, watching television, I was a child watching television.

If you knew it instantly, great. But if not, I'd bet money that you'd still get it in thirty seconds.

### Obvious things may be worth noticing.

There are actually three hints here. Two involve scanning fairly large databases: mythical Halloween beings (goblins, ghouls, ghosts—and that's just under G) and 1960s-era cartoons (*Alvin and the Chipmunks, Rocky and Bullwinkle, Mighty Mouse*—and those are just the ones starring rodents). Wander too far down either blind alley, though, and you're not coming out.

But the third hint is huge and simple: how many Halloween TV specials get repeated every year? I can only think of one: *It's the Great Pumpkin, Charlie Brown*. And sure enough, the title names a mythical Halloween character.

The writers almost always structure Final Jeopardy clues in this you-can-get-there fashion. The worst mistake you can make is not having the patience to read closely, trapping yourself in a dead end as a result. If you ever get on the show: *take your time.* The thirty seconds won't start until Alex has read the clue out loud, so you have an extra seven or eight seconds on top. The whole clue is only fifteen or twenty words. Go *slowly*, and you may find the vital hint before the Think Music even starts.

Electronic pen hits glass. *Clackity-click-whap-clackity.* Done.

Once my response was written down, I had about twenty-five seconds to stand in silence, listening to the rest of the familiar thirty-second musical countdown. I wanted to dance, if you must know.

I thought of my mom back in the small white house in Ohio, and how happy she would be when she saw the game. I thought of my dad, who is still alive in my head, and what he would say if the timeline ever collapsed and we all got to sit together in that living room and watch this very show.

I hoped my sister Connie would be proud. Over the years, despite mystifying health problems, she had married happily, raised two kids, and made the best of discomfort whenever possible. She had given me more reason to be proud of her than I could ever provide in return.

Annika never crossed my mind.

Since I responded correctly, my tie-game second-choice gambit went unnoticed by the universe. Alex came over to shake my hand, and we stood at center stage while random products that *some contestants also receive!* zipped across TV screens thousands of miles away and several weeks in the future.

Sue Bee brand honey! and Scalpicin hair treatment! and the *Jeopardy!* electronic game! later, finally, it was over. While Alex disappeared back into the mists of celebrity, I wobbled off the stage, back into the darkness, and tried to readjust my eyes, ears, and self-esteem.

Susanne Thurber patted me on the back and gently guided me toward a series of forms I needed to fill out. I was walking gingerly, try-

ing to convince myself of what had just happened. Patients leaving surgery are often more sure of their footing.

There was a slip of paper with a large number on it and a place for
me to sign. The number was simply impossible to believe. It was enough
money to pay rent for an entire year. It was twice what I had paid for
rumbling old Max, larger even than the college debt I had worked for
eight years to pay off.

I stuffed my copy of the slip into my thrift-store sports jacket,
grabbed a free Goodie Bag including a *Jeopardy!* home game—which I
still own, almost ten years later, somewhere in a dusty pile in an apartment I don't quite live in—and wobbled out into the Sony lot.

I was proud. I was relieved. I was tired.

I wanted more.

CHAPTER

7

HOW EVERYTHING
IS CONNECTED

Also, Twenty-One
Interesting Uses
for Rubber

Unfortunately, I still didn't have much in the way of actual memory skills.

I often wonder, even now, if I have much of a memory at all. Example: I finished the chapter about taking the *Jeopardy!* test about a week ago. And I still don't remember what year it was the first time I failed.

I've been thinking of going through a large stack of old notebooks and tax receipts, trying to pin down the year. This is no inconvenience. Sometime between six months and six years ago, I again moved in with a delightful and talented woman—for the fifth (or fourth, or possibly sixth) time—and, as you know, all of my stuff is still in boxes and garbage bags, as it has been since you picked up this book.

I've mentioned this woman several times now, of course. Jane, who named Squeema, wink-wink.

The bags and boxes were supposed to be unpacked long ago. But they're still all sort of shoved into the corner of the guest bedroom, which was supposed to have become an office. Instead, it's just storage.

It wouldn't take more than a few days to unpack. I don't have much. I don't like to own stuff. There's a whole explanation for that. The one I usually tell myself involves frugality and charity and even a self-flattering touch of asceticism. But of course that's complete baloney, and you deserve better.

The main reason I don't own many things is that I hate packing up. I've had to do it too many times.

I'm forty-two years old and I've never been married. Came close a few times, but one of us always screwed it up or exploded over Lake-hurst, New Jersey, or something. My series of exes is now long enough that the names have started to repeat like the books of the Old Testament: Ruth, then First and Second Sara, First and Second Kelly, and so on. Eventually you get to Goliath—that was just a phase—and then finally the Ephesians, who seemed nice at the party but didn't even call the next day.

Some of it was youth. I knew *everything*, you should know, at least for a while anyway. Some of it was bad luck or the odd tragic calamity here and there. And some of it was living in Hollywood, where too many people upgrade relationships the way they do cell phones.

Still, I sleep OK. I've never cheated on anyone, my lies have usually been the kind that kept nice little surprises hidden, and I've never once said the words "I love you" without meaning them. I'm still friends with about half of my former One-True-Eternal-Soulmates™, and quite close to a few, if that means anything.

But I still can't quite unpack all the boxes. This late in the game, sometimes I'm afraid I never will.

Jane—the latest book in my personal testament—was probably terrific and smart and funny and kind before she was even born. So maybe *this* time, I said to myself, carrying each heavy box and bag.

Maybe this time. Probably, even, if I had to write down my wager with an electronic pen. Let's just hope nothing truly horrible happens to one of us.

But I just said too much. I keep getting ahead of the story.

■ ■ ■

There are now three large Hefty Cinch Saks sitting empty on the floor, covered in a large pile of notebooks and small slips of paper. I am tired, my throat is dry, and my clothes are covered in dust. Still, there is no record of my first attempt at the *Jeopardy!* test.

However, I have managed to locate my copy of *Speed Reading Made Easy*. So if I can just find a box of nails and some wood, I can make a wine rack as a present for Matt.

I've also stumbled across a large undated receipt from the J. H. Gilbert Company of Willoughby, Ohio. This piece of paper is particularly puzzling. I have no idea what this receipt is for. The letterhead offers some intriguing, even lurid, hints:

INDUSTRIAL GLOVES FOR EVERY NEED
SAFETY EQUIPMENT, RUBBER CLOTHING, FOOTWEAR

For some reason, my eye keeps fixing on the words "rubber clothing." And apparently I once spent almost a hundred dollars there.

I find myself curious.

You're probably scanning through the same set of delicious possibilities that I am right now. But here's the thing: I *really* don't know, and it's me that we're talking about. I was on the road for a long time, and it's gently surprising that I never woke up with inexplicable tattoos promising the secrets of my identity.

What the hell was I doing? How many people were involved? Did we scrub thoroughly afterward?

In the proposal that led to the book you're now reading—facilitated by a fellow *Jeopardy!* contestant named Arthur Phillips, whom you'll soon meet in the green room as an intense young fellow able to send heat rays through his forehead—this chapter wasn't originally about THINGS TO DO IN A CATSUIT. It was outlined as a creativity and lateral-thinking exercise, fleshing out the fun memory techniques we'll need so I can go all Jimmy Neutron in another thirty pages or so.

Looking at the outline, though, a whole separate chapter was supposed to delve into my own life history, so you'll care more about what happens later. But we need a focus and examples for our memory exercise anyway, and so—if only because I'm extremely curious now about this receipt, and giggling childishly at the idea of seeing my whole life through the lens of the word *rubber*—let's have a little fun here, open up a tin of madeleines, and play with everything all at once.

This way, we'll not only encounter exotic maladies, third-world dictatorships, and lovers who flee to South America, but with any real luck, maybe we'll even track down some embarrassing rubber knickers with frilly bits of lace on the side and a thank-you note from the Turkish navy.

I wonder if I've had a more interesting life than I realized.

Close the book, get out a piece of paper, and see how many free associations you can come up with which directly involve the word *rubber.* To keep this brief, let's insist that the word itself has to be in a short phrase: "rubber this" or "this-that-and-the-other rubber."

Don't stop the first time you run out of ideas. Poke around. If you get stuck, change the sense you're thinking with. If you're thinking visually, start thinking with your nose, and then your ears. If you're thinking with your sense of touch, start working with taste and sight.

Take your time. I'll make my own list while you're gone. That will be preferable to cleaning up the mess I just made.

■ ■ ■

Welcome back. Here's the list I came up with.

Rubber bands, which I also heard once as slang for the fan belt on a car.
Rubber stamps, which are also a metaphor for automatic approval.
Rubber cement.
The slab called a pitcher's rubber in baseball.
The rubber arm a durable pitcher is said to have.
Rubbernecking at a car wreck.
Rubber checks that bounce.
Rubber tires.
Peeling rubber with a sports car. You can also burn this kind of rubber.
There's the birth-control prophylactic meaning.
Rubber rooms for the insane.
Rubber gloves, as used in electrical work or in surgery.
The rubber man in a circus.
Rubber galoshes, which we called just "rubbers" when I was growing up.
Rubber balls.
"Rubber baby buggy bumpers," a phrase that made me laugh as a kid.
Rubber chickens, like the kind you find in gag gift stores.
The "rubber game" which decides a series of baseball games.
Rubber rafts.
Rubber erasers—what pencil erasers are called in some countries.
Rubber-tree plants, the kind upon which ants reportedly base high hopes.

Good enough. That's twenty-one. Now let's strip away the rubber bits, and gaze at the incredibly diverse stuff we've just conjured:

| | | |
|---|---|---|
| Elastic bands | Bank checks | Shoes |
| Car parts | Bouncing | Balls |
| Approval | Sporting events | Baby talk |
| Stamps | Tires | Chickens |
| Cement | Peeling | Gag gifts |
| Slabs | Burning | Decisions |
| Durability | Sex | Rafts |
| Arms | Gloves | Erasers |
| Gawking faces | Contortionists | Trees |

If someone had asked you yesterday how to connect "chicken" with "cement," you'd probably have given them a blank stare. But it was already in your head.

This little game of Six Degrees of Your Own Skull shows that nothing exists in your head by itself. In fact, it's hard to find anything that *isn't* connected in a hop or two.

Just for style points, let's look back at the list and pick the three most unrelated words we can find, and see how they also connect in completely non-rubber ways. A few jump right out:

> "Cement" + "trees": there are trees in cement planters near the coffee shop where I usually write.
>
> "Trees" + "shoes": you can find a shoe tree in any department store.
>
> "Shoes" + "cement": OK, that's just an episode of *The Sopranos.*

This is no coincidence; it's a direct result of the structure of the human brain. Visualize it this way: imagine the word *rubber* floating around in the center of the room you're in. Now mentally attach all the connected words, arranged so that they're evenly spaced, floating around the center, flying like kites in all directions. Now try to picture all of these *other* words as the centers of their *own* little kite-spheres, all at the same time, with dozens of their own connections floating around them. And all of these, of course, are centers of their own connection-spheres.

The room gets full pretty damn fast, doesn't it?

It's impossible to imagine how dense all the connections really are. Your brain isn't arranged like a book or even a hard drive, but like the Internet, with millions of interlinking entries and perhaps the same percentage of dirty pictures. You could probably spend a lifetime finding new connections and ideas, just by playing around with what you already have.

Happily, the more you goof around in there, the more connections you'll have, and the faster they'll work. If you've ever wondered how *Jeopardy!* players can find their way to some wildly obscure answers, this is a big part. I'll give some examples from my own games a little later.

And so we reach another step on the Eightfold Path:

1. Obvious things may be worth noticing.
2. Remember the basics: the basics are what you remember.
3. Put your head where you can use it later.
4. Doing nothing is better than doing something really stupid.
5. Admit you don't know squat as often as possible.
6. Everything connects to everything else.

This is handy. When we combine this with the knowledge that visceral, least-common-denominator stuff is incredibly sticky, it really is possible to start uploading data faster than you might have imagined: *Just free-associate until you find a way to connect new stuff to old stuff, using sticky, visceral, primal imagery as the glue.*

You'll see a few examples soon. And don't worry: most of my memory-jogging mnemonic images are perfectly repeatable in front of the kids. When all else fails, however, I'm not above the private creation of some incredibly silly, dirty mental jokes (like the bodice-ripping link between *Moll Flanders* and *Robinson Crusoe*) about everything from Cabinet Departments to Philosophers to Shakespeare. A complete list will have to wait for another book. Written under an assumed name. While I'm drunk.

This book will be bought by undergraduate students at the most respected schools in America, even though it will only be sold in black plastic bags by skeevy men in the dicey part of town.

The movie version, however, will get Uma Thurman an Oscar.

So which rubber-connected item *did* I buy from the J. H. Gilbert Company of Willoughby, Ohio?

We can eliminate a few things from our list right off. They probably didn't sell circus freaks, rubber chickens, or people who gawk at accidents. I'd remember taking those home. Metaphorical uses of rubber are an unlikely retail item, since they're hell to stock. Rubber trees would be a waste of space, especially without little glassine envelopes of highly hopeful ants.

That still leaves at least a dozen things to go looking for.

The J. H. Gilbert Company itself has an address near my parents' house, in a moist area near Lake Erie known as the "Snow Belt," a phrase that should be understood as dry understatement, the way "Mississippi" is the Algonquian word for "Big River."

The first half of my life was largely spent in the Snow Belt, which stretches from the easternmost suburbs of Cleveland to, roughly speaking, Minsk. Our small white house was about halfway in between, at the edge of the watershed of a large sodden marsh that lies on the rim of the vast gray lake.

This was where I first played *Jeopardy!*, tapping my finger against my thigh, every twelve seconds, while shipwrecked on Mom and Dad's couch.

People in the Snow Belt live under a notorious atmospheric quirk: frequently, moisture rises from the unfrozen water, cools in the northwesterly breeze, and gets dumped back on the ground inland as snow. No actual storm is necessary. It could be perfectly clear in downtown Cleveland—close enough to reach by bicycle in a day—but the small white house might be sinking under a fresh new layer of powder.

Winters in the Snow Belt seemed to begin around mid-July, lasting through August of the following year. This was called the "lake effect" by attractive people under warm TV lights downtown. Folks in our neighborhood preferred more colorful terms.

That's not to say there weren't seasons in the Snow Belt. We could always tell when spring had arrived by the sound of the first robin being swallowed whole by a large mosquito. And each autumn, Dad and I would stop cheering for a last-place baseball team, shifting our allegiance to a football team with no hope whatsoever.

Summer days in between (and most years had at least four or five) were marked by torrential downpours caused by the convection currents stirred up by Little League games. Each afternoon the air would turn tropical: thick, motionless, and humid enough that you might expect dinner to be a passing duck that had fallen from the sky, fully steamed and ready to eat.

On summer evenings we kids would play, finally, chasing lightning bugs and splashing in puddles and slapping ourselves, constantly, to stop the mosquitoes. As the night would grow darker and the mosquitoes would thicken, the slapping would slowly accelerate, until we realized that slapping had become our main activity. Then it was time to go in for the night.

Sometimes, in advance, we'd smear ourselves with drugstore-bought sprays. Every new springtime brought bright metal cans adorned with festive pictures of dying insects. These made fine promises. These never quite worked. And every yard had its torches and candles and glowing red spirals, reeking of chemical orange stink, shamanistic totems to ward off the bugs. These never worked, either. Slapping still seemed the most practical method.

That, and the bug truck.

Most of the mosquitoes in the Snow Belt were no larger or more aggressive than, say, a rabid cat with wings. So it was possible to fight off the insect horde with our bare hands. But there was also, eventually, the wholesale approach: our town frequently doused itself and everything in sight with organophosphate poisons.

The fashionable toxins of choice, I would learn thirty years later, were called *cholinesterase inhibitors.* Large chemical companies will proudly tell you that these kill bugs quite dead by shutting down their neurological systems, inducing fatal little insect convulsions, but yet have, mind you, *no effect whatsogoddamever* on the neurology of children whose developing skin and lung tissues might become saturated on a daily basis.

Children like my sister.

I only have the one. Connie. She's five years older than me.

She's a talented musician, reliably able to produce a happy noise by blowing in one end of anything wooden with holes in it. Usually this involves a flute, but over the years I've brought her odd little contraptions from about nine different time zones, and dang if an hour later she isn't close to making some distant python start shaking its reticulated booty.

I just wish she could visit all the places the hollow bits of wood have come from.

One of the highlights of the annual warm summer night was the bug truck coming to spray. This was exactly what it sounds like: a big tanker thing, filled with poison, which would creep slowly down the street, its little nozzles spewing a sickly sweet mist in all directions.

Common sense apparently wasn't invented until some time later.

I still remember kids playing in the street as the truck went by. Their parents were sitting on doorsteps, many of them drinking beer, apparently talking about something other than what their children were being exposed to.

I still remember the smell. I suppose if you were curious, you could take a bottle of bug spray off the shelf, whiz a few blasts around at eye level, and suck in a lungful or two just for flavor. But I do not recommend this, although it would be a good time to wear rubberized safety goggles from the J. H. Gilbert Company of Willoughby, Ohio.

A decade later, Connie posed for a senior prom picture I still have. There's a wide hopefulness in her eyes, and an intelligence sharp enough to cut right through the suburban photographer's arty Vaseline-on-the-lens blur technique.

Not long after posing for that picture, Connie began to feel strangely weak, and her limbs became somewhat less reliable.

I'll spare you most of the following years.

You might be amazed how many different medical tests are capable of not telling you a thing. Most seem to involve large needles. It took almost a decade of probing and poking and lab-coated chin-stroking before finally Connie found a doctor who, puzzled at his first results, didn't reassure his own ego by quietly muttering it was all in her head.

Maybe ten years ago, the symptoms started getting more complicated. We'll never know exactly how it all overlapped or what developed when.

The early symptoms seem to line up with what you'd expect someone with Goddam Idiot Bug Truck Exposure to have. At least as far as we can tell, which isn't far. But later symptoms look more like autoimmune problems of some sort. I say "of some sort" because autoimmune thingies are themselves a medical guessing game.

For a year or two, Connie definitely, absolutely had multiple sclerosis. Until she probably didn't. Insert a new diagnosis every eighteen months or so, followed by a half-panicked home study course in Whatever the Hell It Is Now. Lather, rinse, repeat.

Each time, I would sit up at night, reading and studying and trying desperately to put this three-pound crinkly organ inside my skull to some earthly use. Trying to think even harder was the only defense I could come up with:

*If the cholinesterase inhibitors were the original cause or a complicating factor, maybe it would help if we just did a better job of maintaining her acetylcholine levels . . . there's a study that shows these can be manipulated by dietary intake of choline . . . choline is a component of vitamin B3 . . . I dunno, maybe I should get her a big tub of B3 and see if that helps . . . Oh, wait—is that backwards? Maybe that would just make things worse. I wish I knew what to do . . .*

Too bad the *Jeopardy!* categories rarely include AUTOIMMUNE DISORDERS. I would rule.

Fortunately, sometime between the prom picture and starting to fall down a lot for no reason, Connie was smart enough to marry a fellow named Rich, who has the patient resolve of a lighthouse. He's extremely skilled at driving to hospitals at night in the rain. Somehow in all this they've managed to raise two wise and kind kids who can beat me at any board game in the universe.

So things are more than OK. Things are good. Things are *great*.

Sometimes, though, I notice Connie's prom picture. I look at that young girl, just about to dance off into the future. She's still completely unaware of the hard left turn coming up. I want to warn her, or save her, or at least tell her to memorize how good her body feels right now, so she can replay the memory far into the future.

I think about what my sister has gone through since, year after frightening year. I feel guilty about my own perfect health. I think about how steady Rich has been. I marvel at the kids they've still managed to raise.

Sometimes water comes out of my eyes when I think about it.

Like right now, as I write these words. I'm sad and I'm happy and I'm angry and I'm grateful, all at once. I'm proud and I'm scared. And most of all, I'm so unable to do a goddam thing to change it all.

It's surprising how much water you actually have in your head. Entire buckets can pour out sometimes, spilling all over the floor.

So I might have bought rubber galoshes.

I don't blame anyone for Connie's illness. I certainly don't blame our folks. Our parents were farm people with little formal schooling, then employed in the sort of honest, endless work that requires wearing your name on your shirt and coming home tired with life. They did this since before Connie and I were born, just so we could exist.

Dad lifted things for a living, in a rectangular cavern owned by General Motors. I tagged along once when I was six years old. I remember thinking that there was nothing to read and it smelled like a gas station.

I also remember that the boxes were a hell of a lot bigger than Dad was. He never weighed more than 140 pounds in his life. I think our DNA must have included a few strands of ant.

Most of the time, Dad had to be at work at a very early hour—something like 4:00 a.m. the previous Tuesday—and so had to be in bed sometime early in the previous month. When he was working second or third shift (or both; he was *always* working), he had to sleep in the daytime. Connie and I still have to play very, very quietly in the living room for at least another three or four years.

Dad was a bright guy with virtually no education and no one who ever really encouraged him. So: two kids, house in the suburbs, play by the rules, and if that's not enough, then it's your own fault, and that's why God made beer. But he had a silly and constant sense of humor. If you smile or even laugh sometimes while reading this book, in those moments you're really seeing my dad. I promise.

Up before dawn, mind-numbing days doing backbreaking work, home and in bed. And again. He did this, no exaggeration, for thirty-seven years. For my sister and me.

I believe, although I cannot prove, that he had high hopes.

Mom had a name tag, too. Hers was pinned to a smock handed to her by Newberry's, a five-and-dime in a shopping mall surrounded by a half-mile rectangle of concrete.

In the days before box stores replaced entire small towns, Newberry's was the sort of place you'd run to three times a week, anytime you discovered you needed pliers, a Wiffle bat, a box of plastic party sporks, or perhaps a single staple.

If you went in the doors closest to the 25¢ mechanical horsie, you'd find Mom at a cash register, talking with someone named Bea (or sometimes Ethel).

Someone's dog would be sleeping against one wall. No one would mind.

You'd ask Mom about whatever item you were looking for—tea cozies, toy flutes, brake fluid, baby food, nine-volt batteries, fake vampire teeth, a protractor, baseball cards, or a Halloween mask of Harry Truman. And Mom would ask Bea (or sometimes Ethel) about it, and they would be certain your item was there somewhere.

Wait—Lillian might know where it is. So they'd ask Betty—who was walking by holding a live snake from the pet department—if Lillian was back from lunch. Pretty soon, someone else named Eleanor was asking Doris to page Marian.

About here, Olive would walk up, holding the same live snake from the pet department that Betty had, plus a large box of rubber balls. There would be no explanation.

Doris would ask what's going on, and then either Mom or Bea (or sometimes Ethel) would re-explain the saga in remarkable detail.

An hour later—after you'd bought the item somewhere else, returned home, and ultimately installed it, worn it, or eaten it—you'd find yourself going back to Newberry's, just out of curiosity.

You would find twenty-seven middle-aged women in smocks trying to get a boxful of rubber balls out of a live snake.

Mom would be awfully glad to see you again, though.

This might also explain why I went to the J. H. Gilbert Company. Newberry's was *always* running out of rubber balls.

If you came to our small white house not far from reclaimed marshland in the middle of the Snow Belt, Mom would offer you food.

This is how she tells you she likes you. It is also how she tells you she loves you.

It may also be how she tells you it's about to rain, or that the water heater is acting up again, or that there is a bunny outside in the backyard, quick, come look. There have been offers of food involved with each.

In the kitchen you will find, at all times: bagels in the fridge, pretzels on the table, pizzas and pierogis in the freezer, cookies in the cupboard, pasta on the stove, and lasagna in the oven. You will be expected to eat at least three.

You can make conversation by commenting on the large variety of knickknacks shaped like frogs and ducks. Several of the frogs are holding umbrellas. Discuss.

If Dad is awake and still alive, he will offer you a beer afterward. Then you will sit outside on the porch and not move for several hours. Soon you will fall asleep before you expect to and later awaken under a warm blanket you've never seen before.

If you get up and look around, Mom will be asleep in bed, but Dad will probably still be on the porch, sitting silently by himself. He was one of the men in the neighborhood with their shirts off, drinking beer on summer nights. Some nights there was more beer than Dad available.

I understand now that this was part of how he got himself ready to lift things for the rest of his life, but I was pissed about all the quiet for years afterward. And he was pissed at me for being pissed. But we started talking it all through, bit by bit, in the years after he was diagnosed, and we made our peace just a few hours before he died.

Dad had cancer. The doctors said that they got it all. But they didn't. Then they said the new medicine would make him better. Instead, it made him much, much worse.

When there were only a few days left, Mom and Connie and I took shifts at his side, making sure he would never be alone. I had the night watch.

I remember sitting with him in the silence of the hospital, wishing I hadn't hated all the quiet that had come before.

Of what he and I said to each other on the very last night—and we both knew this was the very last night—I remember every single word. Many were complete nonsense, in fact—silly quotes from Lewis Carroll, Ogden Nash, and Edward Lear—but that's getting ahead of the story again. In any case, it was the last time I ever saw Dad laugh. I'll remember that happy moment as long as I live.

You know how memory kicks in under stress.

The next day, when Dad was gone, rubber galoshes weren't nearly enough. Not for me, not for Connie, not for Mom.

I might have had to buy a rubber raft.

■ ■ ■

That weekend, I had to buy a pair of black dress shoes. I still have them. I've tried throwing them out, but they simply won't go. So they're in the big stack of boxes and bags in the spare bedroom.

I only wear them occasionally, when I have to dress up.

After Dad, I avoided alcohol completely for many years. It would be a long time before I was comfortable around Potent Potables.

A dear friend named Dan Melia would help me with that. But I hadn't quite met him in the *Jeopardy!* green room just yet.

Mom and Dad were both raised in an obscure Appalachian hamlet called Rose Hill, an hour by carriage from Cumberland Gap, the low spot where Tennessee, Virginia, and Kentucky converge. Daniel Boone once blazed a trail through the opening. A few generations later, my parents were born just up the road.

My father's dad taught him how to hunt dinner with a slingshot made from a tree branch and a long slice from a discarded inner tube. This grandfather could kill a squirrel with a rock, a stick, and a car tire from twenty paces. To be honest, he scared the crap out of me.

My mother's dad was a coal miner before becoming a Baptist minister. All things considered, he was very good around brimstone. He was so holy on Sundays that he could damn things for all eternity without even getting out of his chair. This grandfather scared the crap out of me, too.

Rose Hill was the sort of place where any child could stand on a hill and accurately predict the weather in three states for the next week, even if they'd never held a book in their hand.

My dad was one of those kids.

Up the road, you might find a family running its own little dairy farm, requiring a half-dozen children in bonnets to get up twelve hours before dawn to till the soil, gather wood, and rearrange the cows, all before walking three days to school each way with thirty-pound Bibles strapped to their backs, just to build up their strength in the Lord.

My mom was one of those kids.

In Rose Hill, large and hardworking families were a way of life, mandated both by infant mortality and a total lack of birth control. Simply producing enough food to keep all the mouths quiet was a sizable and sufficient test.

As a result, parenting skills—at least in my parents' own experience—were rightly judged by the percentage of children who reached adulthood with twenty fingers and toes, arrangement optional. Providing for survival was all the love there was time for.

So Dad lifted things that were too big for a man of his size. Mom still feeds people too much for their height. It took a long time to be grateful for what this actually meant. It is humbling to realize it now.

Still, our house wasn't exactly the Library of Alexandria. The few books we owned when I was very small featured Jesus as either the star or co-star. The one I remember most was a large, neatly bound *Concordance of the Bible*, which gave unto me a full and ceremonious list of all of the words used in the original, but rearranged by frequency of use into (if I understand this right) descending order of holiness.

If you're curious, the word "unto" turns out to be pretty damn holy—about ten percent holier than "Lord," even. I did the math. In fact, "unto" is almost twice as holy as "thou." But then, "all" is holier than "thou," too, so yes, everything's holier than thou, really.

I was reading the *Concordance*, for some reason, at an unexpectedly pink and squishy age. (My relatives disagree on the exact date; all I remember is the first word my eyes ever understood, under a cartoon of a red "h-a-t." *Hat.* A red *hat.* And a new world opened up.) The *Concordance* was a major interest when I was a small child. It's a bit of a slog, what with the complete lack of plot or character development, but it does have a certain postmodern flair.

Clearly, I would need to be in a place with more books.

A kindly first-grade teacher intervened on my behalf. Phone calls, interviews, and tests followed—fortunately, no needles—until I was finally whisked off on a scholarship to a lush and prideful all-male college-prep mill for the wealthy, twenty miles and three tax brackets from home. Modeled on the English tradition, this was Hogwarts without magic: a private academy with rows of students in little suit jackets, a motto in Latin, ritual morning assemblies, and processionals by Elgar reverberating in every wall.

I was eight years old. I was scared to death. I said OK and just tried not to pee.

There will be times in this book when I exaggerate a little, trying to keep you entertained. You may have noticed this. The next eleven sentences will not be one of those times.

To this day, the school symbol is an interlocking "U" and "S," strongly resembling the dollar sign itself. (In fact, the school was founded in 1890, and this exact symbol was how the U.S. Mint often marked bags of currency in the nineteenth century.) The football team is actually called the Preppers. The most famous alumnus is Jim Backus, the actor who played the tycoon Thurston Howell III on *Gilligan's Island*. You can guess where he found inspiration.

The other kids' parents seemed to own everything in town. The father of one of the kids across the hall owned the Cleveland Browns. Dad couldn't even afford tickets. We never went, although we watched almost every single televised game, year after year.

Mom and Dad were so proud of me for getting this chance. They told their friends, and then told me about telling their friends.

Which was a wow. Dad was so busy lifting things and Mom was so busy helping Marian find the glue gun that getting such intense and vocal approval, so regularly, was a startling and glorious thing. No way was I ever giving that up.

However, some of the wealthier kids at Hogwarts didn't always take kindly to a younger, poorer, smaller kid screwing up the curve in Newberry's-employee-discount clothing. Imagine *Lord of the Flies* with a better supply of underpants, and you've got the idea.

All considered, it was both (a) a frequent source of physical terror, and (b) more than a working-class kid could have hoped for. This is a very confusing combination.

It's too bad that the J. H. Gilbert Company did not sell rubber rooms. I probably could have used one.

To this day I still get quarterly Alumni Notes from the school. Many of my former classmates, after honing their sharpest skills at the best Ivy League schools, are now bankers, civic leaders, and corporate titans. They are well-groomed, square-jawed, fondly remembered, respected by all, and passing their privileges down to their own beloved children.

Who are probably strangling cats.

Revenge, when it came, came always in displays of intellect. Eventually I graduated at the top of my class. This was not because I cared about knowing much of anything, by the end, but more as a way to prove I could not be broken.

I once went to the hospital with a knot on my skull made by the cement locker-room floor. The next week I struck back at my attackers in math and history class, piling facts on their chests until they couldn't breathe. I wanted them to see the emergency room, too, suffering from limited functions and Peloponnesia.

College, after that, was oddly uninteresting. Everything I had ever learned, I had learned as a counterpunch. Every "A" was a right hook unthrown. Suddenly those people were gone.

So was my reason to learn.

Unsure what to do next, I chose what seemed practical, even stable: I majored in electrical engineering. But my college still had rotary phones in the dorms. This was hardly encouraging.

It didn't help that I was two years younger than the others in my class—I was sixteen when I first arrived at college—and convinced that my obituary would include the word "virgin," possibly in the headline. Uninterested in my own major, I spent most of college hanging around the campus radio station, doing an all-night jazz show and trying to pick up girls.

By the time I graduated, I knew a little about music, how to do large amounts of work, and how to chat lightly while nervous without passing out. Do not underestimate the importance of these three things.

Despite my near-ignorance of both Applied Pong and Pong Theory, I managed nonetheless to land a job in the field, working for a defense contractor, learning to show military guys from a friendly dictatorship how to flip switches on things that went *zip, zzzzzap*, and (ultimately) *boom*. It took a while before I understood exactly for whom I was ultimately working. Once I did, I didn't want to. So: lift things, drink in silence, and everyone would be proud.

One morning, however, the car surprised me by bluntly refusing to drive to work. Instead, it just drove on its own, for four solid hours, back to the small white house not far from reclaimed marshland in the Snow Belt.

Mom offered me food. Dad drank a beer.

I can't imagine how many times my dad got through his day by thinking proudly that his son was at least going to attend college, get a useful degree, and make something of himself in the world. Now that was gone.

I was twenty years old and already a complete failure.

I turned to my favorite holy book for words of guidance. But *the*, *and*, and *of* were no use.

If the J. H. Gilbert Company of Willoughby, Ohio, had sold rubber erasers large enough, I probably wouldn't be here right now.

Meanwhile, on almost the very day my car suddenly decided it needed to go home and start over, Merv Griffin had just reanimated a certain defunct quiz show. And for some reason, Mom and Dad would put *Jeopardy!* on and watch it five times a week. Channel 5, 7:30 p.m., right after the Ohio Lottery drawing that Dad lost five dollars on every night.

Usually I'd come downstairs and watch it with them. So this became our routine: Mom, Dad, Alex, and I would play this game. (There were other people playing the game, too, but we only noticed a few.) I was puzzled at the time by my parents' instant loyalty to the show. Every single night. Even though they didn't know many of the answers. Some nights they barely even seemed interested. Strange. Mom would knit something warm for someone to sleep under, and Dad would chew on his three-starch dinner and sip his beer.

Alex, for his part, was always impeccable. He was, after all, Alex Trebek: he of the *Magnum, P.I.* mustache and laser-sharp suits. I remembered him from the daytime game *High Rollers*, which I'd watched as a curious boy just to glimpse Ruta Lee's leg curl when she kissed him on the cheek.

Alex would zip through the clues every night, rolling through phrases in Latin and Urdu with impossible ease. I'd try to fire back, with Mom and Dad occasionally chiming in bits of their own expertise:

"What is Chrysler?" or "Who's Robert Kennedy?" The three of us combined probably knew half of the responses.

Occasionally, Connie and Rich would swing by from their hope-filled newlywed home, but during the game, they'd always find something to do in the kitchen instead. It wasn't hard to see why. Connie had taught me to read *hat*, after all. Soon I got the scholarship to the private school. She didn't. And she didn't attend college, either. There wasn't enough money for more than one of us. I was the prep-school kid.

Slowly I saw that all of the privilege-parading I'd resented in my classmates—the sheer damn self-entitled unappreciation for luck—I had been inflicting on Connie for years. And now the college education she didn't get, I had just wasted.

Some things are so large that even an apology sounds wrong.

Connie and Rich always found a way to spend those thirty minutes in the kitchen, rearranging the dumplings, making sure all the frogs and the ducks shared their umbrellas. I understood, while wishing I didn't.

I never imagined I might someday compete on the *Jeopardy!* stage, or that Connie might watch with delight, or that the results might one day help her recover from having bones rearranged.

Besides, the players were simply too good.

I felt impossibly dumb next to one talented fellow, Chuck Forrest, a law student from a snowy small Midwestern town a short drive from my parents' own house. Chuck was as young as I was, but he won five games in runaways, inflicting severe thumbily harm while lightly maintaining a college-kid grin. Chuck set a new record for winnings while bouncing through clues with a fearless abandon that confused other players, including me in the Snow Belt on Mom and Dad's couch.

Before long, Chuck had also won the $100,000 Tournament of Champions. He was self-assured and well versed and on his way with his life. I could not imagine what that would be like.

A few years later, as my early adulthood was taking the form of long days on the road, I remember also shrinking from Frank Spangenberg, a huge and gruff-looking New York transit cop with a walrus mustache and dark, hooded eyes. Frank was fascinating: he had the body of a linebacker, the amiable demeanor of Captain Kangaroo, and the knowledge of your average talking science-fiction computer. He quickly established a new five-game record for winnings that stood for over a decade.

Like Chuck, the buoyant Boy Wonder before him, Frank could be quizzed in seemingly any category—FRENCH LITERATURE, QUANTUM MECHANICS, PLACES TO DUMP A BODY, THINGS ALEX LEFT IN HIS CAR—and Frank would buzz in, smile through his eight-pound mustache, and answer with the calm, vaguely disturbing assurance of HAL himself. And when the show held a special 10th Anniversary Tournament of previous champions, Frank won that, too. (Chuck, however, was working overseas and couldn't participate. It seemed clear that a cage match would be needed someday.)

Damn. I felt small.

Sometimes I think it would be nice to go back and tell the twenty-year-old me that one day I would actually meet Chuck and Frank. I would join them, in fact, in a tournament at Radio City Music Hall, competing for a million dollars. Then again, I think the twenty-year-old me would have passed out on the spot.

The forty-year-old came pretty darn close.

So I'd sit there with Mom and Dad for that half hour. Every single night.

Then I'd go back upstairs and stare at my future, trying to squint and tilt my head until I could make out some of its details. I couldn't see anything but a giant blur.

The blur would turn out to be an accurate depiction. In the years since, I've had at least six different careers you'd call full-time, fourteen addresses I can remember in four states and the District of Columbia, and more than a few nights sleeping in airports or the backseat of Max. I've lived in shared rooms, fancy condos, tiny apartments, luxury houses, and even the YMCA. (About which: I will confirm that you can get yourself clean, and you can have a good meal. You *cannot*, however, do whatevah you feel. Especially if whatevah you feel is the need to move the hell into a real apartment.)

I have few regrets. But the possible items I may have bought from the J. H. Gilbert Company of Willoughby, Ohio, now seems like a staggering list.

The first time I ever thought about trying out for *Jeopardy!* was also the first time I ever visited California. I was toiling on the edges of the music industry, which is to say I was surrounded by people whose fashion, moral, and business instincts were largely inspired by Colombian crime lords. (From what I understand, the entire music business at that time was much like the illegal drug trade, only with more drugs.)

A business trip had sent me to Los Angeles for a week in November. In preparation, my boss provided careful instructions on how to wear my *Miami Vice*–inspired sport jacket with the sleeves pushed up to show, as he actually phrased it, "just the right amount of forearm." This mattered greatly.

I played along, since it was a chance to glimpse the guidebook version of L.A.: Melrose, Beverly Hills, Venice, the Strip, and always, always the ocean. This was exciting. But that's not the main thing I remember feeling.

I remember feeling warm.

"Comfortable outside" wasn't something we had in the Snow Belt, especially in November. November was eight months into winter, the month we'd usually start getting sympathy letters from the Russian infantry.

So one night, in Santa Monica, I stood on a hundred-foot bluff overlooking the Pacific and vowed that someday I would live here in the sun forever, never be cold again, and devote myself to forgetting things as hard as I could. I'd find a job, or maybe, I dunno, win money on that quiz show, in the process of all that forgetting.

I also resolved that someday I would meet a girl and propose to her on that very spot. I even made a mental note of the location, so I could be sure of finding it again.

As it happened, I was standing between a park bench and a dirt path, about half a block from a fifteen-foot religious statue that looked like a giant penis. It's still there, a singular object even the J. H. Gilbert Company of Willoughby, Ohio, might have found challenging to sheathe.

I didn't know much about memory yet. But I was pretty sure I could remember *that*.

■ ■ ■

This is another one of those spots where I'm not exaggerating for the next eleven sentences:

A few years later I actually did stand on that exact spot with a girl I was madly in love with. Her name was Tonya, and I asked her to marry me. Not only did she say yes, we even went ahead and said the vows, right there, the sea as our only witness, promising forevers, tears filling our eyes.

About a year after that she started sleeping with her boss, although she didn't tell me about it for a while. Not until Christmas Eve, in fact, which she apparently thought was a good time to tell me. We stayed up all night, breaking up, and she left on Christmas morning, shortly before it was time to watch my niece and nephew open their presents.

A few months later she moved to Ecuador. I have no idea why she chose Ecuador. I never saw her again.

The spot we were standing on later collapsed in a mudslide, plummeting over the cliff for good.

I've been a little twitchy about commitment ever since.

I'll skip most of the other One-True-Eternal-Soulmates™. You're already through Leviticus and Deuteronomy. By the time you reach Thessalonians, you see the plot coming anyway.

Clearly, I've been doing something wrong.

Maybe I should stop dating women in eleven-sentence increments.

Eventually, on that first day I was sitting in the makeup chair, my current One-True-Eternal-Soulmate™ was the quiet, pretty, intelligent schoolteacher named Annika, the one motionless enough to wear bees. She had two master's degrees, spoke several languages, did occasional volunteer work for the poor, and was completely trustworthy. We both had rewarding careers, we were in perfect health, and all of our friends approved.

Clearly, this could never work.

Money, or at least my part of our money, was getting tight. I was actually working several part-time creative jobs, all of which paid more in ego than actual cash. The best one was a radio gig I'd had for about a year, doing commentaries and humor for the top-rated news station in

California. I was on every day, in afternoon drive time, and I had even won several awards. Finally. I was doing something Mom and Dad's memory could be proud of.

I didn't usually mention that this paid exactly thirty-five dollars a day. Before taxes and union dues.

I was afraid. I could go back on the road and make money that way, but that would mean more time away. This wouldn't make life any more stable.

I hadn't yet told Annika about my money problems. But if something didn't work out soon, I might not be able to pay the rent. And since I'd let things go this far, that could easily seem like a breach of trust, even meaning the end of our relationship. It might even mean going back to Ohio. Another whole round of failure.

There was no way I could face the family again. Not at this age. It was one thing to return home after college; now my entire adulthood was starting to look like mistake after mortifying mistake.

And then a makeup lady got some goo on the inside of my left nostril.

Less than an hour later, I wanted more. *Lots* more.

CHAPTER

8

EVENING FALLS

Also, A Fifty-Foot Wall
in My Head

My first game had been the fifth and final show of that day. Since *Jeopardy!* is recorded on Tuesdays and Wednesdays, I would normally have had either one or six nights to prepare for the next game. However, because of a scheduling quirk—I had played on a Wednesday evening, just before a two-week Teen Tournament, to be followed by a series of celebrity games played by Washington political figures—my next taping date was still weeks away. (Personally, I wanted to see the teens play the politicos. We all know exactly who would have won.)

I had made it through the first trial thanks to my Jedi buzzer technique and large amounts of pure luck. Now came another amazing bit of good fortune: I had extra time to study.

To win four more games, all I needed to do was somehow simulate a complete liberal-arts education.

I had just under three weeks.

First things first: Remember the lesson of Halloween. Consider the broadcast dates for the next four games: November 24 through 27. My potential fifth game was scheduled for Thanksgiving Day. I was about to become rather expert on the *Mayflower*.

Second things second: maintaining my Jedi state-dependent retrieval buzzer skills would be paramount. I would need to set up the VCR to tape every game, so I could practice several times a day. But for the most accurate rehearsals possible, merely tapping my finger on my thigh or a table would not be enough.

I would need a practice buzzer.

A simple plan: I would just find a ballpoint pen, remove part of the clicky bit so it would simply spring, then wind this in masking tape to the desired weight, shape, and size. That should work.

OK. Now I would give myself bright lights, a podium, and the sound of Alex speaking from my right side. At a minimum, this would involve rearranging the furniture.

I should add, incidentally: I had not yet left the Sony parking garage.

I made the practice buzzer the next day. I still have it. I've used it before every tournament. It's my second-favorite memento of the show.

Still, it's a strange thing to have on a shelf. It feels like a real *Jeopardy!* buzzer in your hand, but it doesn't visually resemble one at all. It looks a lot more like something you'd be caught with in an unseemly scandal involving grainy photos, hush money, and a mysterious blonde fleeing to Mexico. I had to explain it to every woman I ever dated, even if they already knew about my *Jeopardy!* games. This was usually a source of amusement, albeit with some furrowed brows or even mild expressions of concern.

Jane was the only person who ever guessed what it was at first glance. In fact, she picked it up, pushed the button a few times, and turned it over in her hand, as if comparing it with the one she would have made herself. Then she looked around at my overflowing shelves and the hip-high piles of reference books, the ones now jammed into cardboard boxes in her apartment, and grinned as if she wanted to sift through them all, too.

Looking back down at the practice buzzer, she asked an interesting question.

"What do they call these things, exactly? They can't *really* be called 'buzzers' . . ."

You've already peeked in on the rest of that day, involving champagne and the renaming of the Signaling Device.

We had no idea what was coming just a few months later.

For obvious reasons, *Jeopardy!* doesn't allow you to share the outcome, no matter how much you want to leap ahead in your story, with anyone but immediate family and close friends. And they're not allowed to tell a soul. The safest thing, in fact, is not to let anyone you know leave the house until the whole thing blows over.

The first rule of Fight Club is: You do not talk about Fight Club.

This is elaborated in a pre-taping legal agreement, much of it in fifth-century Latin, drafted in lamb's blood on goatskin seized during the Crusades. (Sony's attorneys are *very* well connected.) You seal the folded contract by pricking your buzzer finger with a needle and pressing it down quickly into a blob of hot wax—leaving a clear print, a DNA sample, and a blood oath all at once—and this entire deal goes straight into a positronic vault, where it can be accessed by Sony lawyers at any point in history.

I'm exaggerating mildly, but this stuff really should be taken seriously: the show's very existence, not to mention the jobs of everyone involved and any chance whatsoever of playing in future tournaments, depends largely on the audience not knowing the outcome.

The second rule of Fight Club is: You *do not* talk about Fight Club.

There were exactly three people I was sure I was definitely allowed to tell: my sister Connie, my mom, and Annika.

Since I didn't yet own a mobile phone—this was the Bronze Age, remember—I would have to fight traffic for an hour before I could get home and make some calls.

I passed the time by telling my memory of Dad all about it.

When I finally got home, I called Connie first. She couldn't have been more pleased. She wasn't doing very well physically, though. Marvin was acting up again.

"Marvin," I should explain, is the name we have given to the endless catalog of maladies that meander in and out of Connie's flesh. What the name "Marvin" lacks in clinical specificity, it makes up for in convenience. And since autoimmune diagnoses are largely guesswork anyway, it's just about as accurate.

Marvin's health and Connie's are inversely proportional: if Connie's feeling vigorous, Marvin is very sick or possibly on his deathbed. And vice versa.

When I called after the first game of *Jeopardy!*, Marvin had just learned flamenco, and he was thumping his heels on Connie's last nerve. And still, Connie was truly happy for me. Her voice became noticeably less weary when I told her how things went.

We talked and laughed for a while. I remember wishing very hard I could trade all of my good fortune for a way to make Connie feel better.

I called Mom next. She picked up on the first ring.

She was, in her own word, tickled. And then I told her the broadcast date and a bit of my already-forming plan of attack for the next four shows: weeks of hammering thousands of possible short answers into my skull, rearranging the furniture, buying a bunch of bright lights . . .

"And what does Annika think about all this?"

There are times when my mom can talk for hours about nothing besides an animal that hopped through the backyard two days ago, some new and exciting carbohydrate, or what fell over down at Newberry's.

But sometimes Mom cuts right to the point.

Annika got home a little late that night. This wasn't unusual. She was working as a public school teacher at the time, so it sometimes took an extra hour just to peel off the Kevlar.

I was always amazed that a creature this small and quiet could somehow command an overcrowded room full of strange and hyperactive children. I admire her to this day.

And this comes from a former stand-up comic, mind you. I've worked 3:00 a.m. prom nights in Manhattan, strip clubs in the Ozarks, and biker bars on the Mexican border. And there's no way I'd set foot in the job Annika did. There must have been a much tougher side to her that I never saw.

Or maybe I just didn't pay enough attention to see past my own assumptions, or I was too lost in my own thoughts to care. Maybe the *Jeopardy!* coordinators aren't the only people I just grunted at while thinking ahead.

I told Annika the news about *Jeopardy!* before she'd even gotten in the door. In my hurry, I'm not sure I even said hello. This was ego, of course. I was ready to feel like a hero, and wanted only to see this re-flected in her face.

Finally, a long stare, followed by a slight eye-roll, and then:

"You're really going to rearrange the furniture?" said with equal dollops of bafflement and horror.

I guess even Mom knew that was coming.

Still, the slightest bit of joy might have been nice.

Some moments march upon you with voices shouting and clocks ticking down their arrival. Births, graduations, marriages, prizes on fabulous game shows—all will be enormous, with flashing lights and band music and sometimes even love, and they will carry no surprise. Things will have changed. You will know when and how.

Some moments creep up silently, unannounced. They will be small, and slip upon you before your guard is ready. You will feel a shift and not know why.

Some moments just come.

Sudden, unexpected clarity: Annika and I were becoming strangers.

Looking back, I had known deep down that the relationship was in trouble long before this moment. On some unacknowledged level, it wasn't that big a surprise. But even afterward, I wouldn't admit it to my-self, much less try to do anything about it, for months.

This is a fairly clunky approach to happiness. It's also nothing unusual.

I later learned that the human brain is profoundly averse on a me-chanical level to integrating new connections that cross wires with established neural pathways. When a pathway is large and complex enough to be named, we call it a "belief" or an "attitude" or "that god-damned habit of yours, Harold." But it's ultimately a tangle of well-connected neurons. And these are extremely hard to cross, sometimes as physically insurmountable as a fifty-foot wall. More so, in fact, since they're invisible, and buried inside your own head.

Even trivial thoughts can color our ability to see reality. How many times have you looked in vain for a particular item—car keys, eyeglasses, maybe facial tissue in a green room—convinced that it had suddenly disappeared, only to notice that it was, in fact, squarely in plain view all the time, often in a spot you had looked at directly? This is called *cognitive dissonance*, and it's a common form of this inability of the brain to cross-wire itself. If you don't *think* the keys exist anymore, *poof!*—they *don't*, at least between your ears.

The effect is even more powerful with long-held beliefs, whose neural pathways have had more time to grow and strengthen with rehearsal, developing numerous connections to strong reinforcing emotions. Such beliefs often become filters through which the world is viewed; the only facts and ideas we can even *see* are those that fit into the existing pattern.

Therefore, most of the time, our mental model of the world—including mine as I write this and yours as you read—are less a measure of reality than an echo chamber for existing sensations and emotions. Everything from "I'm doomed to be fat" to "I'm not a good listener" to "I fail under pressure" to "Norwegians are always mean to me" can become cardinal tenets, personal boundaries that we simply cannot cross.

You can actually see this acted out on *Jeopardy!* several times each week. You'll often see a contestant in second or third place get a Daily Double so late in the game that a large wager is their only real chance to win. And almost always—not *some* of the time, mind you, not *most* of the time, but almost *all* of the time—that player will not bet enough to take the lead. Instead, they'll bet small, apologizing to no one in particular with a little shrug.

In that moment, they have *chosen* to lose.

Whether or not they respond correctly, they have guaranteed that they will trail entering Final Jeopardy. And since good players respond correctly to most Final Jeopardys, that's usually that.

On the other hand, most players also respond correctly to most

Daily Doubles. So a large bet makes a win the most likely outcome of a "risky" large wager, even though the game might have seemed out of reach.

Why do people do this? The same reason my father worked for thirty-seven years in a factory he hated. The same reason I stayed in (and, in truth, cultivated) bad relationships. The same reason you probably do something in your life, right this minute, that you wish you didn't.

All change is hard, even good change, like winning something. It's hard for any of us to imagine real alternatives to our expectations, so they're what we often wind up with. Which reinforces the existing pathways in what can become an inescapable loop.

I sometimes wonder if natural selection didn't reward our ability to bullshit ourselves in precisely this fashion. If two hominids were both fleeing a large, fast predator, and one of them was sincerely thinking "I am safe, I am exceptional, the gods are watching over me, and I cannot die" and the other was thinking "AIEEE! I'm an entrée! *AAIEEE!*" it's not hard to guess which one got dragged back by his entrails.

With Annika (and Tonya and Leviticus and Zachariah), I couldn't imagine how things could be otherwise, what I could do differently, or what I could value differently. On the other hand, my high-school revenge-training had put such a value on intellectual competition that, even while *filled* with self-doubt, once a *Jeopardy!* game started, on some level I couldn't imagine *not* winning.

This leads us to our next step down the Eightfold Path:

1. Obvious things may be worth noticing.
2. Remember the basics: the basics are what you remember.
3. Put your head where you can use it later.
4. Doing nothing is better than doing something really stupid.
5. Admit you don't know squat as often as possible.
6. Everything connects to everything else.
7. You can often see only what you think you'll see.

So the night I came home from my first game, Annika and I actually had a pleasant evening. The undercurrents of mutual dissatisfaction stayed where they were. I convinced myself that clarity was not worth noticing.

I told her of my exciting day dodging intellectual bullets. I'm not sure if I even asked about her day, which for all I know may have involved dodging real ones. We ate burritos and laughed reassuringly and went to bed convinced everything was fine.

But neither one of us went back to discussing the furniture.

Next up: gathering study materials.

Fortunately, between the time I passed the test and *Jeopardy!* startled me by actually calling, I had stumbled across a book called *Secrets of the Jeopardy Champions* by Mark Lowenthal and Chuck Forrest, both of whom had impressive successes on the show.

Chuck, you recall, had spooked the crap out of me when I was still sitting on the couch in the small white house in the Snow Belt, watching the show with my silent parents and hoping someday to become a functional grown-up. Chuck was a better player than I could ever hope to be.

Part of what made Chuck memorable was his pure bravado. In September of 1985 he pioneered a technique (still called the "Forrest Bounce") in which he selected clues not in simple vertical lines but by hopscotching back and forth across the game board, continually changing categories.

At the time, the Bounce was a surprising move. Contestants aren't required to play straight down the board, but it's easier for the camera and graphics people to follow, not to mention the folks at home whose viewership pays for the whole shebang. So the contestant wranglers always give the players a little pre-game chat in which the show's technical preferences are made clear. Besides, playing in straight columns is also easier for most players, since responding to a simple $200 clue eliminates one possible answer for the difficult clues to come.

Chuck was the first player to defy convention, careening wildly about the board, with devastating results. His confidence in his own mental agility to change topics every twelve seconds distracted his competitors enough that they never once found their footing. Five wins later, he was $72,800 richer.

Accounting for inflation, that would be over $125,000 in current dollars. (Suddenly the recent doubling in value of the clues seems merely a cost-of-living adjustment.)

Chuck accomplished all this while he was still just a law student.

Meanwhile, I was sitting on a couch in the Snow Belt, my own college years and original plans for adulthood receding from sight.

I played along a few times. Chuck responded to almost twice as many clues as I could.

I could never acquire access to Chuck's education, but dammit, I could still crack his book and cram like hell. *Secrets of the Jeopardy Champions* was filled with long lists of stuff Chuck said I must learn, and fast. And it was still right there on my shelf, intact, and ready for immediate use.

This was to become my new *Concordance of the Bible*: words and facts stripped of context, yet all impossibly significant in mysterious and hopeful ways.

I was ready to receive the holy knowledge within.

I took a deep breath, flipped through the pages, and hoped for wisdom.

Chuck told of U.S. PRESIDENTS and CONSTITUTIONAL AMENDMENTS and KEY SUPREME COURT DECISIONS. NATIONAL CAPITALS and RIVERS THROUGH BIG CITIES and HIGHEST POINTS ON EACH CONTINENT. FAMOUS DRAMATISTS and AMERICAN NOVELISTS and POETS OF THE WORLD.

*Yes*, I said out loud. *Thank you, Chuck*, I said.

So Chuck kept going. I flipped a page, and then flipped three more. Chuck reeled off BRITISH ROYALTY, SPANISH EXPLORERS, and FRENCH IMPRESSIONIST PAINTERS. GREEK SCULPTORS and ITALIAN COMPOSERS.

*OK, this is good*, I said, flipping ten pages, then twenty. *Don't hold back.*

Chuck picked up speed. 18TH CENTURY PHILOSOPHERS, 19TH CENTURY INVENTORS, 20TH CENTURY POPES. GERMAN INVENTORS, JAPANESE GENERALS, OTTOMAN KINGS.

*I can do this*, I said, though my eyes were beginning to tire. *I can do this.*

CHEMISTS and PHYSICISTS and ANTHEMS and ANTONYMS. FLORA and FAUNA and SLOGANS and PSEUDONYMS. TONYS and EMMYS and OSCARS and PULITZERS. DEITIES, DEMONS, and DEMIGOD*dammit, Chuck.*

I was breathing heavily. The room was beginning to spin.

*Give me a second here, OK?* Bright lights and loud noises were starting to swerve through my head. *I think I may need to lie down.*

Chuck didn't hear me.

JURASSIC ANATOMY, SOUTHERNMOST VEGETABLES, TRANSGENDERED ANEMONES. *Chuck, please.* HINDUS NAMED STEVE. TINY DUTCH ASTRONAUTS. *For the love of God! Stop!* ALTERED STATES, INNER BEINGS. *No, please! I'm scared!* BLACK HOLES, BOUNDARY PHYSICS, STRING THEORY, STATE SECRETS . . .

*Chuuuuuuuuucck!*

Finally . . . silence.

The Forrest Bounce had claimed another victim. I made a drastic concession.

I would need at *least* another week of studying memory books first.

It would be nice if we were taught as children a bit about how to actively *use* our brains, instead of just carting them around like spine-mounted lint rollers, hoping a few things stick.

Unfortunately, like me, a lot of you were told *what* to learn, but not *how*: here are your textbooks—*plop!*—and good luck. No operating instructions, no owner's manual, and if you can't figure out where the On button is, then it's your own fault for getting a bad unit.

We all know what often happens next: a staring contest with an inanimate object. The book usually wins. We're reduced to repeating words and formulas like religious chants, hoping that the brute weight of time will somehow crack open our foreheads and allow the information to seep in.

Rote repetition does work somewhat. Repeating any neural sequence over and over will eventually cause the synaptic connections to strengthen, much as flowing water will eventually cut through solid rock. Since this works eventually, a lot of us just get used to learning this way and assume that's the best we can do.

Worse, since we're taught using books with numbered pages, it only seems natural to try to remember things in a fairly linear fashion, connecting the information only to what came on the page before. Unfortunately, as we've seen, this runs counter to your brain's physical architecture and chemical mechanisms.

Now let's try learning some stuff the fast way. (Incidentally, some of what follows has been known for centuries, while some is the result of relatively recent research. Some of this will be found in the self-help section of any bookstore, and some is my own personal amalgam of everything I've read and put into practice concerning memory, neurology, and snickering quietly under your breath in a library.)

We'll start with something very *Jeopardy!*-like, a list of novels by E. M. Forster:

**E. M. Forster novels**
*A Room with a View*
*Howards End*
*A Passage to India*
*Where Angels Fear to Tread*
*Maurice*

Then we'll up the ante with a different task, a series of items you need to remember in a specific order. In this case, we'll use the seven main ranks usually used by biologists to classify living things in a big giant diagram:

**The hierarchy of life**
Kingdom
Phylum
Class
Order
Family
Genus
Species

And just to enjoy a brutal little challenge, let's complicate things with something horribly arcane, hard-to-pronounce, and downright dull enough to resemble the sorts of things we often have to know in school, even against our will:

**UN Secretaries-General**
Trygve Lie
Dag Hammarskjöld
U Thant
Kurt Waldheim
Javier Perez de Cuellar
Boutros Boutros-Ghali
Kofi Annan

Those of you who still advocate rote learning, please repeat all of the above, over and over, until you're certain you'll remember it all perfectly in a week.

Feeling confident already? Good. Close the book. I'll see you in seven days.

Everybody else, prepare to be as childish as possible.

Since anything can be linked to anything else, we can *always* free-associate from the stuff we want to remember, looking for sticky images involving visceral issues of rapid movement and bright color and bodily functions and food and threat and sex and danger.

Take *Howards End*, for example.

Yes, definitely. Let's start there.

Aha! You're getting ahead of me already, aren't you? Yes, yes, I thought so. Very good. (An aside to the prudish or easily offended: go away. Go away right now. We're studying British Literature here. We shan't be disturbed.)

I'll bet there's someone you know named Howard. I'll also assume, for the sake of argument, that your Howard has buttocks.

If not, get another Howard.

If you don't have a good Howard handy, just use someone else's:

Howard Hughes, Howard Stern, Howard Cunningham (the fictional father from *Happy Days*), Howard Alan O'Brien (novelist Anne Rice's real name), or Moe, Shemp, and Curly Howard of the Three Stooges. You can even use Howard University, although this will take some organizing.

Pick a Howard, grab him or her or them by the gluteus, get a good clear mental picture—complete with as much detail as you can stand—and now let's attach that *Howard's particular End* to the rest of the list, one by one.

Let's imagine *A Room with a View*.

Of, obviously: *Howard's End*.

(I'll be misspelling *Howards End* hereafter, including the possessive apostrophe for clarity's sake. Thirty-foot buttocks often require such flexibility.)

So let's picture ourselves in a big empty room with a floor-to-ceiling bay window, and then mentally shove our *Howard's End* into view, filling the window completely, a giant throbbing thirty-foot-wide buttocks of doom.

Do not continue until you see it clearly.

Didn't take long, did it? Notice that "memorable" and "logical" are different and often contrary things. Now we should do something sticky with the room itself.

Let's look at *Where Angels Fear to Tread*. For this, we can use a member of the Angels baseball team (or the halo kind of angel, or Charlie's Angels, or any angel image that pops into your head; it's usually best to trust your own first instinct), and now create a circumstance *Where Angels* really would *Fear to Tread*.

Thumbtacks, maybe. Or—much better, because it involves unexpected motion and danger, always interesting to our inner beast—let's imagine an enormous sucking force threatening to pull our Angel helplessly up and away if he dares set foot in the room. The Angel is now filling with Fear of this whole Treading thing. Excellent.

This is good and scary and odd. So now our *Angels Fear to Tread* in *A Room with a View*. And what is the source of this vacuum-like force?

*Howard's End*, of course. *Whooosh!*

That wasn't so hard, was it?

If you're feeling a little guilty about being amused by thoughts like this, don't. It's utterly human, just your brain doing what it's wired to do. In fact, if you're smiling right now, *that's how you know you'll remember it.* Laughter is a visceral reaction that means your brain is going into Record mode.

Laughter provoked *by* visceral imagery is even more memorable. Ask any drunk to tell you a joke, and you'll get instant proof that even pungent alcohol can't overcome the most primitive neural connections.

So. That leaves just one question: If we let ourselves be pulled along with the fearful *Angel,* and we turn and focus our attention from the *Room with a View,* what do we see in the distance, *in* our thirty-foot *Howard's End?* What, pray tell, are we being pulled so forcefully toward?

*A Passage to India.*

In fact, if you're in the *Room with a View* and looking at *Howard's End* from just the right angle, you can just barely glimpse the Taj Majal.

OK. There's a chance now that you're just appalled. So cover the whole thing up in your mind with a forest—one built by a "forester" himself, in fact—and never, ever go back. Oh, the shame of it all.

Unless a week from now you want your Forster to pull back the trees and reveal *A Room with a View* where *Angels Fear to Tread* because *Howard's End* sucks everything in sight toward *A Passage to India.*

Two or three damn minutes, that took. With a bit of review in the next day or two, you'll probably remember most of it for years.

I swear this on my own eventual grave: If you get good at this, learning the driest subjects can quickly turn into endless outbursts of childish giggling.

If you ever saw me play *Jeopardy!* and wondered why I was smiling at odd moments during clues, now you know why. The other players might have been intensely focused on RUSSIAN BATTLES or FRENCH ROYALTY or ASIAN CITIES or whatever. Me, I was mostly remembering a lot of naked people throwing things on fire at each other's butts.

Years after first creating that image, I learned that E. M. Forster had written a novel called *Maurice* as well.

No worries. I just tossed Maurice Gibb of the Bee Gees into Howard's End—*thwup!*—and sent him on his merry way toward New Delhi.

Took all of two seconds. Whoosh, *glurk*, new knowledge.

Obviously this has absolutely nothing to do with knowing *anything* about Forster himself or his novels or his place in literary history. Not one bit.

But it *is* extremely useful for connecting together and learning any pile of stuff that doesn't have to be in a particular order. And that can often be a real foothold on any subject.

What we've just done, incidentally, is also an example of "chunking," the fancy word for remembering stuff by grouping things together. You do this every time you use a telephone area code or consider a chorus as one refrain instead of four lines or thirty-odd words. You don't need to know the term, but you do want to get in the habit. Organizing and grouping information together so it all sticks at once can be amazingly powerful.

How cool would it be for our world if a first-grade class could quickly learn the names of all the states and their capitals, and laugh in the process? If junior-high kids could buzz through the Bill of Rights and major Supreme Court rulings, making the time spent in the classroom more about discussion and understanding?

In the short term, of course, all I had in mind was only one purpose: getting me through *Jeopardy!*

Long-term, I had no idea how my own world would start to change as a result.

Sometimes you need information in a specific order, as when trying to memorize how scientists divvy up life. No worries.

Given a list, you've probably looked at least once at the first initials, hoping they might spell out a recognizable word or an acronym. Unfortunately, this almost never works, beyond FACE for the notes between the lines of a treble-clef music staff, NAY for the world's longest rivers (Nile, Amazon, Yangtze), STD for the three most senior U.S. cabinet positions (State, Treasury, Defense), and a few dozen others I've come across. You'll make that work perhaps once more in your life, and even then you might have to rearrange the letters a little.

A slightly better tactic is to make up a sentence using the first letters of the desired sequence. The treble-clef music staff is often remembered as Every Good Boy Does Fine. (Inspired, I taught myself how to tune a guitar with Every Bad Girl Does Assorted Extras.) The seven colors of the spectrum (red, orange, yellow, green, blue, indigo, and violet) are often taught in England as "Richard Of York Gave Battle In Vain," which I mention despite the great unlikelihood that Richard III will come up later in the story, over and over.

Better still, just make up your own sentence: "Rabbits On Yo-yos Go Bouncing In Vegetables" or "Radio Orator Yelps: Got Balls In Vinegar" or whatever makes you smile most. You'll probably store it as part of the process. As a rule, if you can make yourself laugh, you're halfway to long-term memory.

If you're dealing with things more complex than individual letters and familiar words—Latin phrases or strange names or foreign words, say—the solution is still simple: cheat harder. Just change the words slightly until you can make a recognizable sentence, preferably something visual. My own chunky mnemonic for the biological classifications of life—

*Kingdom, Phylum, Class, Order, Family, Genus, Species*

—is one mental picture of a minimalist composer with a crown on his head enjoying a good meal with his loved ones:

*King Philip Glass Orders his Family a Generous Special.*

If you're not familiar with Philip Glass and his music, use something else:

*Keith in First Class Orders a Flunky to Genuflect Spastically.*
*Ken Fights the Clap by Offering Frauleins a Gentle Spongebath.*

Whatever works best for you. (And no, the "Ken" here isn't Ken Jennings, much as he enjoys volunteer work.)

■ ■ ■

What if you have a spectacularly long list to memorize? Still, no worries. Just glue each piece to an existing list you already know—anything from the streets in your neighborhood to something as simple as the numbers 1, 2, 3, etc., themselves.

When I first passed the *Jeopardy!* test, I had no idea what order the presidents came in, other than the first few and the recent ones since World War II. Somewhere in between was an enormous void containing William McKinley and Martin Van Buren and even Millard goddam Fillmore. I did, however, know how to count (although if I had thought more about the mathematics of probability, I would have stopped taking the *Jeopardy!* test long before passing).

There's not room here to include over forty separate presidential mnemonics—those would belong in yet another book (or someday, perhaps, a series of books someone will write this way, reducing the basic facts of human history into memorable, bite-size nuggets)—but here are a few at random, just to give you the flavor:

12 = Zachary Taylor. There is a *Z* in the word "dozen." Done.

16 = Abe Lincoln at a Sweet Sixteen party. Make up your own "stovepipe hat" jokes.

35 = JFK, the youngest elected president. Minimum age for the office: 35.

It also helps to link not just to the number, but also to what comes before and after. This is pretty much how I finally sorted out Pierce, Buchanan, and Millard goddam Fillmore, a few days after my first *Jeopardy!* game, using romance as a unifying theme:

13 = Millard Fillmore. What an unlucky name. Completely unlovable.

14 = Franklin Pierce. Valentine's Day (Feb. 14) means hearts *pierced* by arrows. Better still: a burning hail of fiery arrows, piercing a whole field of Valentine hearts. And I am not bitter.

15 = James Buchanan. After any romance, once the hail of arrows is over, you need to Jump Back Again.

This, incidentally, took minutes, once I saw how.

Scan your brain and find connections between the new material and a list already in your head, and you can do the same thing with any new list you like.

The existing list—the target of the gluing-on process—can be anything appropriate to the topic. I once tried to memorize the geographic locations of about fifty major Native American peoples. This was easier than I expected; all I had to do was link each group to something memorable in their physical location.

For example, to remember that the Chickasaw Indians lived along the eastern shore of the Mississippi, near modern Memphis, I just needed to play with Memphis until it connected back with something primal and sticky. This is the thought process that followed:

> *Dr. King was shot there. Hmm. Memphis State, the college.*
> *That Tom Cruise movie where he played a lawyer with Gene*
> *Hackman . . . hmph . . . Graceland is in Memphis . . . Elvis . . .*
> *—and Elvis slept with every chick he saw. Done.*

Like it or not, the Chickasaw Indians and Memphis are now glued together permanently.

OK, now let's take on a real challenge. Let's try that list of UN Secretaries-General, a series of strange names from seven different countries on four continents. In this case, every single syllable is strange, so shorthands can't be used. This is the worst-case scenario; if you can handle this, you can remember anything.

> WARNING: the following list is so dull that attempting to memorize it without safety precautions could cause injury or even brain death. If you are alone, do not proceed with the rest of this chapter. If you insist, please notify a friend as to your location and intentions, then hold the book lightly in your fingertips with your arms extended. In the event of a UN Secretaries-General-induced loss of consciousness, the book will drop to the floor, releasing your brain from its grip, possibly averting long-term damage.

We begin by cheating again, even harder. Let's just say those entire names out loud until they start sounding like English words we recognize. If you don't know how to pronounce one or two, no sweat. Just plow ahead and have fun. You'll make more progress than you think, and the real purpose of mnemonics (outside of obsessive *Jeopardy!* study, anyway) is to help begin learning new data, not as an end in themselves.

Your list will differ, but here are some half-baked pronunciations that came out of my mouth:

| | |
|---|---|
| Trygve Lie | *Truck Valet* |
| Dag Hammarskjöld | *Dug Hummers Cold* |
| U Thant | *Ooh, Taunt* |
| Kurt Waldheim | *Cured For All Time* |
| Javier Perez de Cuellar | *Heaver Prays To Clear Off* |
| Boutros Boutros-Ghali | *Butt Rose, Butt Rose, Golly* |
| Kofi Annan | *Coffee, Anyone?* |

Again, stop and appreciate the omnipresence of the human butt, no disrespect intended to the former Egyptian Foreign Affairs Minister, a Fulbright scholar with a doctorate from the University of Paris.

To remember these in sequence, all we need to do is make up a story. Again: hold the book loosely in your fingertips, preferably with someone else in the room.

Let's start with a bad-tempered *truck valet*, a bullying jerk who really likes Hummers (*dug Hummers cold*). He passes a gorgeous woman out on a date with a smart but tiny little man. Naturally, the *truck valet* who *dug Hummers cold* stops to wolf-whistle at the girl and pick a fight with—*ooh, taunt*—the scrawny guy.

However, the little guy is also a flyweight kickboxing champ. The *truck valet* soon gets the crud beaten out of him (*cured for all time*). The bully loses his lunch, then begs to leave (*heaver prays to clear off*). But the little guy finishes the job by kicking the truck valet's nether regions high into the air (*butt rose, butt rose, golly*), then finally relaxes by sharing a delicious iced mocha with his girlfriend (*coffee, anyone?*).

So if you can remember the seven key bits of that one little story—

*Truck valet*
*Dug hummers cold*

*Ooh, taunt*
*Cured for all time*
*Heaver prays to clear off*
*Butt rose, butt rose, golly*
*Coffee, anyone?*

—you now know the complete list of United Nations Secretaries-General. Please put down the book, thank your assistant, and hug your loved ones. Wipe their tears. It is over.

With practice, something like this takes about ten or fifteen minutes to dream up. Granted, you don't have it slammed into your head like the other stuff, but this is the Armageddon example. And even so, with just a little review, you can now keep that unlikely-looking list in your head, in order, as long as you live if you choose.

(There were a few blind alleys, of course. Kurt Waldheim, for example, came out variously as Good Valid Ham or Card Vault Time. These were fun to play with, but didn't fit. No biggie. It always takes a few tries.)

Notice that the story is intentionally extra-sticky because of the use of violence, a primal fight to display male dominance for a potential sexual partner (this is the entire function of the date in the story), and even the sensory satisfactions of the taste of strong coffee and the presence of a desirable mate at the end.

You could flip the narrative a hundred ways. I chose a fairly familiar one; in fact, you'll see this exact story in multiplexes next year as *Speed Reading Made Easy II: The Kick-Boxening.*

This probably seems like a lot more work at first. Make no mistake: it absolutely *is*. A lot more. There's an initial investment of time here that you needn't bother with in the bang-your-forehead-while-clocks-spin approach. The time you'll save on the far end is enormous, but that can be hard to see at first.

Worse, studying this way means you have to practice and develop a new set of skills while fighting against old habits. And if you have inhibitions—if you're afraid someone will mock you, perhaps, if you someday admit that your knowledge of Classical Mythology is (like mine) originally rooted in a lengthy series of unrepeatable dirty jokes—you just won't want to try this.

Some folks may even have invested so much time and effort in rote learning that they'll feel angry at the very suggestion that there's any other way.

Since we're not wired to adopt strange ideas easily, some folks reading this will sniff dismissively, shake their heads, and possibly emit a series of uneasy *grrrr* noises. I probably would have, too, honestly, if I didn't have tens of thousands of dollars riding on the need to learn whatever worked fastest and bestest.

It is not, in fact, a cheap shortcut to encode and recall information in a fashion compatible with your brain's physical structure, any more than using a highway map is cheating when you're trying to navigate the layout of a strange city. You're just helping yourself find the fastest route possible.

Again, knowing a list of British Monarchs doesn't make you even slightly expert in English history. Of course not. But having the raw material already stuffed into your brain *does* make picking up all the details and context a lot easier. Eventually, with use, the memory aids begin to fall away, and the information itself has been recorded in your head.

When I started writing this section, jotting down the names of the UN Secretaries-General was the easy part. I had to look up the story in my notebooks.

I never would have believed this a decade ago.

*OK, Chuck.*

I had gone to the supermarket and bought a five-subject college notebook with a blue cover, the first of four I would eventually fill. It was open to the first blank page.

I had a pen in my hand, a large supply of caffeine in the fridge, and a willingness to create as many gratuitous anatomical jokes as necessary.

*I'm ready.*

And so began a daily routine: up at 7:00 a.m. In the books until 7:00 p.m.

At 7:00 p.m., I would stop, grab my masking-tape buzzer, and play along with the *Jeopardy!* broadcast. Sometimes I would play along with the tape again a second time or as a break during the following day, simply practicing the timing during the afternoon, the time of day when my games would be played.

At seven-thirty back in the books. Snooze at eleven.

At no time did I ever work this hard in high school or college. Of course, at no time in high school or college did studying ever involve making up dozens of dirty jokes and scribbling down large, amateurish, slightly insane-looking drawings.

Glancing at my notebook entries for Chuck's list of the major works of American Novelists, for example, we find:

- Piano-shaped people throwing TVs at mountains (James Baldwin);
- Elmer Fudd shooting arrows at a dodging Bugs Bunny amid downtown buildings, while a slender green dinosaur looks on (Sinclair Lewis); and
- A near-death slalom skier in a bow tie being retrieved from a pile of sawdust after hitting it with explosive force in bright sunlight (William Faulkner).

I could explain these, but I think you'll have more fun bouncing them around, working out why each image is there, and possibly questioning my sanity. (There's a secret decoder ring below if you're curious.*)

---

*Piano-shaped people throwing TVs at mountains (James Baldwin):*
    Baldwin is a brand of piano. The image of mountains, at least near Baldwin-shaped people, prompts the Baldwin novel *Go Tell It on the Mountain.* The throwing of TVs invokes the movie *Network,* in which Howard Beale inspired millions to hurl their TVs out the window, presumably after *Jeopardy!* had aired in their time zones. "Howard Beale" connected to *Go Tell It on the Mountain* leads to another Baldwin work, *If Beale Street Could Talk.*
    Remember, this is *my* mnemonic; yours may differ. These might seem random and hard to follow; yours will seem intuitive and obvious. You might connect the same words and images with Alec *Baldwin* and Jennifer *Beals* falling into a *mountainous* volcano. (A fiery volcano would even point to another Baldwin work, *The Fire Next Time.*) Or *bald twins* could chase Ally *McBeal* into the volcano. Or a dozen other possible variations. Whatever strikes your fancy.

*Elmer Fudd shooting arrows at a dodging Bugs Bunny amid downtown buildings, while a slender green dinosaur looks on (Sinclair Lewis):*
    Elmer Fudd invokes *Elmer Gantry.* The arrows stand for *Arrowsmith,* while Bugs the rabbit, shortened, is *Babbitt.* The "dodging," indicated by more arrows (zigzagging around his feet), means *Dodsworth,* although sometimes all I see here is more *Arrowsmith,* to be honest.

Those of you who actually *can* eventually decode these should either try out for the show or seek professional help.

Probably both.

Getting ready also meant bowing humbly to the gods of state-dependent retrieval.

The local office supply store had no shortage of cheap pedestal halogen lamps. Five of them were soon scattered across my living room, transforming the ceiling into a blinding source of studio-intensity re-flected light.

My air conditioner, set on "purée," chilled the living room to a studio-like sixty-five degrees. Videotapes of *Jeopardy!* played silently on the TV, associating all new information with the show's colors and scenery. The TV was shifted as far to one side of the room as possible, the better to simulate the actual distance of the game, and the waist-high top of a small bookcase became my makeshift home podium.

And, of course, as much as possible, I studied while standing up.

Annika, who had two master's degrees and spent her days providing basic education in difficult environments, was not enthused.

Every evening, I would excitedly tell her of the new things I was surprised to find sticking in my head. "Eighty-eight constellations! Twelve birthstones! Four elements named for Greek deities!" I would babble. "Goa was Portuguese! Matisse was a Fauvist! Little Orphan

---

The buildings point to *Main Street*, although not particularly well because they're not mov-ing or eating or exploding. And the slender green dinosaur is the Sinclair Oil logo.

*A near-death slalom skier in a bow tie being retrieved from a pile of sawdust after hitting it with explosive force in bright sunlight (William Faulkner):*
This is the Imperial Death Star of mnemonic cartoons, a demonstration of either what's possible or how unhinged I can be. You decide.

The near-death bit, drawn by giving the skier Xs for eyes, equals *As I Lay Dying*. Above this, a brutal Mr. Sun looks down, as *Light in August*. The explosion, drawn as explody-flashy-flamey triangles in the air, is *The Sound and the Fury*. The "slalom" skier, indicated by a series of flag thingies, invokes *Absalom, Absalom!* by sound. Two stick-figure guys retrieving the body: "retriev-ers" lead to *The Reivers*. The skier himself, buried in the sawdust, is *Intruder in the Dust*. The bow tie? It's a sartorial touch. Thus, *Sartoris*.

As for linking all this to the name "Faulkner"—what expletive would you say, if you were skiing out of control and about to hit a giant sawdust ball with explosive force? Just asking.

Annie had a dog named Sandy!" If I ever asked Annika how her day was, I don't recall it specifically.

Looking back, I must have sounded like the world's most sophisticated Tourette's patient: "Sphenoid Bones! Pygmy Shrews! Die Fledermaus! Monkey monkey monkey monkey!"

Annika usually went to the next room to read.

The new knowledge, even shorn of all context, was exhilarating.

Shakespeare, for example, had always somehow been outside my expectations. I knew the plays were *great* and all, sure; everyone said so. But I also assumed they also would be above my station in life. I never saw a single moment of a Shakespeare play until I was two years out of college.

It's not that my parents had anything against the guy; it's just that he rarely visited the Snow Belt. The closest thing we ever had to highbrow literature was my father's love for the surreal, silly works of Ogden Nash and Lewis Carroll.

To put food on the table, Dad spent too many hours lifting things bigger than he was to have much time for reading, but this seemed almost a verbal advantage. For him, words existed as collections of sounds and images, passports to realities skewed from our own.

While he was alive, it is possible that not a single month of my life went by—ever, during the thirty-two years, one month, eight days, six hours, and forty-five minutes that we shared this planet—that Dad didn't recite the first words of the poem "Jabberwocky" to me, just for the joy of the apparently meaningless syllables. "Twas brillig, and the slithy toves," he would begin, and a rare delight would begin to sneak across his face, appreciating each moment of transcendent goofiness, watching my eyes to see if I shared his delight.

I believe, although I cannot prove, that he had high hopes.

One evening, when there was only a day or so left of our time together, I recited the poem back to him for the very last time.

He was sort of asleep at the time, but I wanted to believe I could see him smiling.

■ ■ ■

In high school, we barely brushed against Ogden Nash, Lewis Carroll, Edward Lear, or any of the other so-unserious writers who delight everyone they touch. This was, after all, a very expensive and important school. Instead, I was force-fed a few of Shakespeare's Greatest Hits, although the English always needed translation, the broad comedy and wrenching drama were lost, and none of the magnificently dirty jokes were ever explained. (Incidentally, *Romeo and Juliet*, fully appreciated, might be banned in some U.S. states.) This was the *Concordance* again, and little more. So we'd read all the lines aloud, resign ourselves to a ponderous struggle, and soon give up the plot completely.

But in the blinding glow of my stage-lit living room, I started sucking down Cliffs Notes and Chuck's notes about scepter'd isles, pricking thumbs, and miscellaneous Ides of March. This went much more quickly than I once could have imagined. I was kicking Shakespeare's *ass*.

The more I read, the more I could hear a distant voice, repeating every line playfully, savoring every rhythm and pun, enjoying these sticky new stories. As I crammed in each new quote, locale, character, and basic plot point, I also promised to go back someday and study more.

The voice in my head was pleasant to hear.

I'd never realized: Dad would have *loved* Shakespeare.


Sometimes Annika would emerge, squint through the halogen glare, and ask, with some sincerity, if and how I was managing to remember all this stuff. I would invariably respond by proudly describing a new mnemonic construction in full and glorious detail.

Perhaps I would describe an important Supreme Court ruling in terms of a dancer with bananas on her head being handcuffed by a cactus. Or maybe I would discuss art history by describing ballet dancers on laughing gas, a man who has just lost one ear gargling the word "Arrrrrrrl," or Doris Day being blown to thousands of colorful bits.

(In case you're curious: *Miranda v. Arizona*. Also, the frequent subject matter of Degas; the French town of Arles, where Van Gogh was famously visited by Gauguin; and the pointillist technique of Seurat, whose last name sounds like the lyric in "Que Sera, Sera.")

To Annika, I might as well have been describing subatomic physics in terms of billiard balls, tangles of string, and possibly dead cats. I am certain I sounded—and am starting to sound to some of you, reading this—like a complete loon.

So Annika would look around the living room-turned-soundstage, roll her eyes slightly, and sigh.

I was sure she'd understand once I became a five-time champ.

Game day. Already becoming a familiar experience.

All I wanted to do was try to relax and pace myself. It wouldn't do to breeze in, win one game in a surge of mental energy, and then flame out before lunchtime. This wasn't a sprint, the way my single end-of-day win had been weeks before. *Jeopardy!* was going to be an endurance sport.

I had three changes of clothing with me, as contestants are always asked to bring. All three of my sport jackets had Kleenex stashed in the right pocket.

No way I was climbing back into that makeup chair unprepared.

From the moment I walked into the green room, I could feel the dozen other contestants furtively scrutinizing me, just as I had so recently measured Matt, the returning champion of my own first game. I should have expected this, but it was a surprise nonetheless.

On camera, *Jeopardy!* had been a test of knowledge, judgment, timing, and coolness under pressure. Backstage, however, I realized there was another, more primitive, unspoken game already under way.

I don't remember the exact details, but I made some small comment about professional sports. Two of the men eagerly displayed how much they knew in response, announcing their prowess to the room. One of the women pooh-poohed the exchange, claiming that *Jeopardy!* rarely asks about sports. This was attempted display number three.

A little later I got up to fetch a diet soda, and another player began talking about how bad the chemicals are for you. Another swore he never touched the stuff, claiming such drinks always had an effect on his concentration. And therefore, he seemed to be saying, *my* concentration would falter, if I cared to notice his comments.

Bizarre. Were these people all that focused on beating me? Obviously, *yes*—not me personally, of course, but winning is why we were all there.

Still, I wondered if maybe I was cracking slightly, if my pre-game jitters had caused an unusually high spike of self-absorption. These people all seemed too friendly and bright and good-humored to be engaged in this sort of gamesmanship.

At least consciously.

So I made some open joke about *Jeopardy!* being bloodsport—roughly that once we got onstage this would be like the James Caan movie *Rollerball*, with motorcycles and spiked gloves on our buzzer hands. The *Jeopardy!* theme would even be replaced with Bach's creepy Toccata in D Minor (the *Rollerball* theme, high on the meager list of classical pieces I could recognize). Immediately, the conversation moved to one-upping tales of listening to, attending, and playing famous Bach pieces. And all of these comments seemed spoken carefully loud enough for me to hear.

Oh, my. Yes. The game *was* afoot.

This wasn't Sony, this was the Sahara, and only the fittest would survive. Twelve sets of ears pricked up when I spoke, seeking out weakness. Twelve pairs of eyes scanned my every move.

As I scanned them all back, I began to feel confident: their body language and vocal tones were all about seeking status and reassurance. There was no sign of an Ivy League Serial Killer to fear, no Berkeley assassin, no cold-blooded genius of general knowledge. I only saw stress, as intense as my own had been while waiting to play my first game.

What had worried me most about Matt was how calm he appeared to be. I had feared his experience as much as his head. I had feared my own nerves even more. Appearing relaxed, therefore, was a tool I could use.

I sank back in my chair and made a point of laughing at everyone else's jokes, letting them see me smile. And I said little else. How I wish you could have seen the effect: in this green room octagon, a single jiu-jitsu maneuver was throwing the others off their feet.

Soon, I actually *became* more relaxed. I just grinned and begged them to go on, delighting in whatever they said. So they said more. Probing and displaying, hunting and regaling, tiring themselves out with nervous energy. I listened intently, nodding in agreement, begging for more detail, giving back nothing but calm and a smile.

Resting. Ready for a long day ahead. Smiling was almost easy now.

I was already winning.

Seconds before we all marched out for the first game, I turned to my opponents—a law student from New York and a librarian from Iowa— and in a reassuring voice, instructed them not to be nervous.

I'm a little ashamed of this now. I'm not a big fan of mind games. Notice that this was a triple cruelty: reminding them both of my own previous experience *while* focusing their attention on their own nerves— and looking like a nice guy in the process.

I was shocked at myself, honestly. This may have been the single most manipulative flourish of my entire life. I regret it now. Someday I will be attacked in the street by a gang of well-educated people in suits and dresses. They will slap me to the pavement, steal my wallet, and clean out my bank account, all while reciting the monarchs of Spain in chronological order. And perhaps I will deserve it.

But in that moment, it seemed obvious at the time, the game had already begun.

And I wanted more.

Alex came out. No costume. Just his usual serious business suit. Halloween was over. In broadcast time, this show was a Monday.

It was time to go to work.

The luck I assumed would run out sometime soon showed no sign of abating at all. The first round included the following category:

STAND-UP
COMICS

I attacked the category instantly, since I had personally worked with, opened for, or spilled something on at least a few dozen possible responses. The very first clue, in a coincidence I wouldn't appreciate until writing this book, was this:

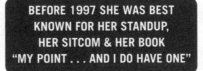

BEFORE 1997 SHE WAS BEST
KNOWN FOR HER STANDUP,
HER SITCOM & HER BOOK
"MY POINT . . . AND I DO HAVE ONE"

I hadn't met Jane yet, and won't for a few more chapters, but at the very moment this clue was revealed, she had stopped naming carbonated beverages that rhyme with "Squeema" for a living. Instead, she was working as a writer on a particular TV sitcom.

Starring Ellen DeGeneres.

Everything really does connect to everything else.

I later realized that attacking STAND-UP COMICS (while possibly a good idea in general, especially if they use a guitar or a large box of props) was for me a tactical *Jeopardy!* mistake.

Many players dive straight into their strongest subject, hoping to run up a score before hitting a Daily Double, thinking this is the best way to maximize those opportunities. I know that's what I was thinking, anyway. But I was also just trying to get comfortable, and thus reaching for the familiar, so the strategic explanation was really just a rationalization.

I had not yet realized that by attacking your weakest category immediately, you'll probably get the hardest clues off the board with the least possible amount of money at stake. If there's a Daily Double in the weak category, it will barely matter, while hitting it late puts you in a difficult betting situation. And if the Daily Double is in a stronger category, you'll be more likely to hit it when it can do you the most good. If you hit this Daily Double late in the game, you'll have significant control over the outcome.

I'm tempted to elevate something like "attack your weaknesses" to a step on the Eightfold Path, but it occurs to me that attacking your weaknesses is sort of what the Eightfold Path itself already does. And I have a real weakness for metastuff.

On the second clue, the librarian from Iowa actually beat me to the buzzer. However, when he made his first choice on the game board, his voice wavered, and his hand reached up to touch his face. This odd gesture of intense stress is the sort of thing any good poker player would recognize as a "tell."

A few moments later he was actually working *up* the game board, not down, seeking the comfort of easier clues. He was very, very nervous.

So I probably owe the guy dessert, too.

During the first commercial break, I mentally played ahead again, letting my mind roam the category THE OLD WEST while making small talk with Glenn, Grant, and the twenty-three makeup commandos keeping my forehead de-shined. I continued thinking all the way through the contestant interviews, a habit that might account for the fact that I always wind up blithering, no matter what Alex asks.

This paid off moments later on the $300 clue:

> **CIBOLA, AS IN THE 7 CITIES OF CIBOLA, IS THE SPANISH WORD FOR THIS LARGE ANIMAL OF THE PLAINS**

At the time, I spoke almost no Spanish, and so the only hint for me was this:

LARGE ANIMAL OF THE PLAINS

How many large animals actually roamed the plains of the Old West? There's only one obvious response, of course: the buffalo. But that's assuming there weren't also vast herds of, I dunno, oversize something-elses following the Sioux back and forth. Normally I would have needed another second to double-think my response. I would have scanned my mental inventory of old movies for stray packs of rhinos, hippos, or giant albino squirrels roaming the Dakotas, buzzing in only after finding nothing *but* the buffalo. I would have been a second late.

But I'd been thinking ahead, and this had included a two-second replay of Kevin Costner stumbling around on his knees hollering *"Tatonka!"* in *Dances with Wolves.* This word had been crucial in the film as the single initial common ground between his character and the Lakota Sioux. So, buffalo had to be *the* large animal of the Plains.

*What is the buffalo?*

—forever cemented my intention to play ahead in every spare moment of any game.

At the first commercial, I had $3000 after responding to only six clues, again keeping my hand off the buzzer for roughly a third of the game so far.

The other two players, each of whom had buzzed in on expensive clues and missed, had $400 combined.

As the first round ended, this was the $500 clue in the category "NUT"s TO YOU:

IT'S CONNECTICUT'S
"SPICY" NICKNAME

I knew nothing about spices, and a few weeks earlier had known only about half of the state nicknames. Even given the letters N-U-T as part of the response, this would have been impossible for me.

But there had been a complete list of state nicknames in Chuck

Forrest's book, which I had just glued into my head with enough gratu-itous action to fill Jerry Bruckheimer's dreams for a decade.

*What's the nutmeg?* I responded, my mind flashing pictures of *Little Women*, giant scissors, and insurance adjusters trying to protect their groins.

The law student from New York and the librarian from Iowa, on the other hand, seemed to be well-adjusted people living normal lives.

They didn't stand a chance.

In Double Jeopardy, my Festival of Chuck continued.

*Who is Poseidon?* for $200.

*Who is Ares?* for $800.

*Who is Anubis?* for $1000.

Two grand in the first category, on three responses I couldn't have guessed at just one month before. The first two were straight from Chuck's book. Not bad for a twelve-dollar investment.

This particular clue would have been completely impossible a few weeks earlier:

THE TYBEE LIGHTHOUSE
AT THE MOUTH OF THE
SAVANNAH RIVER IS NAMED
FOR THIS GEORGIA FOUNDER

But there I am on the tape, confidently banging in: *Who is Ogle-thorpe?* for $800.

To this day, I couldn't tell you Oglethorpe's first name. No idea. But I did have a clear mental picture of Ted Turner—a famous Geor-gian—founding a state as a good place to leer lustfully while getting drunk and throwing up. Georgia. Ogle. Throw-up.

Chuck's book and a few others, my study of how memory works, and a gleeful mental shamelessness were providing about one-third of my entire score.

My good fortune continued as well. Thanks to one particularly un-hinged romance, a couple of the clues in PSYCHOLOGY were entirely too familiar.

Suddenly, even my truly horrible experiences were popping up and proving themselves useful. I was starting to wonder if it was possible to screw up your own life so frequently and memorably, in so many different ways, that eventually you can only succeed on *Jeopardy!*

That's probably your call more than mine.

Still, keeping my hand *off* the Jeopardy Weapon was again the only way I could win. I had no idea whatsoever of the responses for a full one-third of the round. However, when I did ring in, state-dependent retrieval did its stuff: checking the tape, my light came on fourteen times out of eighteen attempts.

I didn't know the exact numbers during the game, of course. But I do remember noticing that my light coming on wasn't even surprising anymore.

As the game wound down, several clues were "triple stumpers," leaving all three of us staring vacantly into the middle distance. This sort of Zombie Jeopardy slows down the game considerably. Rounds with multiple triple-stumpers often run out of time before all of the clues have been played.

Soon, only six clues were left on the board: four in AROUND THE HORN (about brass musical instruments) and two in MOVIE BIOGRAPHIES. I had $11700, the librarian had $5200, and the law student had $2500. I was nearing a second runaway, and it seemed that only a few of the remaining clues would be played.

But then I made yet another tactical error: I forgot to consider the remaining Daily Doubles. Both were still hidden somewhere on the board. It had not quite occurred to me to keep track.

However, since *Jeopardy!* never puts two Daily Doubles in the same column, there had to be one in AROUND THE HORN, and the other in MOVIE BIOGRAPHIES. To finish off the game, I only needed to take them out of play—just hunt around the bottom where Daily Doubles live, making small, safe bets—and the game was over. Since MOVIE BIOGRAPHIES only had two clues left, I had a fifty-fifty chance of finding a Daily Double immediately.

Instead, because we had played slowly already, I glanced up at the game board, saw the scores, and decided to try to run out the clock by playing cheaper clues. For just a moment—a period of perhaps three seconds in real time—I was no longer trying to win; I was trying not to lose.

Less than ten seconds later, the law student had control of the Daily Double in AROUND THE HORN; she would also have a fifty-fifty chance of finding the other on the very next clue.

Even as far behind as she was—she now had $2900—two correct responses could bring our scores roughly level, with just a few clues left. I had let my fear of losing control over the outcome lead directly to losing control over the outcome.

That's so philosophically perfect I could just plotz.

And so, our next step on the Eightfold Path of Enlightened Jeopardy, one that quite plainly belongs at the end:

1. Obvious things may be worth noticing.
2. Remember the basics: the basics are what you remember.
3. Put your head where you can use it later.
4. Doing nothing is better than doing something really stupid.
5. Admit you don't know squat as often as possible.
6. Everything connects to everything else.
7. You can often see only what you think you'll see.
8. Just play each moment. Let go of outcome.

You've probably already noticed that most of these steps are applied over and over, and that my own successes and failures correlate generally with how closely they're followed. This will continue.

I'll only point it out occasionally, but it's there all the time if you look.

You might have also noticed a few similarities between the Path of Enlightened Jeopardy and certain Eastern philosophies. Maybe by now you're starting to think that's what this book is really all about.

I refer you to step number seven.

Still, you might wonder if I'm covertly trying to share some ideas that extend beyond learning stuff and being a good quiz show contestant.

Maybe I'm even planning to start a cult. Perhaps I hope someday to have a squadron of smooth-skinned young devotees mindlessly chanting inside my armed compound, while aging celebrities burn their infomercial money seeking my counsel during the moments I can spare between bribing politicians and taking unseemly advantage of pert new initiates. Before long, I'll dissolve into hedonistic twilight, finally dying surrounded by people who adore me for all the wrong reasons, trading cheap constant pleasure for what could have been greatness.

Come to think of it, that sounds *fantastic*. I'll get right on it.

On the other hand, it's possible that useful ideas are inherently universal, and so of course there's some resemblance. Similar bland counsel about being observant and modest might exist in books concerned with everything from hair care to jet repair. But that's still not the explanation.

In simple fact, most Eastern philosophies descend directly from *Jeopardy!* (n., uncert., prob. deriv. from ancient Pali *Djeh-paa-deh*, ca. 550 BCE, lit. "buzz of life"), a Tibetan Zen-like tradition of students providing answers in the form of more questions, leading them on a path toward wisdom, liberation from suffering, and a new Chevrolet. In each generation, one master—the Merv—reincarnates to spread the teachings, which are written on fig leaves and preserved in a set of hollowed-out coconuts. The Merv, it is said, will announce himself to the world in song.

You know the rest of the story from there.

You may choose not to believe this. But it's more fun if you do.

The legend also speaks of a trickster-mentor who will stand at a Podium of Judgment. About this figure, little else is written, but according to tradition (and I quote):

"You will know him by his Oooh."

The Oooh came soon for the law student, who received her own Zen-like clue requiring close observation of her surroundings.

> FROM THE GERMAN FOR
> "WING," THIS HORN, HEARD
> HERE, WAS POPULARIZED BY
> CHUCK MANGIONE

This was followed by the familiar Think Music itself, played on a trumpetlike instrument with a fatter, mellower sound. I'd heard this horn many times while doing all-night jazz shows at a college radio station back in the Snow Belt.

The librarian, however, had probably been doing productive work or enjoying functional relationships on those many cold nights. "What is the flugelhorn?" eluded her. And for the second time, I had won.

A total of $3300 worth of responses—the margin that clinched the runaway win, in fact—were the direct result of speed-cramming my head full of horny philosophers, popes on rampages, and every one involved being eaten.

For the second time, I was standing with Alex and the other contestants at the center of the stage, letting the some-contestants-receive list roll by.

Bruce's Yams! and Phazyme gas medicine! and Breath-A-Sure endorsed by George Kennedy! and a Honeysuckle Roast Turkey! caressed in a disturbingly sensual massage by undulating female hands! later, it was over.

Two down, three to go.

When this game was broadcast, it was preceded by a commercial for the Anthony Hopkins film *Amistad*, which I never saw because I was too busy studying.

This may seem like a stray and unnecessary fact at this point.

On the other hand, maybe there's no such thing as trivia; maybe there's only knowledge we have yet to fully grasp.

Either way, I've never seen *Amistad*. Just saying.

Back to the green room.

Ten pairs of eyes watching now.

I knew that the waiting contestants would be even more curious and worried now than I had been. Matt, on my first day, had won only one game. Now I had won two games, and everyone knew it. This was an edge I could press. But any bravado would now play as insecurity, so I just smiled and laughed as before.

Still, stuck in the green room, they had no way of knowing I had just racked up my second runaway. I would have a more commanding position if they knew. I tried simply to let a confident walk tell the story so far, and hoped that one of the departing players might share the full outcome.

One did.

Everyone in the green room would now think I was a dominant player. I considered this insane. But they had no way of knowing that.

Change the shirt. Comb the hair. Put on a different sport jacket, this time a ratty green corduroy mess. Pee.

Get ready to do it all again.

But first, make sure the other players can see you smile on the way to the stage.

And remind them, in the spirit of kind fairness, that they should absolutely *not* be nervous.

Enlightenment, my ass. I wanted more.

My third game of *Jeopardy!*

Now batting: a jury consultant from Chicago and a grad student from Columbus.

*What is Uranus?* for $400.

*What is the Sunflower State?* for $500.

*What is bioluminescence?* for $500.

Before the first commercial, three of my eight correct responses came as a direct result of study. By the end of the first round, my total was as much as the two other players' combined. It almost seemed easy.

I came across *bioluminescence*, incidentally, while flipping through a dictionary, the sort of thing I had taken to doing as a rest break from Chuck-a-palooza at home. Bioluminescence, you will begin telling friends, is the phenomenon where meat becomes so rotten that it actually starts to *glow*.

Wow. You barely even need a mnemonic. Glowing meat? Are you serious? Bright red, rotten meat, glowing with blue and green light? I'm less worried about remembering it than not having a camera when I see it someday.

■ ■ ■

Halfway through the Double Jeopardy round was this clue:

> **THE HUGO AWARD FOR THIS TYPE OF LITERATURE HONORS HUGO GERNSBACK, WHO COINED THE TERM**

Annika never came to a *Jeopardy!* taping. Other players had friends and family in the audience for support. I didn't. It didn't even seem strange at the time, which tells you how alienated Annika and I had become.

What I couldn't have known was that one day, years later, I would return to the stage with someone at my side who had actually won a Hugo award.

*What is science fiction?* could describe how this felt.

This Hugo Award winner would meet Alex, and she would be slightly starstruck, enough that when I mentioned her award, she would explain what a Hugo Award was to Alex, modestly thinking it was too small a trophy for anyone to know. Alex would know, of course, but he would smile and nod, a congenial host even when the cameras are off.

Jane would be a lot of fun to be with that day.

This game was my third runaway. Entering Final Jeopardy, I had three times the score of the nearest competitor.

Center stage with Alex. The Remington Dual Microscreen Shaver! DeWitt's Pills, the affordable back remedy trusted by millions! And (as every day now) a Honeysuckle White Turkey brought near physical climax by two lascivious hands!

Green room. Eight pairs of eyes watching. Shirt, jacket, pee, all smiles.

I wanted more.

Game four.

A management consultant from Virginia and a vice president of marketing from Pennsylvania.

*What are barrels?*

*What is polo?*
*What is a carpenter?*
*Who are the fishmongers?*
*What is a scrivener?*

I have just locked up my fourth straight game by running an entire category called LONDON CITY GUILDS, something I never once studied or thought might come up on the show.

To this day, I am not exactly sure how this happened. Honest.

I saw the word *fishmongers* in *Mad* magazine once. I know that for sure.


During the third commercial break in this game, wrangler Glenn made a friendly remark about how I was doing, using Frank Spangenberg's name as a touchstone.

Frank, you recall, was the New York transit cop with the walrus mustache and the efficiency of a Borg-like computer, the highest-scoring five-time winner in the show's history.

Glenn's remark was something like: "You're doing well. Not quite *Frank Spangenberg* well. But not a bad run so far."

Years later, Frank's name, like Chuck's, is still a gold standard. In *Jeopardy!* terms, this is like being told as a writer, "You're pretty decent. Not Mark Twain, but not incoherent."

I was glad not to face Frank Spangenberg on this day. Even as well as I was doing, I knew I would have been stomped.


Center stage. Mrs. Butterworth's Syrup! Caltrate Pills (because it's never too late for Caltrate)! The Libman Wonder Mop!

Green room. Six pairs of eyes now greeting me, looking more downcast by the hour.

I wanted more.

But I was starting to tire. So I was starting to get nervous.

Nervous is not what I was prepared to be.


After the third game of each taping date, *Jeopardy!* breaks for lunch. This does not, however, mean that you get to relax.

For security reasons, *Jeopardy!* must quarantine the surviving contestants from all human contact. Otherwise, an audience member from an earlier game could theoretically tip off the challengers, passing along notes on the categories already played or the champion's propensity for shoving things up his nose.

We were therefore marched to a commissary across the Sony lot, escorted by a watchful Glenn and Grant, who set a light and airy tone, roughly ninety percent Cub Scout parade, ten percent Luftstalag. This was delightful, given the stress involved. We sat at tables carefully placed away from all other living things, and munched on our sandwiches and salads in nervous silence.

The remaining contestants continued to scrutinize me slyly. I had to maintain the act of cool, quiet, confident reserve.

This was more difficult with each passing minute.

The next game was for more than just cash. After five wins, *Jeopardy!* awarded the retiring champion a new car and a guaranteed spot in the annual $100,000 Tournament of Champions.

I *so* didn't want to screw this up. I was starting to stress, fearing my own anger at myself if I did.

At the same time, I was looking forward beyond the final game to come. I suddenly had over $43000. While this was modest compared with the prizes now routinely handed out, it was more money than I had ever seen in my life. *Screw* cool reserve: I wanted to turn cartwheels across the restaurant floor. I was out of debt again. I could pay the rent for a while, no worries. I could call Mom and Connie and tell them I done good. I wanted to dance and sing and scream in fear and run around in circles shouting *boogety-boogety woop-woop-woop yah GAAAH!*

Instead, I just nodded when spoken to, and listened, and smiled, and tried not to show my nerves, fatigue, and excitement.

Under the table, where no one could see, I was snapping my fingers back and forth, over and over and over.

I knew that if I let the stress take over, I would lose my fifth game. While extreme stress can jump your memory into high-speed Record mode as a survival skill, it also kills your recall. Imagine your brain as a bit like a VCR, which can't both record and play back at the same time.

Think back to any moment of real, genuine, *I'm-gonna-die* danger: a car wreck, or an earthquake, or tripping headlong down a marble staircase toward a pack of hungry weasels. Would remembering that Franklin Pierce was associated with Valentine's Day through a hail of arrows, and was thus the fourteenth president, have been any help whatsoever? Probably not.

Your body knows that. And so in those *I'm-an-entrée!* moments, while it's busy paying close attention to everything that's going on *right this freakin' second*, it ditches your ability to remember anything that isn't.

This is why even the brightest and most talented people can still sometimes choke under pressure. It's just biochemistry. Believe it or not, your body reacts to stress—virtually any stress—with almost exactly the same biochemical changes it would use to evade a horny ocelot. The differences are pretty much a matter of degree.

You already know how your body reacts to any decent-sized freak-out. Your adrenal glands do the lambada, secreting adrenaline with every step. This opens up the main supply pipes to your liver and muscles, while narrowing your smaller blood vessels. Your heart rate and blood pressure jerk upward, and you breathe faster, flooding your tissues with oxygen. Meanwhile your adrenals also pump out steroids called *glucocorticoids*, which tell your liver to get busy with the conversion of fat and proteins into sugar to rocket-fuel your muscles and brain.

You can see where all of this is going. In the next few seconds your body will be prepared to kick ass, run like hell, or simply start screaming your lungs out.

None of which, you notice, would do much good on *Jeopardy!*

Of course, all this sudden spidey-strength comes at a price. Say a brief farewell to your digestion, immune system function, assorted reproductive processes, and (here it comes, yes): higher mental abilities.

Major buzz, dude.

And this is how your body *always* responds to stress, from any source.

Ever have the feeling that your stress *itself* was what was keeping you from thinking? Maybe you've brain-locked during a job interview, or while taking a test you knew you should have passed. Everyone, at some point, becomes lamely tongue-tied around cute members of the desired gender.

Now you know why. These are your glucocorticoids talking. *You* just want to remember a physics equation or charm the hottie down the hall into a date. Your *body*, meanwhile, thinks you're fighting off a pack of wild baboons. Thus the confusion.

I was starting to get more nervous than I had been in any of the previous games.

If I won: the car alone would be worth as much as the first four games combined. If I lost: I didn't want to get this close to my goal and fail. I was afraid of my own frustration. Which I knew, of course, and trying not to think about it was frustrating in itself. Death spiral. As I felt my stress continue to climb, I was afraid I couldn't control it.

Under the table, where no one could see, I was snapping my fingers back and forth, over and over and over and over and over and over. *Snappity-snappity-snappity-snappity.*

This was another state-dependent retrieval strategy, a highly targeted type called *anchoring*. I had read about this, too, in the previous weeks, and hoped it might help to reel me back in if I started flipping out.

You see anchoring in sports all the time, although the word is rarely used. Basketball players have careful routines before free throws, golfers may have precise sets of practice swings and waggles, and some baseball players have whole Kabuki ceremonies when stepping into the batter's box. These routines may not seem to bear directly on the act to be performed, but they do, absolutely: consciously or not, these athletes have created physical triggers to invoke desired sequences—e.g., glove-twiddle, hip-shimmy, crotch-grab, and spit, now *go!*—which help topple the neural dominoes they need most: concentration, relaxation, confidence, etc.

As an emergency measure, I had tried to create my own ball-bouncing, hip-waggling, crotch-grabbing, get-ready-now routine, only targeted to create a desirable emotional state of not-flipping-out. (And with less crotch involved than most athletes use. It's a family show.)

The recipe for creating an anchor is simple: just create your desired emotional state—say, "calm and in total control," for example—by using conventional memory of previous experiences in exactly that state, until you start feeling the state returning, intensely. Then pick a physical movement to which no meaning is yet attached—the "anchor" you'll use later—and start burning in the connection by practicing the movement while you experience the emotional state.

Since your brain is already on Record, the feeling and the physical anchor will automatically start connecting. If you're anchoring an intense emotion, the process is pretty quick, since that's precisely the crashing alien roller coaster that gets Homer Simpson turned on at the bullfight. (If you just opened the book and read that last sentence out of context, it cannot be explained. But trust me: the tour group knows what that means.) Later you can put the anchor to work just by throwing the process in reverse: the anchor itself will fire the neurons that invoke the emotional state.

So, about two weeks before *Jeopardy!*, I needed an inconspicuous, personally meaningless motion, one specific enough that I could always repeat it. That particular night, the film *West Side Story* was on cable, so I whimsically chose the odd left-right-left finger-snapping motion used by one of the dancing gangs. I'd never personally been in a dancing gang in New York, so the neurons controlling this movement had no existing emotional connections.

Every day, I spent a few minutes in a quiet, darkened room, closing my eyes and remembering times when I felt confident, relaxed, and in control. This wasn't a huge list. Once I had the desired set of feelings cranked up pretty intensely, I began and repeated the *West Side Story* finger-snapping movement, intentionally ironing in a physical trigger for calmness.

*Snappity-snappity-snappity-snappity.*

I felt like an idiot, incidentally.

I didn't even tell Annika about it. I really didn't need another eye-roll.

Sony cafeteria, a few minutes before my fifth game.

Fingers under the table, low enough no one can see, over and over and over and over and over. *Snappity-snappity-snappity-snappity.*

I did not, in fact, instantly experience a sensation of control and complete personal serenity.

However, I also didn't run around the room shouting *boogety-boogety woop-woop-woop yah GAAAH!* even though I really, really felt like it.

So I think the anchor was working.

Game five.

This time I can't turn to my fellow contestants, reminding them not to be nervous. I'm snapping my fingers, closing my eyes, trying to take my own advice.

A physician from Anchorage. A tour guide from L.A.

We march out. I stop snapping my fingers. Feeling OK, but not great. Nerves coming back.

Less than thirteen minutes and one Final to go.

Alex emerges, calm and relaxed. I envy him those feelings. "Happy Thanksgiving, ladies and gentlemen" are his first words.

*Yes!* I am thinking, *yes!*

Reviewing my Thanksgiving pages: *Mayflower . . . something. Squanto. Um. Bradford. Somebody. Shit. Shit.* My brain has begun to shut down.

On the tape I am smiling. I giggle nervously, laughing with Alex. Inside, I am fighting an oncoming flood. *Glucocorticoids, damn.* Notebooks in flames in my head.

Alex reminds me of the stakes. "If he wins today, he will qualify automatically for our $100,000 Tournament of Champions coming up later this year, and he will have his choice of some fabulous GM cars," Alex says.

If.

*Chuck! Can you hear me, Chuck? I seem to have misplaced your book! Chuck!?*

The very first category:

**PILGRIMS**

*Mayflower . . . um . . . Plymouth Rock . . . Squanto . . . Bradford somebody . . . Squanto. Who the hell is named Bradford, for crying out loud? Shit.*

The entire category goes by. I respond once. I win on the buzzer not a single time. My timing is off. My reflexes aren't normal. My body thinks I am being towel-snapped by a ravenous badger.

While the badger and I wrestle mightily, I don't win on the buzzer until the eighth clue.

At the first commercial, I am in second place. It is the first time I have trailed in five games. My body mistakes the situation for a dozen more badgers, hungry, and armed with wet towels.

At the end of the *Jeopardy!* round, I'm in a distant third.

During the two-minute commercial break, I turn slightly away from the other players, facing the back of the stage.

I know damn well that I'll have no idea of one-third of the responses to come. With my reflexes shot and memory failing, there's a limit to how much I can expect.

*It was a good run*, I tell myself. *This was a blast. The money will be a big help, and you'll remember doing this for the rest of your life. What the hell.*

This moment of surrender allows me to breathe deeply for the first time since the green room before the first game. I start enjoying the moment instead of freaking out about the future. And then I notice: I am actually relaxing.

So I fire my anchor, snapping my fingers, left-right-left-right *snappity-snappity-snappity-snappity*, a one-man dancing gang.

I am hoping to crank up my serenity.

The sheer absurdity of all this strikes. I can't tell if it's working, or a placebo effect, or if I'm just amused now at feeling so silly. But I can breathe while I'm laughing. *Something* is working, anyway.

This is the last round I will play today, win or lose. And whatever happens, I intend to enjoy it.

This brings us to the ninth and final step along the Eightfold Path to Enlightened Jeopardy, one worth an extra exclamation point for emphasis:

1. Obvious things may be worth noticing.
2. Remember the basics: the basics are what you remember.

3. Put your head where you can use it later.
4. Doing nothing is better than doing something really stupid.
5. Admit you don't know squat as often as possible.
6. Everything connects to everything else.
7. You can often see only what you think you'll see.
8. Just play each moment. Let go of outcome.
9. ! Seriously. About this last part. Just get each moment right. Let go.

It may bother you that there are nine steps on the Eightfold Path. In which case you *really* need step number nine. This is one of those things you should let go.

And if that doesn't work for you, get your own damn enlightened path.

On the other hand, if you'd like to memorize the nine steps, you already know how to invent a half-dozen different mnemonics.

If you really get stuck, try something that almost never works.

Shortly after the second round begins, I stumble into a Daily Double:

> **THE NAME OF THIS WESTERN WISCONSIN CITY ON THE MISSISSIPPI RIVER HONORS A NATIVE AMERICAN SPORT**

When I lived in Chicago, I used to date a girl who played this particular game. She showed me how to play once, or tried to. After about three catches, using the odd netted stick thingies, I missed the ball and it hit me squarely between the eyes.

Oh, and how she laughed.

Also, as a comedian I once got booed off the stage by a bunch of drunks in this particular town. Since we tend to remember being chased by growling animals, I remember the place well.

*What is Lacrosse?*

Maybe you really *can* screw up in so many ways that eventually you get good at *Jeopardy!*

■ ■ ■

With about thirty seconds to go, I am $600 behind. But in the moment, I am playing the game, enjoying the fight, not looking so much at the score. Relaxed. My state-dependent timing returns.

*What is badminton?*

*What's the Moral Majority?*

And finally, in the category FEDERATIONS:

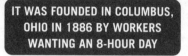

IT WAS FOUNDED IN COLUMBUS,
OHIO IN 1886 BY WORKERS
WANTING AN 8-HOUR DAY

My father lifted boxes almost as big as he was, as a member of the United Auto Workers, for over thirty years. Our corner of the Snow Belt was big on labor unions. And so, thanks to Dad, I knew about the American Federation of Labor.

*What's the AFL?*

Three in a row to end the round. I didn't know this until I looked at the videotape: it was only on the very last clue that I finally got control of the lead.

If I had known it at the time, I'm sure it would not have happened.

This was the first time I did not win in a runaway. Instead, I would be forced to make an enormous wager and then respond correctly to Final Jeopardy.

In a few moments, one clue would be the fulcrum around which would turn a large pile of money, a sports car worth almost as much as all the cash winnings combined, and possibly a trip to the Tournament of Champions. This one final response, by itself, would be worth as much as the small white house in the Snow Belt, where I used to sit with Mom and Dad and watch the show.

The Final Jeopardy category—*p-TING!*

20TH CENTURY
HISTORY

*Well*, that *narrows things down*, I thought. *That could only be anything that happened anywhere to anybody over the course of a hundred years. Piece of cake.*

The final commercial break had arrived.

I tried to relax. I tried to relax. I tried to relax.

*Snappity-snappity-snappity-snappity.*

Before the last break is over, long before the Final Jeopardy clue is revealed, the wranglers always tell you which interrogative to write. As I scrawled down the word "What" I noticed my hand was shaking. I managed to get the four letters out of the light pen. But there are drunks who can write their names in the snow—without bending over—who write more legible characters.

*Snappity-snappity-snappity-snappity.*

Moments later, wrangler Glenn came over with one of the strangest questions I have ever been asked.

The awarding of new cars to retiring undefeated champions had only begun a few weeks earlier, at the beginning of this broadcast season. Champions were to have their choice of a Chevy Suburban, a Tahoe, or a Corvette convertible. One thing they didn't expect: none of the champs liked SUVs. Everyone wanted the sporty Corvette.

So now they were out of Corvettes.

This is what Glenn asked: Would I mind, then, if they just gave me two Camaros instead? One would be a convertible, at least. I could think of them as "his & hers" Camaros if I liked. Would that be all right?

Umm . . . OK.

*Snappity-snappity-snappity-snappity.*

A moment before the game resumed, one of the makeup commandos told me I looked paler than usual, roughly one shade darker than transparent. Naturally: all of the blood in my body was rushing to my heart, lungs, liver, and fast-twitch skeletal muscles.

After all, I was now wrestling entire herds of ravenous badgers.

*Snappity-snappity-snappity-snappity boogety-boogety woop-woop-woop yah GAAAH!*

Finally: *p-TING!*

> THE NKVD, WHICH LIQUIDATED ITS OWN FIRST 2 CHIEFS IN THE 1930S, DEVELOPED INTO THIS GROUP IN 1954

I started thinking of my mom, who would soon be sitting on the couch in the Snow Belt, watching this strange moment. I thought of all the years we had watched this show together. And I still didn't know why she and Dad had sat there so many nights.

*Three letters*, I thought. *Take your time. Three letters.*

I thought about my sister Connie, and hoped her family would enjoy seeing this. I wished she could have had the chance at my formal education, which wound up being less useful to me in practice than a lifetime of screwups, a couple of books, and a boatload of weird off-color jokes. I wished there was more I could do to make her feel better.

*Take your time. You can do this.*

I really missed my dad. I wished he could see this.

*Don't screw it up. It's only three letters.*

As to the clue, I had first heard the correct response while attending Lord of the Flies Academy. Not from books or classes. A couple of the rich kids whose gym lockers were near mine sometimes compared the school to this organization whenever they couldn't get their way.

*Make sure it's spelled right. Is it spelled right? Look at it. Make sure.*

In college, the radio station where I had hid from so many classes had a Ukrainian nationalist program director. We once had a long conversation about the correct response.

*OK. It's spelled right. There.*

And just in case, I even had a mnemonic for the acronym in the clue, in case it was asked the other way around.

*N.ikita K.hruschev's V.D. came from . . .*

*What was the KGB?*


Center stage, stand with Alex. Sweet'N Low candies! Tiger Balm liniment!

I wobble off the stage. They remove the cordless mike I've been wearing most of the day. I sign some papers and hug the crap out of Susanne and Glenn and Grant and possibly twenty or thirty total strangers.

And then I'm alone again. Bright sunshine.

Back in the outside world, less real now than the stage. Walking on the cement of the Sony lot, the same old and hard concrete trail back to the parking garage.

This was exactly the trail I had walked five (or four, or possibly six) times before, back when I couldn't even pass the test. Every echo of my feet in my funeral dress shoes, clop-clop-clopping on the unchanging pavement, reminded me of failure so intensely I wondered if those five games had really occurred.

Finally, Max was waiting there for the ride home, just as he had been every time before. I wondered if he would be jealous of the two new Camaros.

This might have been a wise moment to pause and appreciate what had just happened.

But I had not even reached the garage before I started thinking about the Tournament of Champions. I still wanted more.

I was halfway home before I even realized that someone else would be there.

CHAPTER

11

THE WAR
COMES HOME

Also, Detaching
My Althing from
My Knesset

Blink, blink.

Annika was staring at me as we met in the doorway, waiting for me to say something. I had already told her the news of my undefeated run. It had only been a half-second or so since her immediate reply, but her eyes were already starting to narrow, measuring every instant as it passed.

"Can I quit my job?" she had asked. These were, in fact, her first five words.

I was already late ringing in with an answer.

This wasn't what I'd been expecting. Not that I had expected anything specific. But I had just won $58,000 and two cars, something I had *not* done, it should be said, on most prior days. In Annika's previous experience, in fact, I had not been a winner of $58,000 and two cars with disconcerting frequency.

Her day, meanwhile, had revolved around force-feeding third-grade knowledge into eighth-grade children given second-rate books but first-rate weaponry. So I don't wish to judge her response harshly.

But there she was, waiting expectantly. Not a word of excitement, curiosity, or even genuine interest. Just: "Can I quit my job?"

Blink, blink.

I had met Annika in a coffee shop in Cleveland a couple of years earlier. Her eyes were the same color as my drink that day, and are now the color of whatever type of coffee you like best. (No matter what I write, you'll conjure your own private Annika anyway. All I ask is that you make her anatomically correct, petite, and extraordinarily lovely. Whatever shade of coffee you would find prettiest, that is the correct color for your Annika's eyes. Her hair, however, is the same color as the hair of someone you loved once and no longer know.) My own personal Annika had eyes which were one cream with a touch of cocoa. Which is to say: eyes you'd consider spending your whole life looking at.

On our first dates, her eyelids would sometimes curl at the outer edges, revealing just the tiniest extra bit of perfect white eyeballs. This was always just a buzzer-flash instant before she would toss her head back and laugh. This was a delightful millisecond. I would always see that glint of white and immediately feel the pleasure of pleasing a beautiful woman.

When Annika moved in, I studied those eyes for hours on our first night in my bed. Even in the half-dark of reflected Hollywood street light, there was still a flash of eye-light just before the sound of her laugh.

I had not seen that glint of light in a long time.

I was reminded of all this, as she stood there, looking up at me with those eyes that you have imagined. They were flashing again, but in a different way.

Her voice was calm. But in her eyes—my Annika's eyes—your Annika's eyes—was, of all things: *anger.*

On some level, I understood. Between the two of us, after all, she was the educated one. I was the traveling comedic screwup. She was the more calm and composed and capable under pressure. I was the one with the scars. Annika was, after all, the teacher, whose job it was to know how much a person can and cannot learn in a limited period of time. What I'd just done must have seemed not possible, like somehow I was cheating in life.

So, in the eyes you've imagined, framed by the hair of someone you once loved: *Do you love me, and if so, to what immediate financial extent?*

Blink, blink. A distinct lack of flash-before-laugh.

And here I'd been expecting something akin to "congratulations."

I didn't have the slightest idea how to answer.

I did, however, know that after taxes, the seemingly giant pile of *Jeopardy!* cash was enough to get myself out of debt, pay the rent for a while, and disappointingly little else. I had no idea what to do about the cars yet. Annika could quit her job, but I couldn't support her for long.

And it wasn't like she'd been on my side in all this in the first place. If she'd been eagerly making flash cards or something, hell, I'd have happily given her a kidney, not to mention either one of the his & hers Camaros.

Clearly, Annika and I would have to talk through all these unspoken feelings. We'd have to confess our anger, accept our own mistakes and shortcomings, and develop new habits so we wouldn't repeat the same cycles. This would be a great deal of work, and at the end we might still fail.

Then again, *another* hundred thousand dollars would be just the ticket. Winning the Tournament of Champions seemed like it could solve everything.

Compared to the alternative, this seemed like the easiest option by far.

And so, back to the books. More books. Books about languages, history, theater, and music. Reference and sports books. Fashion and art books. Books about cooks, crooks, and coastal Chinooks.

The Tournament would be played in just four months.

There wasn't a moment to waste.

My first five-subject notebook had already been filled: 300 pages of half-legible scrawls. I started a second. Eventually, a third and a fourth would be filled, all of which I still own. There are also a half-dozen thinner notebooks on especially useful subjects. One page in ten has a lurid, half-competent sketch combining references to the highest creative arts and the rudest of bodily functions.

When I began to study ANATOMY, there was a gleeful irony: I now started memorizing obscure body parts by linking *them* back to classical subjects. The ankle bone, for example, is called a *talus*, easily remembered by thinking of Achilles getting shot in his famous tendon while wearing flip-flops decorated with all sorts of talismans. What kind of talismans? Whatever you find stickiest. I used little keisters, dangling on strings, slapping against the ankle bone, talismans hitting the talus and making me snicker with every fresh tap.

The road between antiquity and thirty-foot buttocks turns out to be a two-way street.

Flipping through this second notebook at random, you would find the following:

Foreign Films & Directors
Animals
Body Parts
Fashion Phrases
Famous Women
Flags of the World
Abstract Art
Ancient Geography

All in the first eighty pages or so, often accompanied by diagrams that seem drawn by a madman.

Some subjects were surprisingly fascinating. ANCIENT GEOGRAPHY, for example.

I had never particularly cared that Alexander the Great once conquered Asia Minor. I mean, big whoop. The thing about Ancient History is that it might as well be ancient history. I didn't even know where Asia Minor *was*.

It's not like I was ever going to visit Asia Minor on vacation.

But wait—it turns out Asia Minor is the biggest chunk of modern-day Turkey. Oh. *That's* where that is. Hmm. And Carthage, why, that was in what we now call Tunisia. And Thrace—who knew that Thrace was a place? Roughly speaking, it's what we call Bulgaria at the moment, although in another century or three it'll probably be called something else. Like everything usually is. Countries and peoples are temporary things. They come and they go, but they're as permanent to us as a storm to a fruit fly.

This was all kinda cool to think about.

There's an actual hill, not far from a town called Çanakkale, where archaeologists think they've found the ruins of Troy. *Troy*, as in big giant horse, and ship-launching-faced Helen, and (somewhat more recently) Brad Pitt pirouetting in a leather skirt.

Troy. Is still *there*.

I wondered how it might feel to see that in person someday.

As a young boy trapped on a long family car trip, I had once been to the Civil War site of the Battle of Bull Run. The guide told of Washington socialites traveling for hours to enjoy the view of a simple skirmish, hoping to sit on a hillside supping on tea and madeleines while young men were slaughtered below.

This story stuck with me for life, partly for the appalling idea of well-off people enjoying a picnic holiday while delighting in carnage, and partly because the tour guide could point to the exact hillsides and grassy fields where both kinds of ugliness raged.

Unmarked by the years, those hills could have still been in the previous century. Forgetting the timeline, I could almost hear the gunfire and see the panicking petticoats scurrying back to their carriages. I was no longer looking at grass and trees and hills or a story in a book. I was looking at a real place, and real events, and thinking about what they meant in ways I hadn't expected.

This was my first glimpse of Trebekistan.

Trebekistan is a location unfixed in physical space and time. It's a place of pure learning, where hard playful work can bring sudden shocks of unexpected perception. In Trebekistan, art and math and geography and science stop pretending to be separate subjects, and instead converge in a glorious riot. Every new detail creates two fresh curiosities, so you know less as you learn, and yet nothing seems unknowable. Trebekistan, oddly, is a place of expanding dimension yet increasing connection, both growing and shrinking with every new step.

Of course, even the best places can be screwed up. Toured foolishly, I would learn, Trebekistan can become a place of self-absorption, where knowledge has no purpose but the accretion of other knowledge. One can sin with intellectual greed as self-destructively as one who hoards wealth, love, or pride itself.

I have gotten ahead of the story again. But the timeline in Trebekistan can be surprisingly flexible.

As I continued to work, I kept seeing details that gave breath and blood to dry names and events that had once seemed like dust on the page. This was often a great source of glee.

A key breakthrough in physics was the Michelson-Morley experiment, meant to measure a pervasive invisible space-goo called the *luminiferous ether*. If you've never heard of it, that's because Michelson and Morley so definitively *didn't* find space-goo that soon it was clear that it didn't exist. In other words, their work so thoroughly discredited their own ideas that they radically leapfrogged our understanding of the universe. (Coincidentally, they were working in Cleveland, at what became my alma mater, in what became the department where I got a degree.) Failure, taken far enough, can be brilliant success.

The greatest logician of the twentieth century, Kurt Gödel, pioneered entire fields of mathematical reasoning that brilliant minds take years to comprehend. However, much of what he proved with indisputable math was that many things cannot be proven. *That* much, you can prove. Outside of his work, he was a schizophrenic convinced he was being poisoned by unknown beings. So that's humankind's greatest logician.

Mark Twain (a distant relative, it turns out, but then aren't we all) suffered great personal tragedies, could not handle money, and slowly became depressive with age. He was rescued from ruin when he started to drink with the ruthless head of Standard Oil, Henry Rogers, a robber baron so merciless he was widely known as "Hell Hound," a man Twain's characters might have once held in the deepest contempt. Rogers, in turn, was humanized by the great humanist, and donated small fortunes to the education of black Southerners and numerous others in need. So Twain's distressed kindness, returning the friendship of a man he could have judged harshly, was redeemed many times over, in the end.

Fun to contemplate: Twain's financial woe may well have indirectly led to the education of Helen Keller. It can be hard to know good news from bad.

The world is far stranger than I could ever have hoped. So are all of us in it—spectacularly mixed bags, varying less by absolutes than degrees.

Gandhi, great soul, disowned his own firstborn. Einstein's first published paper asserted deep significance in the action of drinking straws. Arthur Miller, sensitive dramatist of family issues, pretended his youngest son didn't even exist.

Ancestrally speaking, the Windsors of England are more German than English. George V switched to "Windsor" (from "Saxe-Coburg-Gotha") in 1917 when England was warring with Germany. It would be hard to persuade young men to die in the trenches to prevent Germans from taking over if it seemed clear that they already had. So, Windsor it is. Carry on.

There seem to be as many examples as there are human beings.

How fragile and brilliant and vain and sad and vulnerable and ludicrous everything started to look. A strangely familiar world began to open. No one had ever told me this, but the whole of humanity seems to be mostly a bunch of screwups who do their best, get it right most of the time, but often don't.

Yes, yes, *of course* plans fail, leaders are corrupt, and self-proclaimed paragons get caught with their pants down. History screams: this is *normal.* That's just what we humans often do. But we also learn and recover and rebuild and nurture each other in magnificent ways.

Which is why striving to be better, every day, and with all of our energy, is so damn difficult, rare, and admirable.

It's why pride is a sin and humility a virtue. And so at least four words in the *Concordance* were now making more sense.

Very slowly, my *Jeopardy!* notebooks started changing, from a list of dry information I needed to memorize to outlines of things I wanted to know more about, field guides to a world I'd barely even seen.

When I first saw Trebekistan in the midst of a battlefield, Bull Run had been made into a park. My parents paid to get in, and some guy led us around, so it all had a special-world air to my child's mind. It never occurred to me that the whole planet is actually like that hillside in Virginia, if you learn to start seeing with more careful eyes.

I wanted eyes like that. I'm still trying to see to this day.

As was becoming habit now, I checked the air dates for the Tournament games. Only the two-day $100,000 final, pitting the three remaining contestants from a field of fifteen, fell on significant dates.

The first game would air on February 12: Abe Lincoln's birthday. The second game would air on a Friday the 13th.

A notebook soon filled up with everything Lincoln. Phobias took over another.

Of course, it would be useless if I didn't make it through the first two rounds.

The gods of state-dependent retrieval received proper tribute.

The bright lights and bookcase-turned-podium would remain in place for the next four months. (Even if Annika, on the other hand, might not.) My never-rest study habits would continue. If it was good enough for *A Clockwork Orange*, it was good enough for me. But I realized there was still more I could do.

The effect of physical state on recall has even been proposed—with some good evidence—as extending to the foods you eat, the medicines you've taken, and how much sleep or caffeine you have had. Rats who are given an intravenous drip of alcohol before learning to run a maze will later repeat the maze better when drunk than sober. (They'll also be more comfortable wearing little party hats, doing Jell-O shooters off each other's tummies, and flashing their tiny rodent breasts while squeaking "whoo.")

Such is the power of physical state.

On a taping date, I would have to be awake at 7:30 a.m., and I would play my actual games sometime between noon and 5:30 p.m. During the day at Sony, I would have access to a limited menu of food and drink, although I could surely sneak protein snack bars into the green room. So: with rare exception, every day for four months, I awakened at

7:30, studied most intensely between noon and 5:30 (often standing at the bookcase that doubled as my practice podium), and ate exactly the green room snacks and protein bars I would eat on a game day, plus a Sony-lunch-style sandwich around 3:00 p.m.

Annika was usually at work. But not on weekends. So two days a week, I shared my life with someone who definitely thought I had completely lost my mind.

This was entirely possible.

It's also likely that I was involuntarily responding to another type of programmed retrieval: classical conditioning.

We all remember Pavlov's Dog: ring a bell when you're feeding the dog, and soon the dog starts salivating at the sound of a bell, even in the absence of food. (Pavlov himself, incidentally, was as trained as one of his dogs: he rose, ate each meal, and slept at the same time every day, vacationed each year at exactly the same place, and always left on the same day on the calendar—*p-TING!* indeed.)

I had just spent weeks on end training myself to push a button and feel smarter a few seconds later. And then, on national television, I had pushed a button and gotten rewarded, pushed a button and gotten rewarded, and pushed a button and gotten rewarded, over and over and over.

In some sense, I'm not sure the Tournament of Champions—or any external stimulus—even mattered. Of course I was still pushing the button.

Perhaps I was Pavlov's Contestant.

Further on in my notebooks, you'd also find the following lists of information:

State Flowers and Birds
Different Shapes of Seashells
Diacritical Marks
Names of Foreign Parliaments

And so on.

Looking back, I'm not sure what I was thinking. Or if the word "thinking" even applies. *Jeopardy!* asks for STATE CAPITALS, sure, but I've never seen the flowers or birds without some sort of hint.

Seashells? Wow. Was I really expecting to be asked to reel these off? *What are—left to right—a chiton, a cowrie, a whelk, and a limpet?*

Diacritical marks? What the ellipsis was I thinking?

I was certain, however, that the parliaments would be helpful. Knowing my Knesset from my Althing would matter someday.

More important, though: I *wanted* to know this stuff.

I couldn't imagine *not* wanting to know everything about everything. Every day was a rush of excitement, new knowledge and worlds and perceptions unfolding. I was an eager captive, unable and unwilling to leave.

I was imprisoning myself in Trebekistan.

Halloween came. On the calendar this time. The air date of my very first game.

My phone started to ring at 4:30 p.m., just as the show was ending back east.

Mom thought I looked nice. Connie thought I looked healthy. Old friends who knew me called just to catch up. I didn't realize there were so many, or that it would feel like such a prize when they called.

Surprisingly, most people commented on how very confident I looked, how calm and in control, how completely relaxed. How bizarre. I was "the funny one," that odd *Jeopardy!* player who seemed comfortable onstage. Clearly, my Midwestern years of doing comedy in VFW halls, dance clubs, and other near-combat conditions were finally starting to pay.

Other callers and e-mailers had other agendas. A cousin I didn't know needed money for business. An old boss called me up for a loan. A girl I had dated perhaps twice in college thought I looked better than I had in school. She mentioned the exact total of money I had won in that day's game. Twice.

Another round of calls came around 5:00 p.m. Chicago friends now. *Jeopardy!* was moving across the map like a storm front.

A series of Frequently Asked Questions was already developing. What is Alex like? (I dunno. I'll ask him next time.) Do they give you anything to study? (No.) Really? (Really.) They don't give you anything to study? (No.) Then how do you know all the answers? (I don't. And I study.) Well, how do you know what to study? (Excuse me while I stab you in the lungs with my phone antenna.) Because it seems to me— (URKuhhhhhgh.)

At 6:30 p.m., I heard from a waitress I'd known briefly in Michigan, now living in Arizona. She only mentioned the money once.

At 7:00 p.m., our local broadcast began. I was almost as nervous watching as playing. Perhaps this time I would lose.

Annika and I plopped on the couch for the show. She was nervous, too, almost giddy. She blurted out answers and rooted and wagered and played along eagerly. She mentioned how confident I looked on the show, and smiled proudly at last when I won.

The buzzer-flash glint in her eyes had returned.

The week of Thanksgiving was more of the same. Friends calling friends, and those friends calling me. The phone rang a bit more every night. Men tended to point out a response they knew that I didn't, asserting themselves competitively. Women more often pointed out responses that no one knew, creating safety. Rarely are stereotypes so grossly confirmed.

A few friends came over to reinforce these stereotypes over pizza and soda while my games aired four nights in a row.

Me, I ate protein bars.

My next-door neighbor David had a lot of pizza and soda that week. We'd met a few months after I moved to L.A., when he knocked on the door, hoping to borrow a hammer from a stranger. I invited him in for a beer, offered him any speed-reading book in the toolbox, and pretty soon I had a best buddy in town.

You've seen David on TV, even if you don't watch much TV. He's not famous, but he's constantly working. I've seen him in a lot of roles, but mostly he's on a certain show about crime scene investigators in Las Vegas. He tends to get splattered with blood a lot.

On the show, I mean. If he does this in private, I don't know about it.

David has the honor of being the first person to introduce me to someone as a *Jeopardy!* champion. He did this about once every three seconds, possibly in his sleep. "Hey, this is my friend Bob. He won on

*Jeopardy!*," David would say. And then, sometimes, just to prove the point: "Hey, Bob—what's the capital of Namibia?"

I would smile, pleased for his affection and proud to be called smart, but a little embarrassed at the trained-monkey moment. It was like being my parents' child again. But not answering was never an option. Pavlov's subject was well-trained.

David would know this. David would love this. "Come on, Bob. What's the capital of Namibia?"

*Windhoek*, I'd say, and then would come laughter. I'm not sure how often the show-off-ee was amused, but for us the game was a fun one.

I don't remember who he introduced me to this way first.

The last person he introduced me to this way was Jane.

After millions of people had seen my five games, for a time I was recognized with surprising frequency. For a few days, it was almost every time I left the house. Each time, I reviewed the *Jeopardy!* FAQs once again from the top, with occasional slight variations.

While eating a burrito, I was once asked to repeat the $500 word for meat so rotten that it glows. *Bioluminescence*, I replied. I never finished the burrito.

Unfortunately, public discussions of dazzling meat, even brief ones, meant more time spent away from my studies. Leaving the house would have to become the exception. My own personal Ludovico Technique wouldn't allow it: I had notebooks to study and straitjackets to wear and pried-open eyes to have droplets plunked into and *It's a sin! It's a sin!* to cry out.

I told most of my friends to pretend I had left the country for a few months.

David called a few weeks before the Tournament and asked me if I wanted to attend the movie *Amistad*, with Anthony Hopkins. I said no; I was too busy studying American Presidents that day.

You may notice that this is the second time *Amistad* has been mentioned, and for no obvious reason. Perhaps you even sense the presence of connections unseen.

Well. With that kind of buildup, if *Amistad* doesn't pay off somehow, I suggest you get your money back.

■ ■ ■

Annika's appreciation for the project again cooled.

One day, almost out of the blue, she actually said this while I was poring over a list of Famous Inventors:

"You *do* realize that the other players probably have real educations, right?"

As a matter of fact, I did. I also realized that I just couldn't imagine Annika as the "her" for the his & hers Camaros.

(Actually, I couldn't imagine sharing the his & hers Camaros with anyone, including me. I was, after all, well into my thirties. Camaros are for high-school quarterbacks with easy hair. At my age, driving a Camaro projects an entirely different image. To look the part fully, I would need to start wearing aviator sunglasses, shiny shirts unbuttoned to the navel, and someone else's head entirely.)

When the breakup with Annika finally comes—very soon now—it will only be a couple of sentences long. You've been way ahead of that, anyway, since the first mention of Jane. The end of love can be as gradual as its beginning is sudden. But after a certain point, the rest of what follows is just moving furniture.


Whatever mistakes or flaws in our relationship may have been Annika's doing, my own were much larger. She wasn't the one trying to study the world by scrupulously never leaving the house. She wasn't the one transforming our apartment into a well-lit Skinner box. And I certainly wasn't the most attractive guy at the moment.

As the last weeks before the Tournament passed, I began playing my practice games wearing my clothes for the show. This makes perfect state-dependent sense. Theater groups do exactly the same thing. But theater groups are probably a bit more careful about doing laundry in between. The spare hour required seemed a luxury. There was so much to learn.

My diet became even more focused on green room cuisine: danishes, muffins, cola, and protein bars mostly, plus the Sony-lunch tuna croissants. My body was well trained for a *Jeopardy!* day. It was also well trained for washing up on a beach, huffing for air, and being carted back to sea on a pallet by concerned marine biologists.

I hadn't exercised much. An extra hour of review always seemed more important than, say, maintaining my cardiovascular system or supplying oxygen to my brain. A spare hour of sleep seemed luxurious, too. When you're trying to learn everything that ever happened anywhere to anyone, it's hard to know when to stop.

By the night before the first Tournament taping date, I had put on almost fifteen pounds. I was sleep-deprived. I was constantly exhausted. I was depressed because I was losing my girlfriend.

And all I had to do *now* was overcome fourteen players who knew more than I did. Then, finally, all of my problems would be solved.

Clearly, I had everything under control.

*Jeopardy!*'s standard tournament format was devised by Alex Trebek himself, when the show ended its first season with fifteen five-time champs. The format works, so it remains:

- The fifteen top players of the year are invited.
- Taping takes two five-show days, creating two weeks' worth of games.
- The first day is a preliminary round. Nine players survive: the five winners, plus the top four remaining scorers, who advance as "wild cards."
- On the morning of the second day, these nine contestants play a semifinal round of three games.
- That afternoon, the three winners play a two-game, cumulative-score final.

At worst, you play once and go home. At best, you play four games and win.

Part of what makes the format intriguing is

that it doesn't actually require four wins; the only game you *must* win outright is the semifinal. With a wild card in the first round and close second-place finishes to different opponents in the two-day final, it's conceivably possible to come in second three times out of four and remain standing at the end.

On the first day, in fact, you shouldn't even care about winning, but focus only on finishing well. If this reminds you of the eighth and ninth steps on the Eightfold Path, you're thinking ahead like a champ.

I was thinking ahead myself on exactly this point at about 6:00 p.m. the night before the first game. I was walking through the lobby of the Beverly Hilton, where *Jeopardy!* bunked all of the players. I was trying to stay calm and focused. I was just going for some coffee, one last jolt of caffeine, and then I would try to relax for the night.

I had everything under control.

Surrounded by the hotel's metallic gold fixtures and weaving through the metallic gold clientele, I was thinking about how the tournament format might affect my wagering.

And then I noticed I was feeling kinda woozy.

I had studied FAMOUS ATHLETES. I had memorized MAJOR BATTLES. I had immersed myself in THE BODY HUMAN, ANATOMY, and PSYCHOLOGY.

One thing I had forgotten to brush up on, amid all the overwork: HUMAN LIMITATIONS. By bedtime my body temperature was well over 100.

I had once again gotten something in my nose.

Being sick in a posh hotel does have its advantages. If you cannot even rise to walk down the hall, for example, you can pay someone wearing a metallic vest to bring you a large shiny ice bucket.

You can then lie on your back and stare at a roomful of gloss, or look out a window at Los Angeles's metallic gold air, and try to take your mind off the fact that you have managed to destroy any chance of winning, before you have even reached the studio.

By morning, my fever was simmering quietly. I dressed and just tried not to panic. I was moving as smoothly as a fifty-foot fiberglass Hiawatha, and feeling about as intelligent.

The green room began in the golden-trimmed lobby. The *Jeopardy!*

wranglers assembled the sixteen of us (fifteen plus an alternate) and led us to a Sony-supplied van. We all piled in, wondering who would survive, and made small talk in rush-hour traffic.

There was little one-upmanship this time, however. Everyone here knew that everyone else here was good. The tone was quiet, focused, reserved, tense, and unrested. Saving it all for later.

I did the same, even more.

As we stepped onto the *Jeopardy!* soundstage and began the morning rehearsal, no one was dazzled. No one was surprised by rotating in and out. We'd all done this before. So the rehearsal was now a chance to assess the competition.

Everyone was fast. Everyone was good. Everyone in the room was in peak combat condition, muscles rippling and bulging from their sleek thumbs of steel.

Whether it was my fever disrupting my timing or the others' equal ability, I couldn't ring in at all. My buzzer advantage was gone.

My light just kept staying off.

Any edge I had gained from my studies also seemed to dissolve. Tournament clues are a notch harder than normal. At this level, all of my work had still only brought me up to perhaps average in this group. And I was slower of mind on this day by some margin.

I was beginning to panic. If I lost and went home, I would feel stupid for months. I was frightened of losing in public. I was frightened of facing Annika. I would lose her, possibly from my own selfishness, and very likely for nothing, in the end.

The players filed back to our seats in the green room, where the day would soon tick by. We would be led out in threes, not knowing when we would be called next. The rest would remain, waiting.

Those left in the green room could know nothing of the games under way, lest later players gain an advantage in knowing the wild card totals. Based on past years, however, the amount needed to feel certain of advancing would be about $10000.

To me, it might as well have been a million. Everybody here had played like brilliant assassins, and everyone knew it, so a collegial atmosphere floated over my enveloping dread. I shrank into a corner chair, trapped in a room with Lee Smarty Oswald, Lynette "Clicky" Fromme, Sirhan Buzzerer Sirhan, sharing professional respect for their infamous skills.

I imagined they all had concealed backup buzzers in holsters strapped to their shoulders and ankles, just in case shit went down bad.

Even without the genital-sniffing primate behavior of earlier green rooms, however, one player projected a high-powered Confidence Field, the same one I had projected on the day I won four games, only stronger. His relaxed smile and pressureless humor inflicted light psychic damage in every direction. He was slightly older than the rest of us, and he smelled of freshly inked manuscripts and tenure. When he spoke, his eyes inspected the listeners' reactions as if he were grading their response on a curve.

When Berkeley arose in conversation, it soon emerged that he was a professor there. This concerned me. I leaned forward, closer, playing ahead, looking for clues.

His necktie was adorned with a motto in Latin. It was a Harvard school tie.

*An Ivy League Serial Killer was in this very room.*

His name was Dan Melia.

I could feel my fever rising again.

Worse, I knew it would rise further as the day dragged along. Every minute was harder. I hoped for the earliest game. I just wanted to play first and lie down. Failing that, I would hope not to get stuck with the cold-blooded Killer, or at least that he would show mercy, and not track down my family in Ohio and defeat them all, too.

I would hope for a miracle.

One other player bears mention here, although we barely spoke on this particular day: Arthur Phillips, now a best-selling novelist, author of *Prague* and *The Egyptologist*, well known for his intense mind and quiet dry wit.

In the green room, his powers of concentration were on display. He prepared himself mentally by retreating to the northeast corner, where he sat, eyes closed, listening to music in a pair of headphones, focusing focusing focusing as if trying to move test objects in some remote parapsychology lab. Except for the occasional twitch of his brow, only his heart and lungs ever moved.

The rest of us didn't want to distract him, but if you waved a piece of notebook paper in front of his forehead, it would burst into flames.

This was hours of fun.

Finally, Susanne called three names:

*Come on, come on, come on . . .*

"Kim! Fred! Lyn!"

*Crap.*

My temperature throbbed up one degree.

Nearly an hour passed. Routine production cramps, contestant turnover, between-show resetting of every doojobbie, and the time-distortion field generated by my own throbbing head were all conspiring to create a series of tiny enormous delays.

Finally, Susanne called three more names:

*Come on, come on, come on . . .*

"Paul! Claudia! Josh!"

I got hotter.

An hour later, three more. And I no longer cared who I played. Even Dan.

*Come on, come on, come on . . . I do not fear Jeopardy! death . . .*

"Dan! Peter! Craig!"

I got hotter.

Then lunch. And again. Three more names. None was mine.

I would have to play last. It was almost five in the afternoon already. By now I was lying on my back on the carpet in the makeup area. I had given up on advancing, and was only trying not to make the other two remaining players sick.

They couldn't have been kinder. Wes Ulm was a med student from Boston working on a gene therapy project. I believe one day he will find a way to deliver cures for cancer at the cellular level. Grace Veach was a librarian from Decatur and a new mom. Someday she will find a way to deliver all the information in the library into her young boy's lucky head.

They were both also funny and genuinely sweet. Wes, true to the

Hippocratic Oath, was more concerned for my health than for the game we would play. Grace got me cold water and made me laugh. I would cheer for them both. I was glad at least one would advance.

This was the first time I ever met anyone else who had studied in the weeks before the show. Wes hit the books, of course, simply by getting out of bed in medical school. Grace studied, in her own words, "too much, obsessively, every spare moment." The three of us watched another hour tick by, punctuated only by the soft gurgle of my will to live trickling out on the floor.

Finally: "Grace! Bob! Wes!"

Dead Man Walking again.

Even with video to review, the game's just a haze that I don't recall very well. You can see on the tape as we walk out, however, that the three of us are rooting each other on, glancing and smiling at each other in the introductions.

This was so much better than my "don't be nervous" bullshit. I began the game feeling like an ass for having done that in my earlier games. A sleep-deprived ass, in fact, with slow reflexes, still little real knowledge, and a cranium pounding with fever.

I just wanted to go home. Except Annika would be there.

The game begins.

Wes quickly whips out the Forrest Bounce, swerving from category to category. Against a guy whose head he knows is already spinning.

I am relieved. I feel like much less of an ass. At the podium, all oaths are off.

After months of continuous study, I know few of the responses. It feels like I'm back on Mom and Dad's couch in the Snow Belt. In the first dozen clues, I respond exactly once on a lame $100 clue. I keep my hand off the Weapon and wait for my doom.

I glance up at the scoreboard, involuntarily curious to see the results of nearly three solid minutes of textbook futility. I have, in this moment in this game, exactly one hundred more *Jeopardy!* dollars than you do.

And I am, I discover, in the lead.

■ ■ ■

Wes and Grace still must play each other, of course. They are still under considerable pressure. So they are ringing in with bad guesses. I'm the only player with any money at all. One *Who is Danny Bonaduce?* later, I am practically pulling away at the first commercial break.

*Keep your finger off the button,* I am thinking. *Just don't shoot yourself, and maybe Grace and Wes will nail each other in the crossfire.*

Since I know even less here than usual, maybe the way to win is by *playing* even less than usual. This may not seem logical. But you'd have to ask Gödel, and he'd just think you were trying to poison him.

In the interview segment with Alex, I seem surprisingly lucid and animated on tape, talking even faster than normal. I do not remember a glimmer of this. When I look at the video, what I see are my unsteady hands, visibly shaking when I gesture.

The game resumes. In the first minute I give two wrong responses. So much for not shooting myself. I am so discombobulated that I can't even reply to this $100 clue in the category PETS:

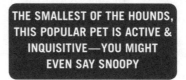

THE SMALLEST OF THE HOUNDS, THIS POPULAR PET IS ACTIVE & INQUISITIVE—YOU MIGHT EVEN SAY SNOOPY

In my first game, against Matt, I deduced the Great Pumpkin by detecting multiple hints and making a snap analysis of the relative database sizes. Today (and your internal voice should slow for comedic effect here), I cannot remember that Charlie Brown's dog is a beagle.

Still, a category on celebrities plays to the only slight advantage I might have over a librarian and a med student. At the end of the *Jeopardy!* round, I find my timing and quickly reel off:

*Who is Bob Vila?*

*Who is Erik Estrada?*

*Who is Anthony Edwards?*

Take *that,* smart healthy people with real educations!

My superior knowledge of WATCHING TV WHILE KILLING TIME IN

MOTELS carries me back into the lead, with more points than Wes and Grace combined.

Six minutes to go and I can lie down and sleep. Possibly right at the podium.

The Double Jeopardy round feels much more like six hours. I respond to the first clue—*What is a bake-off?*—and am thereafter beaten on the buzzer to every single response for over two full minutes.

Grace seizes the lead, and by the twelfth clue, I am a mute, distant third. My thought process is so slow that I'm not even completing some of the clues in my head. For example:

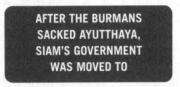

AFTER THE BURMANS
SACKED AYUTTHAYA,
SIAM'S GOVERNMENT
WAS MOVED TO

Two podiums to my right, Wes buzzes in, while my eyes are just reaching

THIS CITY

at the end of the clue. My brain scrambles to catch up: *Siam is the old name for Thailand,* I think, *and the capital of Thailand is Bangkok.* But I hear Wes responding "What is Bangkok?" correctly.

Wes and Grace both open fire without mercy:

"Who is Ken Follett?"

"Who was Frederick the Great?"

"What's a portcullis?"

*Yes,* I say to myself. *What IS a portcullis?* To this day, I have not the slightest idea.

As a piercing headache sets in, I realize that I am nowhere near winning or even reaching a wild card. So I feel compelled to guess. Several times.

This is a transgression against all that is Enlightened Jeopardy, an unwise straying from the Eightfold Path. Punishment comes swiftly. I spiral downward, giving four wrong responses in the last eight clues, driving my score almost all the way back to zero. It is surely among the least-competent seventy-two-second periods in the history of the show.

Alex gives the scores at the end of Double Jeopardy as follows:

"We have Grace at $8300, Wes with $5700, and Bob—faltering slightly there, winding up with $1600."

*Faltering slightly.*

The first question in the *Jeopardy!* FAQ is "What's Alex really like?"

I don't know what "really" is. It's not like we hang out up at the lush *Jeopardy!* Mansion, kicking back Potent Potables in a Jacuzzi with left-over groupies whom Johnny Gilbert turned down. I've never met Alex outside a *Jeopardy!*-related context, and for show security reasons, I assume I never will.

But I have stood a few feet away from him for a total of several hours now, conducting a strangely disjointed conversation while trying to keep two other people from butting in. And I do know this much: the guy is always rooting for every contestant to do well. Always. I rarely glimpse his face during a game, with my eyes locked on the game board, but I hear the joy in his voice whenever any tough clue is conquered or a big Daily Double pays off.

After over twenty years, he still gets excited when the games are close, and he appreciates it when people play well. He often seems to wish everyone could win.

He's good at the rest of the job, of course. He's too modest to admit it, for example, but I am convinced he really does know most of the responses. But there's a much more important aspect of Alex's job that I've never heard anyone fully appreciate.

Every day that Alex Trebek goes to work, he has to deal with five batches of three bright but nervous people competing for piles of cash that could change any of their lives. He can offer just the slightest encouragement to anyone, lest it appear he is taking sides, and he can provide only an occasional bit of gentle humor without risking throwing a player off stride.

Since the best players work from the rhythm of his voice, his smoothness is completely essential. He often goes entire shows without blowing a syllable, sometimes with phrases from five different languages. His gig is a bit like a referee's job in football: you only notice he's human when something doesn't go right. If he mispronounces even a single rat-a-tat word, be it in Latin or Chinese or Russian, it can disrupt the game, breaking a player's timing. But perfection will not even be noticed.

And at the end of all that, almost every single day, there will be a moment where Tilly from Phoenix or Walter from Yakima or Bob from Cleveland will suddenly *not* respond correctly. This will cost them dearly. And it is Alex's job, then, to explain gently that, no, sorry, they will *not* be buying a decent car, they will *not* be paying the mortgage off early, they will *not* be sending their kids to college. I have never seen this appreciated, and it should be: Alex's job, as much as anything else, is to be a graceful bearer of bad news to most of the people he meets. Day in, day out. And Alex has to communicate this bad news in a matter of seconds, projecting both authority and compassion, with a wink and a smile, and see you next time on *Jeopardy!*, so long.

It's not coal mining like my grandfather did. It's not lifting stuff like my dad. But in its own way, that's a hard job for anyone with even a decent heart, no matter how much you get paid.

This is the role of the *Oooh*.

You have seen the Oooh. And the Oooh is good.

"Faltering slightly" was Alex's way of saying, "It was a good run. Sorry it didn't work out. Good luck to you." This was a somewhat elaborate Oooh. And I appreciated it.

Still, it wasn't so bad. With Grace already nearing the coveted $10000 mark and Wes at $5700, there was a good chance they'd both advance to the next round. And they're both cool people. So, OK. I'd worry for their safety, knowing the Ivy League Serial Killer might be lurking nearby. But I was glad for them.

At $1600, I knew I had no shot whatsoever. So when it was time to wager before Final Jeopardy, I bet it all. There was no real risk, anyway. Besides, the Final Jeopardy category was U.S. CITIES, and my many years on the road wouldn't hurt.

However.

*p-TING!*

> **THIS HISTORIC CITY WAS NAMED
> FOR THE BISHOP OF HIPPO
> ON WHOSE FEAST DAY THE
> AREA WAS FIRST SIGHTED**

I had not the slightest idea. While the Think Music played, my mind wandered again. What follows is what I thought about for the first ten seconds or so, written in prose perhaps more lucid than the inarticulate panic I was feeling, given that my brain was about to ignite.

Annika would think I was a fool. And perhaps she was right.

Trebekistan is a fine place to visit, but not at the expense of your actual home. I had driven myself to exhaustion in what was really nothing but a massive feeding of my own ego. No wonder I was thirty-five and still so chronically single.

My sister, back in Ohio, would see once again what I'd done with the one college education between us. I still would have done little to make her life truly better.

My mom would have to see her son go down in flames on national TV.

And then I realized: since I was feeling so bad, that meant the reflected pride she and Dad always basked in when I was a kid was still important to me, so much so I would turn myself inside out to get it.

Two decades later, I was after all, despite everything I thought about myself, still eight years old and trying not to pee.

Was I actually still showing up the guys I hated in school? Yes, *yes* I was, in fact. Was I still dating women for how they salved my insecurities, and not because of actual love? Yes. Was I still, in the end, wasting my abilities, just to massage my own ego?

Well.

I had learned so much without ever learning a single goddamned thing.

So this was the end of my *Jeopardy!* career.

Unless things were about to get even stranger.

CHAPTER

13

FACING THE
THINK MUSIC

Also, Strangers
Seize Me by the Udder
and Yank

The Final Jeopardy Think Music consists of two repeated choruses of a happy little tick-tocking melody, not unlike "I'm a Little Tea-pot" conducted by an atomic clock. After thirty seconds, the music ends with the two dramatic tympani thumps—bum-*BUM!*—signaling (a) the response period has ended, and (b) Merv is get-ting another royalty check.

Maybe they should replace the bum-*BUM!* with a cha-*CHING!* now and again.

For the first chorus of the Think Music, you already know what I was thinking. But I didn't want to just leave my little electronic screen empty. A dead man could do as much, and I wasn't one yet. So as the second chorus began, I tried to invent a reasonable enough wild guess that I could escape and go home without looking like a complete idiot.

So, giving up on answering entirely,

*Let go of outcome.*

I read the entire clue again a second time,

## Slow down and see the obvious.

looking for any hint I could free-associate from.

## Everything connects to everything else.

*"This historic city"* . . . *OK, and the category is U.S. Cities* . . . *well, the oldest city in the U.S. is St. Augustine; that's in my notebooks somewhere . . .* *"Was named for the Bishop of Hippo."* *Hippo, singular. A place, not the animals. Good, I didn't think hippos had bishops. Where the hell is Hippo? Still, any city named for a Catholic might start with "St." or "Santa." Good enough. St. Augustine, fine . . .*

Electronic pen on glass. *Clackity-click-whap-clackity.* But I am second-guessing my response before it is even finished.

*"On whose feast day the area was first sighted."* *So it's either on a coast or near a mountain pass. Shit. Santa Fe is really old, too. And it's in the mountains. Crap. I wonder if somebody named Fe was from Hippo. Shit . . .*

Bum-*BUM!*

The lights come up. It's over.

Because I'm in last place, my response will be revealed first. It's a formality anyway, since I only have $1600 more than Annika does at home. I'm curious, hoping to double this fictional total while it exists, but mostly just relieved to have been wrong in a face-saving way.

Alex smiles gently at my response. He sees the resignation in my body language and measures how to phrase what he'll say next.

I fear the Oooh.

But *Who is St. Augustine?* is correct.

Fred Ramen, an undefeated champion who actually went to his classes at NYU, will tell me more about St. Augustine later, on the way back to the hotel. Fred will have the slightly distant carriage of a Luxembourgian prince, but will speak like a kid showing you a hidden cache of squirt guns. I will like him immediately.

Fred, I will learn, grew up watching *Jeopardy!* with his father and was too nervous to sleep before his first time on the show. He spent

much of that day loading up on caffeine and hoping not to face the returning champion, a certain Harvard-trained Berkeley professor causing
much fear in the green room. Fortunately, Dan Melia won his fifth
game just before Fred's name was called. Fred soon won five games himself, but he put it down to good luck. He will still dread Dan, as we ride
back to the Hilton.

Hippo, Fred will inform me, was an area ruled by the Romans,
roughly where Algeria and Tunisia are today. And St. Augustine, I will
learn, was a fourth-century utopian with influential sexual hang-ups, another fine mess joining Mark Twain and Gandhi in the grand human
pageant. I will smile and resolve to learn more.

Fred will later confess that he studied obsessively and even created
a computer program to time his Go Light reactions, comparing different techniques to the nths of a second. The forefinger is fastest, Fred
will be certain. I'll agree.

I will feel a great deal less alone.


Once I'm done reacting with hapless surprise at being correct, Alex
moves over to Wes, whose $5700 current bankroll is (a) nearly twice my
$3200 final score and (b) still not quite enough to feel confident of a
wild card spot.

Wes's Final Jeopardy response: "What is Santa Fe?"

His wager: large enough to clinch a wild card if his response had
been correct. Large enough to eliminate him now.

Wes hears the Oooh. He looks even sicker than I feel. I'm bummed
for my erstwhile caretaker, his Forrest Bounce and all.

Alex turns to Grace. She has a big smile, the correct response, and a
conservative bet. She's into the semifinals. We hug, and Alex invites her
to join him at center stage.

Wes and I are happy, envious, and thoroughly defeated.

As the audience applauds, videotape versions of other advancing
contestants introduce themselves to the home audience. Their mortal
equivalents, meanwhile, are led to join Alex and Grace onstage. Since
nine players will advance, it's quite a brilliant little herd.

Wes and I helplessly watch them assemble. Our buzzers are limp and powerless now. We smile wanly at each other, wordlessly communicating a mutual desire to get drunk somewhere.

I turn to exit.

This, finally, was the end of my *Jeopardy!* career.

*Jeopardy!* is a TV show, however. Appearances matter. So contestant wranglers Susanne and Grant and Glenn ask Wes and me to remain on-stage at our podiums. We only need to be good sports for just another minute or two. There is some commotion offstage, perhaps a minor technical glitch. Hushed voices handle whatever it is.

I let the long seconds pass. I am already thinking of Merv's big hotel, where a solid gold bed and a platinum pillow await. My fever is peaking. I need to lie down.

The camera comes on. The show is almost over. Finally.

Alex turns to the other contestants. I only have to stand here for a few more instants. But instead of congratulating the winners, he does something unusual, something I never once saw him do while watching back in the Snow Belt.

Alex starts, of all things, to *count*. He points to each contestant at his side, one by one, speaking aloud. "One-two-three-four-five-six-seven-*eight*," Alex says. And then he looks in my direction. I cannot fathom why.

But $3200, as of that final instant, becomes one of the lowest scores ever to advance through the first round of a tournament in the history of *Jeopardy!*

I want to celebrate, either by jumping up and down or by curling up on the floor and moaning softly.

Instead, my body averages the two. I lumber dizzily toward Alex and the other winners, a pasty-skinned Irish guy in a discount-rack corduroy sport coat, grinning and joking and just amused enough to remain standing and talking for another few minutes.

It feels like being given a surprise party by people I have never met.

Of course, this means some unseen producer (I have a few suspects in mind) with a wicked talent for improvisation has figured out how to frame those moments to capture my authentic response on camera. So one could say this is as manipulative and cunning as anything in "reality" television. More so, in fact, since "reality" contestants fully expect their emotions to become fodder. My feelings, arguably, are being milked.

To which I can only say: *Moo.*

More to the point, I would like to add, with a few years of perspective: *Moo moo moo, moo moooooooooooo,* and, on considered reflection, further *moo.*

I glance at Wes, still standing politely at his podium, watching from a great distance. Of the eleven people now crowded onto the stage, he is the only one who will never return.

He and I will stay in touch for years afterward, and I will come to know him as generous, vastly better-educated than I am, and yet modest to an extreme. We've lost touch of late, but from what I can find out he is improving his foreign-language skills, with aspirations of becoming one of those sainted physicians working in insufferable Third World conditions to bring health and hope to the destitute. That's, um, after his gene therapy project is finished.

Here is everything you need to know about Wes: when I catch his eye, he just smiles back at me. "Enjoy it," he is saying. "I'm happy for you." This will be the only thing he ever says about it.

I believe he actually means it.

Before the cameras click off and the doojobbies stop whirring, I half-jokingly rest my head for a moment on the shoulder of a fellow contestant named Lyn.

Lyn doesn't look too happy about it. Justifiably so. If Lyn ever reads this, I apologize. If I am her, and some strange guy carrying a contagious booger just three notches down from Ebola, something even Wes couldn't cure, playfully puts his head on my shoulder less than twenty-four hours before I'm playing for $100,000, I reach into my ankle holster, pull out my backup buzzer, and click the poor bastard into the next life.

Lyn doesn't do that. I owe her some thanks.

The nine survivors are all facing another day and two more rounds of play. And Dan Melia, the Ivy League Serial Killer, is still lurking in the field.

Wes goes out to dinner with Grace and her husband. I go back to the hotel to lie down.

In the lush Beverly Hilton, a plush little thermometer reads a golden 102 degrees.

I assume a shiny fetal position and groan myself to sleep in a satisfyingly self-pitying way.

A nice quiet blackness follows.

Morning.

Fever down.

My body suddenly moves with a novel ease.

The day before, while certain of losing, I have had glimmers of useful insight, thoughts of failed loves, and failing loved ones, and of losing track of the purpose of knowledge, reflections of failures greater than anything a game show can offer.

These are instantly forgotten.

I am awake and alert and excited and ready to win.

I want more. And I want it now.

CHAPTER

14

WE'RE
MALAYSIA-
BOUND

Also, Why People Are
Looking at Me Funny
in This Coffee Shop

In the green room, the nine of us are quiet and focused. I munch on my protein bars in careful state-dependent increments, thinking about Go Lights and timing. I am dreading the pre-taping rehearsal.

Yesterday I survived only through three gifts of fortune: a lucky Final guess, Wes's incorrect response, and freakishly low wild card scores. Today I am again on my own. Even with my fever subsiding, I doubt that a mere Jedi buzzer trick can work against fellow champions. Perhaps at this level, everyone has fully integrated the Go Lights, Borg-like, into their central nervous systems.

I will know very soon.

The rehearsal begins. We're switched in and out quickly. I'm not called right away, so I watch from nearby, more carefully and alertly than ever.

And to my surprise, I catch almost everyone at least peeking once or twice at the Go Lights, trying the difficult feat of honing their timing on the day of play. This is akin to timing a 90-mph fastball after only a few swings. I have no idea if they can, or how—I certainly can't—but I find this all slightly encouraging.

I have a chance. There is hope.

Although one guy does not seem to need the practice: Dan Melia.

Dan Melia, who has written, edited, and perhaps inadvertently eaten more books than I've ever read. Dan Melia, whose snoring has footnotes, whose sneezes are quoted in theses, whose belches are bagged and numbered by the Library of Congress.

The Ivy League Serial Killer is loose. His buzzer is sharp, and his brain has big jaws. I have no natural defense.

We return to the green room. Soon, Susanne enters, calling names for the first of three semifinals.

"Some Guy! Dan! . . ."

I sit in one corner and try to hold very still. Maybe she won't call me if she doesn't see me. *Don't say Bob, don't say Bob, don't say Bob . . .*

". . . Some Guy!"

*Whew.*

Bizarrely, one of the other contestants and I discover that we have actually met in passing, many years before.

In my days as an unknown comedian, playing every bowling alley and American Legion hall between the Atlantic and the Rockies, I once worked a weekday one-nighter in a bar in Wisconsin that smelled of armpits, cheese, and back hair. Standing before flashing neon beer logos and wood-paneled walls decorated in dead Green Bay Packers and deer, I struggled mightily to amuse working-class men who were only there to drink and be left alone.

These men, you notice, in no way whatsoever resembled my own father. Not even slightly. After all, they were in Wisconsin.

Usually on such nights, I remained onstage just long enough to collect a paycheck and be left alone myself, often in the company of another comedian with unrealistic dreams, or perhaps a waitress smelling of cigarettes, cleaning products, and cherry lipstick.

This particular night, one of the other comedians was a tall, thin guy with laser-beam eyes and the sort of large flowing hair the Bee Gees would have envied. His act was particularly memorable, filled with literary and historical references I was sure must have been funny, if only I knew what he was talking about. The jokes were all clever, with recognizable structures, but seemed to be drawn from a Ph.D. database I couldn't quite access. The few jokes I *did* understand were brilliant. In another place or era or space-time dimension, this guy would have been huge.

The crowd responded, of course, with the intense kind of indifference normally reserved for Indonesian earthquakes, Iranian apartment collapses, and other such faraway tragedies. If bodies had washed up on the foot of the stage, it wouldn't have changed the mood noticeably. And here's the thing: the guy just smiled, kept on going, and truly enjoyed himself.

I envied that. I don't know if it was a kind of courage, or perhaps the lunatic sort of self-reliance that must come from being smarter than everyone you've ever met. He seemed to know his situation, too, taking a dark glee in the experience. We didn't speak more than a few words before the show, and I was long gone by the time he finished, probably somewhere gathering a fresh cherry stench. Besides, the next act (I swear to you) was scheduled to be a guy with a toilet plunger on his head. My will to live was sapped enough as it was.

But the image of this well-coiffed beanpole cheerfully citing Proust over the clacking of pool cues and the wafting aroma of fermenting piss never left me.

His name is Kim Worth. He remembers me first, and I am happy to recognize him. "Long way from Wisconsin, isn't it?" we say.

The lights are sure a lot brighter here.

I wish him good luck. And I try once again to get focused.


On a side note, neither Kim nor I can remember the name of the Wisconsin town where we first crossed paths. Not to this day. Can't even guess.

If anyone else once went to a comedy show in a bar smelling of cheese and armpits and saw two comedians working in mortuary silence: please, for your own sake, alert the town elders. Please hand them this book, with the next page's corner turned down.

Town elders, attention: Your town is so nondescript that two *Jeopardy!* champions, trying with all their might, have no idea what it's called or even what part of the state it's in.

Maybe it's time to consider a pumpkin festival.

An hour passes.

Susanne enters the green room, calling names for the second of three semifinals.

"Lyn! Peter! Bob!"

So Kim and Grace will play each other in the third semi. I wish them both the best.

And suddenly I'm at a podium again. Alex walks out.

And it's time to see how far the extra study, my Jedi buzzer trick, and a normal body temperature will carry me.

Lyn is at the champion's podium, so she calls the first clue. She dives directly to the bottom of the board, hunting amid high-dollar amounts for the first Daily Double. This is also a demonstration of confidence. This first clue, in a category called THE LAW, is surprisingly easy:

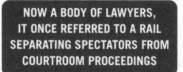

NOW A BODY OF LAWYERS,
IT ONCE REFERRED TO A RAIL
SEPARATING SPECTATORS FROM
COURTROOM PROCEEDINGS

Two separate hints in the clue. Even if you're not sure about the "bar" in "bar exam" also referring generally to lawyers, you've got confirmation that the word they're looking for is a physical barrier.

I focus my eyes on the "-ngs" at the end of "proceedings," and wait, wait, wait, wait, trying to remember just how to time the buzzer. Thinking only about the timing. Readying myself. Seeking just the right instant. Finally, *cliklikikkitylikkityclikit.*

*Crap.*

Lyn beats me on the very first clue. I'm early on the buzzer. Adrenaline affects your reflexes. Maybe my perception of time is skewed. While Lyn responds, I take a breath and force myself to think about the categories again. Maybe focusing on the game will calm me, letting good state-dependent stuff kick in.

Lyn stays at the bottom of the board, playing THE LAW for $400:

> FAILURE TO PAY A BUILDING
> CONTRACTOR MAY RESULT
> IN HIS LEANING ON YOU
> WITH THIS TYPE OF LIEN

*Crap again.* I don't know the response to the second clue. I just stand there, trying to relax and put myself back in all the games I've played at home.

Peter beats Lyn on the buzzer. He responds incorrectly, and the clue passes unwon. ("What is a mechanic's lien?" is the response we don't know.) For an instant, I mentally focus directly on Alex, something I have very rarely done in any game, imagining that I'm seeing him on TV. As the third clue begins, I am trying once again to merge where I'm standing with my living room.

*I am not standing at a podium. I am standing at a low bookcase. And this is not a buzzer in my hand. This is a ballpoint pen rolled in masking tape . . .*

> THE EISENHOWER CENTER IN
> THIS KANSAS TOWN HOUSES
> NUMEROUS MEMENTOS OF
> THE PRESIDENT'S LIFE AND CAREER

I don't even need notebooks filled with haunting mental images. There are American Legion halls and bowling alleys and lonely people drinking in Kansas, too. Those are haunting enough. So:

*What is Abilene?*

With almost no thought to the buzzer. And my light comes on.

Then, rapid-fire:

*What is Easter Island?*

*Who was Stu Sutcliffe?*

*What are cigar bands?*

*What is Independence Hall?*

*What is* Mother, Jugs & Speed?

My light comes on. And on. And on and on.

I reel off ten correct responses before the first commercial. It's like Alex and I are just chatting in a hallway, with a few interruptions as others pass. I'm *back*.

At the first break, my score is three times higher than Lyn's; Peter has a negative number. I'm ringing in on over 80 percent of my attempts. To my right, I can glimpse Peter clenching his jaw, growing frustrated. Lyn's voice, two podiums away, is already slightly urgent.

Of course, Lyn is a working mother, and Peter runs his own business. Unlike me, they have lives.

So again, they have that particular disadvantage.

After the commercial, Alex asks about my fever, slyly letting the audience know why last week's (that is, yesterday's) cartoonish incompetent can suddenly wield his buzzer like the hammer of Thor. I blither as always, not sure if it's appropriate to thank Wes and Grace for their kindness on camera, so much that I almost keep Alex from sharing a stunning note of encouragement.

Once upon a time, Alex tells me, another bottom-rung wild card stood exactly where I was standing. And *he* managed to come from behind and win the entire tournament.

Well. Pretty thrilling thought, I must say. I am secretly starting to think it's just possible. But certainly that could never happen twice.

I mean, you've read this far. Can harbingers ever be this obvious, either in real life or the retelling?

Thank goodness you're letting me step out of the narrative so often to screw with your expectations a bit. I appreciate that. Otherwise, you'd already know how everything turns out. And that's a very bad thing to presume.

You'll see this sort of thing again, later, when Jane, the best friend I have ever had, whom you will meet and love right along with me very soon now, is diagnosed with a particularly scary form of cancer.

Yes. That was a bomb just now. Cancer always is, you know.

If you're angry in some weird way, you should be. *It's not fair,* you say. *I was having a good time a minute ago.*

Trust me. I do know how that feels.

Just six months after meeting her, just a bit ahead in our story and while she and I (and vicariously, you) are all curled up happily in bed together, Jane will find a lump.

The lump will be bad.

Of course you do not expect moments like this. They come while you are in the middle of things, in exactly this way. During exciting things, maybe, or sad things, or contented things, or whatever things you are doing. You never get up one morning and say, "Today I will fall in love." But one day you do. You never get up one morning and say, "Today I will learn how I will die." But one day you'll do that, too. We all do.

I'm pretty sure Jane never got up one morning and said, "Today I will discover I have cancer." But one day, she did.

None of us expects a day, later on, when we will get up so early that it's still the coldest, blackest hour of the night, and then drive to a hospital to find out whether we will live or die.

But one day, that day came for the best woman I have ever known.

A doctor was about to cut her open—again—and grab another chunk of her from another specific spot and peer at it closely amid furrowed brows and a dozen growling gadgets. By that afternoon we would know if her particularly scary form of cancer had spread.

That particular morning came for Jane. It began at precisely 4:00 a.m. one day.

I would not be able to imagine what one does to pass the time on a morning like that, except that Jane and I actually did it once.

We sang.

Imagine that in your own car, with someone you love, on a similar drive to your nearest hospital.

We *sang*.

Jane started it. She gets most of the credit. In the empty early morning, we passed a drugstore with its lights on. It said GIANT DRUG STORE.

Jane made up a little ditty on the spot:

*It's a Giant Drug Store, but they don't sell giant drugs.*

I made up a second line:

*They don't sell drugs to giants, so what the hell kind of drugstore is it, anyway?*

And then we laughed. And we sang it again and again and again and again. Trying to hold on to the song and each other and what it feels like to be alive in just one good moment, even once, with someone you love. Maybe if we just kept singing, the hospital would never come.

We sang.

The tune Jane chose for the song, if you'd like to sing it yourself for a moment, is the same one Judy Garland sang in her last MGM film appearance: "Sing Hallelujah, come on, get happy, we're gonna chase all your cares away."

You should have seen Jane's face. Laughing in the passenger seat of my car, streetlights reflected in the tears on her cheek.

You know how memory kicks in.

If you need to put the book down now, reassess, and feel sad or angry or confused for a bit, go ahead. We'll get back to the game in a minute, I promise.

That's another thing you do around something like cancer. It reminds you that all the things you treat as so damned important usually aren't. You completely reassess. But that takes time. Meanwhile, you get on with things anyway. You just take a breath and go on ahead with what you were doing, probably even some things that seem like they barely matter, at least for a while.

There is comfort in routine. The firing of any familiar neural pathways can feel like a letter from home. So we'll get back to the game in a few more paragraphs, and pretty soon it'll probably even be fun again, almost like nothing ever happened.

Still, I'm about to take a break myself, right now, as I'm writing this very sentence. Other people in this coffee shop are looking at me kinda funny.

One thing I've heard from people who've seen me on *Jeopardy!* is that while I hide nervousness well, they can always see everything else I'm feeling.

■ ■ ■

*What's a foot fault?*
*What's a referendum?*
*What's* Serial Mom?

For the rest of the first Jeopardy round, I remain in command. The one audio clue is a TV science-fiction star singing a ludicrously over-acted version of "Lucy in the Sky with Diamonds"—a track I played a dozen times at my college radio station.

*Who is William Shatner?*

I'm winning on the buzzer, and of the thirty clues in the round, I've known the responses to twenty-eight. The game is turning into a run-away: I'm at $6000, Lyn is at $2700, and Peter is still in negative num-bers. All I have to do is stay the course, play and wager conservatively, and I'll have a great shot at a runaway win.

The remaining Daily Doubles are my only concern. If Peter or I find them both, I'll be fine. But if Lyn lands one and nails a big wager, I could still be in trouble.

Double Jeopardy begins. Alex announces the categories. I think ahead along with him.

HARRY GUYS *(Okay: Truman, Belafonte, Houdini, Reasoner, Carey . . .)*
WE'RE MALAYSIA-BOUND *(Kuala Lumpur, um, some islands, um . . .)*
FETAL ATTRACTION *(Crap. Lyn's a mom. This is hers.)*
TOP 40 BONUS *(Mine.)*
FROM THE JAWS OF VICTORY *(Uh-oh. How many harbingers can I have in one game?)*
POETS' RHYME TIME *(Chuck? Notebooks? Don't fail me now.)*

Peter starts off the round at the bottom of the board, hunting for Daily Doubles on the $1000 row of TOP 40 BONUS and WE'RE MALAYSIA-BOUND. Each time Peter or I call for a clue, I hope to hear the *Bweed-wooo, Bweedwooo, Bweedwooo-dwoo-dwoo-dwah* sound of a Daily Double being revealed.

Lyn hunts for a Daily Double in the $1000 row of POETS' RHYME

TIME. I dread the *Bweedwooo, Bweedwooo, Bweedwooo-dwoo-dwoo-dwah* when she's in control. But it doesn't come here, either. Instead:

SIR PHILIP'S
RENAL ORGANS

And my light comes on. *What are Sidney's kidneys?* I blurt, with barely a second thought.

This is something I would never have known a few months ago. I am starting to feel like a very different player from the terrified guy bouncing around with Lancôme up his snotter. I still don't know much about who Philip Sidney *was*, of course. But now I can recognize him as a poet in less than two seconds.

I'm way ahead again, with $9200 to $2100 and $1700 for Lyn and Peter.

But then Lyn, the second librarian I've played in twenty-four hours (and third librarian in seven games), impressively rips through the rest of POETS' RHYME TIME, whipping off

"What are Blake's snakes?"

"What are Pope's hopes?"

"What are Pound's hounds?"

all in a row.

I realize I'm just lucky our game board has been far stronger on pop culture than the classics. Lyn's command of literature is as good as her silly rhymes.

*Where are those damn Daily Doubles?* I wonder. Peter gets a correct response and selects from the board. No Daily Double. Peter gets another and selects. No Daily Double. Lyn gets a correct response and selects . . .

*Bweedwooo, Bweedwooo, Bweedwooo-dwoo-dwoo-dwah.*

Lyn's Daily Double is in the category FROM THE JAWS OF VICTORY. This is more harbinger, um, -ish -ness than I would prefer.

Lyn looks up at our scores. She has $4700. I have $9200.

HEAVY ARMOR & HEAVY
RAINS DEFEATED THE LARGE
FRENCH ARMY AS MUCH AS
HENRY V'S MEN AT THIS
1415 BATTLE

One "What is Agincourt?" later, Lyn is at $8700. All I can do is smile, applaud, and hope for some heavy armor and rain of my own.

Lyn chooses again, and finds the last Daily Double on the very next clue. *Damn!* She now has the option to try to put the game away. Instead, she makes a conservative wager, essentially rendering the clue meaningless, choosing to fight on the buzzers for the rest of the game.

Still, my easy runaway is now a battle. And while the TOP 40 category—my strongest—is gone, all of FETAL ATTRACTION remains.

Fortunately, we split what I thought would be Lyn's strongest category three ways. Peter has kids, and thus personal fetal experience. I am lucky again. I then knock off three of the HARRY GUYS—including Harry Belafonte, one of the names I've thought ahead to—and manage to name an island that is much less obscure than it once would have been:

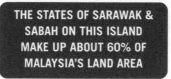

THE STATES OF SARAWAK &
SABAH ON THIS ISLAND
MAKE UP ABOUT 60% OF
MALAYSIA'S LAND AREA

Because three different nations occupy portions of this same island, *What is Borneo?* is in my notebooks at least half a dozen times.

I now have a $2800 lead over Lyn. There are seven clues left, worth just $3200 combined. Lyn will need every clue to take the lead entering Final Jeopardy.

It is time to loosen my grip on the Weapon. The worst possible move is an incorrect response.

Doing nothing is better than doing something really stupid.

I choose a $400 clue in MALAYSIA, since Lyn hasn't seemed strong on geography. If I get it, I've clinched the lead going into Final Jeopardy. If Peter gets it, I've clinched at least a share of the lead.

ENDAU-ROMPIN PARK IS
ONE OF THE LAST HOMES OF
THE SUMATRAN SPECIES OF
THIS HORNED MAMMAL

*Could be a rhino*, I think to myself. *But who knows what the hell lives in Sumatra?* I keep my hand off the buzzer. The only way Lyn is going to pass me is if I start guessing incorrectly.

Peter rings in. His "What's a rhino?" is correct. I've now clinched a tie entering Final Jeopardy by doing absolutely nothing.

Peter selects a clue in FROM THE JAWS OF VICTORY:

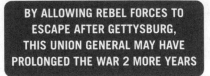

BY ALLOWING REBEL FORCES TO
ESCAPE AFTER GETTYSBURG,
THIS UNION GENERAL MAY HAVE
PROLONGED THE WAR 2 MORE YEARS

*George G. Meade was the Union general at Gettysburg*, I think. *But wasn't that a* good *thing? Maybe somebody else was the screwup.* Again, I leave my Weapon uncocked.

Peter rings in. His "Who is Meade?" is correct. I've now clinched the lead entering Final Jeopardy by doing absolutely nothing, well-aimed.

There are still five clues—an entire category's worth—on the board, but the rest of the round is superfluous. Lyn's high second-place score will compel me to make a large wager *and* answer correctly to guarantee a win.

If I answer Final Jeopardy correctly, I win. If not, I probably don't. Nothing else really matters right now.

As the last few clues roll by, one strikes me as absurdly obscure, the sort of thing that no amount of study or normal experience could fill in:

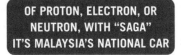

OF PROTON, ELECTRON, OR
NEUTRON, WITH "SAGA"
IT'S MALAYSIA'S NATIONAL CAR

Lyn, Peter, and I just stand there, staring. Zombie Jeopardy. Who knows what they drive in Malaysia?

It's not like someday I'm gonna be hitchhiking in Malaysia in a steaming rain. It's not like I'm gonna accept a ride to Kuala Lumpur from a man I don't know driving Malaysia's national car, revealing the correct response in a way I'll remember as long as I live. It's not like I'm gonna go off wandering around strange countries for months trying to learn the right lessons after how things turned out with Jane.

Even Trebekistan isn't *that* strange a place.

Right?

*p-TING!*

The Final Jeopardy category:

**BRITISH LITERATURE**

This may be Lyn's strongest subject. It may also be my weakest. Alex briefly glances at Lyn. I can't see Lyn's face, but her expression reflects noticeably on his.

Two podiums away, I can tell that Lyn is grinning.

■ ■ ■

Back in the Snow Belt, Dad and I spent many autumns watching the Cleveland Browns in the years they were known as the "Cardiac Kids," captivating our frogs-with-umbrellas neighborhood.

The quarterback was a tiny man named Brian Sipe. He stood only three-foot-two and weighed just nine pounds, the only NFL Most Valuable Player I've ever seen who was smaller than the opposing team's cheerleaders. I believe he now lives in a tree, making cookies.

But damn, that teeny man had heart. When the fourth quarter came, Brian Sipe would stand his ground while 300-pound carnivores lunged and ripped at his flesh. Cleats hammering the frozen earth would thunder out threats of his imminent doom, and Brian Sipe would hold his place manfully. And at the last possible second, just before having his bum blown to pieces, Brian Sipe would sling the ball heavenward, seemingly at random. More often than not, this laced-leather token of prayer would fall into the arms of a guy wearing the same-colored helmet, not far from some unlikely goalposts.

Then my dad and I and everyone in the Snow Belt would all scream as if our testicles were coming unspooled. Including the women.

This was even more fun than it sounds.

If you were driving through Cleveland on a Sunday afternoon in the 1980s and thought you heard the sound of 250,000 people being force-fed into a paper shredder, that was the extra point being kicked.

And so, from September to December every year, our neighborhood would festoon itself in brown and orange, the Cleveland Browns' colors, amid the endless coatings of snowy white.

Someday, just once, I wanted to be like Brian Sipe.

Even if we always, *always* lost the last game.

■ ■ ■

After the commercial, Alex even comments on Lyn's visible delight at the Final Jeopardy subject:

"When we revealed the category—ENGLISH LITERATURE—a few moments ago, Lyn Paine smiled broadly. I think she likes this category."

*Ulp.* My *Jeopardy!* career could be over for good in exactly thirty seconds.

*p-TING!* comes the clue:

> THE 5TH EDITION OF THIS WORK,
> PUBLISHED IN 1676, INCLUDED
> A SECTION ON FLY FISHING
> BY CHARLES COTTON

"Good luck," Alex says. The Think Music begins.

I have absolutely no idea. None. So, back to the basics:

### Slow down and see the obvious.

What follows is my actual thought process, as verbatim as possible amid a pre-verbal spasm of neural chaos. Hum the Final Jeopardy Think Music to yourself if you like:

*OK. "Fifth edition." Is that the hint? New Edition was a band once . . . Ummm . . . "1676." Is that the hint? 1776 was a movie I saw in junior high. Guys in powdered wigs singing about Abigail Adams's combustibility . . . Errm . . . Is "fly fishing" the hint? The writers went a long way to get there. Hmm . . . Could be this Cotton guy, but I'm running out of time. OK . . .*

The first chorus of the Think Music is ending. I have to begin writing in a matter of seconds.

## Everything connects to everything else.

*Fishing. Old books about fishing. Wait*—Moby Dick! *Yes!* Moby Dick!
On the tape, you can see my hand start to write.
*Hold on. Wait. You can't fly-fish Moby Dick.*
My hand stops.

## Doing nothing is better than doing something really stupid.

The second chorus of the Think Music begins. I physically slump, putting one elbow on the podium and resting my chin on my hand. I still have no idea.

*OK. Fish. Rods. Reels. Hip waders. Ice fishing. Angling. Bait. Boats. Back up*—*there's an old book called* The Compleat Angler. *And it's spelled funny, like "The Compleat Beatles" was, that documentary I saw on cable once. Must be old and famous. Good. Go!*

Electronic pen on glass. *Clackity-click-whap-clackity.* Racing the Think Music to the end. *Write, come on, write,* write *you bastard . . .*

I drop the pen just as the tympani thumps the final *bum-BUM!* whump.

Peter has written "What is the *Encyclopaedia Britannica*?" Alex reads this with surprise in his voice, not recognition.

Peter and I will stay in touch for several years. We have lunch and encourage each other. He will eventually co-write a parody of both the L.L. Bean catalog and modern business practice that will make me laugh out loud. But it is instantly clear that Peter will hear the "Oooh."

Lyn, too, has written "What is *The Compleat Angler*?"

If she is correct, I have won.

Alex looks at Lyn . . . and he *smiles* at her.

Somewhere on a distant football field, Brian Sipe is on his tiny little ass. And another man is holding a football under a pair of goalposts.

Somewhere back in the Snow Belt, my mother and sister and the memory of my father are cheering.

■ ■ ■

The game we have just played is only the second of three semifinals. Glenn and Grant wrangle me directly into a cordoned-off section of the audience, where I will sit next to the winner of the first semifinal. For security reasons, the two of us must be carefully sequestered. Together we will watch the third game, speaking to no one but each other.

We will make small talk and pretend that we are not measuring each other, although in truth we will have immediately begun to compete under our breaths in a private head-to-head for pre-final supremacy.

As I climb the stairs, I recognize a familiar face smiling back at me. Dan Melia.

I will be left alone in the dark for an hour with the Ivy League Serial Killer.

And then I will confront him twice that afternoon in a two-day final.

I have no idea in this moment that one day the result would be played as in-flight entertainment.

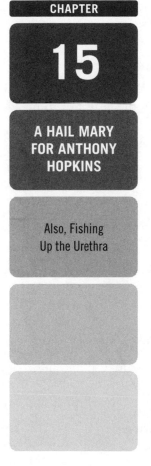

CHAPTER

15

A HAIL MARY
FOR ANTHONY
HOPKINS

Also, Fishing
Up the Urethra

Dan and I spent the better part of an hour alone in the cool Sony stillness, illuminated only by blinding stage lights, able to hear nothing but the sound of Grace and Kim clawing and slashing at each other's jugular, fighting over the third spot at our side.

I would like to tell you that I discovered my opponent to be cruel of hand, uncaring in heart, and of questionable dental hygiene. I would like to tell you that my first real conversation with Dan made me want to defeat him even more.

I'd like to tell you that, but I can't.

Dan seemed genuinely happy for me. He could tell by my face that I hadn't known *What is* The Compleat Angler? and he was delighted that I'd figured it out. When I explained my thought process, zigzagging through 1980s R&B, Herman Melville, Broadway shows, and the Beatles, Dan erupted with the same half-admiring, half-baffled laugh I'd have wanted to hear from my best friend right then.

Dammit.

So my attention turned from trying to find any edge against the professor, and toward rooting for Grace and Kim, who were busily crushing each other's mental rib cages. Besides, I wanted to conserve energy, lest the prior day's fever return.

Grace led the match entering Final Jeopardy, but Kim came through with a correct answer in the Final for the win. Kim will later describe this to me as "like one of those World War One things—I just climbed out of the trench with two fellow soldiers, and when I got to the next trench, they were gone. I didn't know why or have authority to question the orders. I just knew I'd have to gear up and climb out again in a few minutes anyway."

I would face Kim and Dan for the $100,000 grand prize.

I reviewed the broadcast dates: the first game would air on Lincoln's birthday, and the second was set for a Friday the 13th. For a nine-show run that had begun the previous Halloween, this seemed a fitting way to close.

We had the usual Sony escort to the cafeteria before the two-day final would begin. Kim, Dan, and I sat together, eating lunch, wondering which of us would walk away as the best player of the year, not to mention $100,000 richer.

During our conversation, I learned that their pre-game rituals were at least as careful, slightly absurd, and necessary as my own. Kim went for long swims on the night before every taping, then carefully prepared himself a high-protein fillet of cod. Dan, the Berkeley professor, felt completely unable to play without going to Disneyland the day before.

Since the show had no higher-level tournaments, these games really would be the end of my *Jeopardy!* career. Finally.

Win or lose, I was glad to share my last games with these two.

Thanks to a high final score compelled by Lyn's Daily Doubles, I'm assigned to the champion's podium. I realize while we're walking out that it feels like Dan really belongs there.

This is a very Cleveland thing to be thinking.

Game one begins with the following categories:

ARCHITECTURE *(Excellent! Notebook stuff—but I'll need the break to think ahead on that.)*

LITERARY POTENT POTABLES *(Great; let's combine my two weakest subjects.)*

MOVIE DEBUTS *(This could be any actor or director in the world.)*

BODIES OF WATER *(More notebook stuff—but I feel pretty good here.)*

PEOPLE OF THE MONTH *(What the heck is this?)*

WORD ORIGINS *(Eek. This sounds like one for the Berkeley guy.)*

I pick up my Jeopardy Weapon, hefting the black plastic, rubbing my index finger against the tiny button, marveling for a moment at the fraction of movement in the clickity instants, an eighth of an inch that can feel just like miles.

I plunge with blind faith into BODIES OF WATER. We begin.

"What's the Mediterranean?"

"What's a hansom cab?"

"What's a cowslip?"

"What are jack straws?"

"What's a filbert?"

These all dash by in a blink. Unfortunately, I do not give any of those responses.

"What is beer?"

I do not give that one, either.

After the first seven clues, I have known fewer than half of the responses. I pass the time by moving my finger without touching the buzzer, keeping the rhythm of the game in my body. I must remain patient, and detached, playing each passing moment. But for now I am only an observer, watching the show from third place in the distance. My only solace is that Dan's voice has wavered in asking for more clues. I remind myself that he and Kim are nervous, too.

Finally:

*Who is Gatsby?*

After eight clues, I have given two responses and won on the buzzer exactly once. In desperation, I briefly peek at the Go Lights, trying to figure out if I'm early or late. But they barely illuminate.

■ ■ ■

Let's zoom in on the single split-second before the flash of a Go Light, to feel the fineness of good *Jeopardy!* timing.

Sometimes you will see a trio of players whose exact buzzer movements are visible. Maybe all three thumbs are in view, or the clenching of one player's hand causes her arm to twitch. (In my own case, my right shoulder drops slightly before I ring in, preceding my actual Weapon volley by roughly one video frame. Also, there is a puff of smoke on the grassy knoll.)

In advanced games, multiple players often twitch within three frames. In the United States, standard video zips by at 29.97 frames per second. (The missing .03 frame is collected by the IRS, which has a secret storage facility of fractional video frames, said to be used by the Pentagon for sinister purposes overseas.) So, in tournament play, all three thumbs might go *cliklikikkitylikkityclikit* in under one tenth of a second.

Just for comparison, a 90-mph fastball takes about 0.45 seconds to reach the batter. Most coaches think it takes about half that time to recognize a pitch and begin a good swing. Therefore, the reflex of a .300 hitter takes two tenths of a second. Twice as long. (Of course, we're not comparing athletic ability—whoa, hey, heck no—just the *bang-bang*iness of timing. *Jeopardy!* clues are not curving in flight, nor do they slip out of Alex's mouth occasionally and bean us, so we rarely flinch and hurl ourselves to the ground. Although I've come close a few times.)

On rare occasions, two or even all three contestants will twitch within a single video frame. One third of one tenth of a second. About 30 milliseconds. I would not believe this myself if I hadn't seen it on tape. At these times the player who comes closest to when the Go Lights *actually receive electricity*—without being early—is the one who gets in. And tungsten filaments take a glimmer of time to heat up.

Studio audience members sometimes notice that the Go Lights occasionally seem to stay off or barely illuminate, as if skipping a clue here and there. Now you know why. Obviously, nobody is reacting that quickly. It's just rhythm and state-dependent retrieval and a touch of good millifortune, nothing more. But that's how on-target the best Jedis can be.

I would discount this occurrence as utterly random, especially since the whole process is triggered by *another* imperfect human being, invisible offstage, listening to some internal rhythm of his or her own. With four people pressing buttons, there's too much margin of error for these single-frame moments to be more than a crapshoot.

Except for one thing: some players really *do* seem reliably better at blanking the Go Lights than others, game after game.

This may be luck—an anomaly of insufficient trials, the unlikely flip of a coin that lands heads ten straight times—but it's also possible that some Jedis are simply that good. *Jeopardy!* clues end in a limited number of rhythms and sounds, a few hundred combinations at most. Maybe someone with particular talent, watching the game in the months before playing, might preconsciously sense the unseen buzzer-person's own internal clock.

This would not be different from my own Jedi skills. Just much better.

In any case, by the end, you will meet one player whose name has become synonymous with tungsten destruction.

However, as Dan and Kim have begun the $100,000 two-day grand final by making the Go Lights vanish repeatedly, there is not even a word for what is happening.

It occurs to me that one ought to exist.

But there is not much time to think about it.

*I am not standing at a podium. I am standing at a low bookcase. And this is not a buzzer in my hand. This is a ballpoint pen rolled in masking tape . . .*

Finally, ten clues into the game, I find my way in BODIES OF WATER:

SITTWE, BURMA, &
CALCUTTA, INDIA ARE
MAJOR PORTS ON THIS BAY

I've never heard of Sittwe, and the only Burmas I know are the country and the Shave. But there are three big hints: First, we want a huge body of water, since it serves ports in two countries. Second, the clue explicitly says we want a "bay." So we just need a giant wet spot near India. Fortunately, I once drew a cartoon in my notebooks depicting, right to left, a Bengal tiger eating an Indian guy swearing in Arabic, representing the layout of the Bay of Bengal and the Arabian Sea. Thus:

*What is the Bay of Bengal?*

is correct. (And if you ever see a rerun of one of my games, and I'm jabbing the air with my left hand just before a response, I'm working my way across a cartoon just like this.)

The next clue takes similar seat-of-the-pants logic:

THE KAGERA RIVER IS THE
LARGEST AND MOST
IMPORTANT TRIBUTARY
OF THIS AFRICAN LAKE

I've also never heard of the Kagera River. But there are only a few big lakes in Africa, and this was just a $400 clue with no other hints at all, so the writers can't be going for anything tricky. The obvious answer, then, would be the biggest lake in Africa, which is fortunately as round as its royal namesake:

*What is Lake Victoria?*

Finally comes this Daily Double:

NAMED FOR AN EXPLORER
IT'S CANADA'S LONGEST RIVER

I flash to a cartoon in my notebooks—a hurried blue scrawl of Dave Thomas and Rick Moranis of SCTV dressed as Canadian hosers and drowning in a river of beer—and without hesitation I blurt:

*What's the Mackenzie?*

I'm climbing back into the game.

Alex, for his part, seems to be having a fabulous time, decorating his lines with Hindi accents and Scottish brogues where appropriate. He seems at least as stoked as we are.

As we reach the first commercial, Kim, Dan, and I have played a nearly perfect game, responding to all fifteen clues correctly with only one missed guess.

Despite letting seven of fourteen buzzing opportunities pass—still surrendering half of the game so far—I am tied with Dan for the lead.

During the break, I am playing ahead furiously. I still have no idea what PEOPLE OF THE MONTH is, and MOVIE DEBUTS is too broad of a category to consider. But my notebooks do have a large section on ARCHITECTURE.

In my mind, the first important English architect loves dashing in and out of royal doorways (Inigo Jones). A German pole vaulter gropes a small dog (Walter Gropius, founder of the Bauhaus school). A hundred dancing corpses shout "Yay!" while poking the holes in a block of Swiss cheese (Swiss architect Le Corbusier). The greatest trophy in the field is shaped like a building wearing a pretty skirt (the Pritzker Prize).

On the tape, as Alex moves through the contestant chats, I'm staring intently at the board, still trying to sort out which Finnish guy—Saarinen or Salonen—designed the JFK airport and the arch in St. Louis. *Ah, wait—it was Saarinen, because he was soarin' in.*

I am also trying not to notice that my hands are becoming sweaty. I am wiping them on my suit, attempting to keep my buzzer dry.

We begin again. I blast through two in a row, then Dan rips off four in a row. I fight back with two more:

*What is Rococo?*

*Who is Le Corbusier?*

The latter, of course, is an ARCHITECTURE response I've called up just moments before.

This last clue—

> THIS SWISS MAN WHO
> USED A PSEUDONYM
> WAS KNOWN FOR HOUSES
> ON STILTS LIKE THE SAVOIE
> HOUSE IN POISSY

shows you how little I really know at this point. I do not know that "Le Corbusier" was a pseudonym, I have never heard of the Savoie House nor Poissy, and I have no idea why you'd put houses on stilts. Instead, I see only this, in the category ARCHITECTS:

BLAH *SWISS* BLAH BLAH
BLAH BLAH BLAH
BLAH BLAH BLAH BLAH
BLAH BLAH BLAH BLAH BLAH
BLAH BLAH BLAH

Thanks to months spent with notebooks, I find the correct response, barely reading it off the image of the word in my head, stumbling through the pronunciation of "core-booze-yay" as if I've never seen it before in my life. This is not far from reality. And yet the game against the Berkeley professor with a Harvard education is still a virtual tie.

PEOPLE OF THE MONTH turns out to be a category asking for people with names matching calendar months. Asked for a Swedish playwright, the only one I can think of is "Strindberg," a name in my notebooks connected to Sweden and little else. I don't see any link to a calendar month. Instants later, Dan replies:

"Who is August Strindberg?"

I am left only shaking my head. Still, on the very next clue, in MOVIE DEBUTS, I respond with

*Who is Johnny Depp?*

HA! Take *that*, guy who actually knows Swedish playwrights' full names! But I'm starting to realize that Dan has actually *read* all the books whose titles I have merely memorized. This is not going to make my life easy.

In the remainder of MOVIE DEBUTS, Dan gets Valerie Harper. Kim gets Kiefer Sutherland. I get Jennifer Beals. So I get the best end of that deal. And finally, on the last clue of the round, I take an unusual risk:

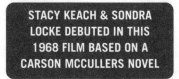

STACY KEACH & SONDRA
LOCKE DEBUTED IN THIS
1968 FILM BASED ON A
CARSON MCCULLERS NOVEL

I ring in, naming the only Carson McCullers novel I can remember, knowing there are others on my list. But sure enough,

*What is* The Heart Is a Lonely Hunter?

—puts me back in the lead at the end of the round.

I still feel outclassed, however. I begin to believe I will have to continue gambling where I can in order to win in the end. You may notice that this is a departure from the Enlightened Path. Ahem.

As soon as the round ends, Dan and Kim and I are having so much fun in the competition that we immediately turn to chat, not realizing that we're barely paying attention to Alex doing the outro for the folks at home. It's both the hardest I've ever played and the most fun I've ever had in a game. The feeling seems entirely mutual.

During the break, I make a point of saying out loud to the others that my temperature is still down and I'm still feeling much better. More than once.

I am saying out loud something I am trying to believe, something I am just wishing were actually true.

I can feel my fever returning.

As an aside, I caution you to consider any malady I suffer here as (a) nothing that will ultimately affect any outcome, and (b) affirming little more than my own status as a certified, MedicAlert-bracelet-wearing Weenie. In fact, my status as a PWW (Person With Weenieness) is so advanced—and so uncontaminated by actual disease—that it will one day be described in sophisticated journals.

My sister Connie, on the other hand, has been diagnosed over the years with Acute Chronic Hyper-Everything. You've already met "Marvin," her variety of baffling unwellnesses, and Marvin's possible origin in the tank of a Bug Truck atomizing its neuroactive piss through the watershed of a marsh in the Snow Belt.

However, over the years, my sister has also been positively, definitively diagnosed (or misdiagnosed) with the following, among others:

- Erythema nodosum
- Fibromyalgia
- Environmental and chemical allergies, various (see "bug truck")
- Asthma
- Myasthenia gravis

- Multiple sclerosis
- Inflammatory arthritis
- Guillain-Barré syndrome
- Lupus

You don't want to know the invasive procedures Connie has endured in order to receive such diverse explanations. Rest assured, however, that she is deeply familiar with a half-dozen -ipsies, a variety of -opsies, and one unforgettable expedition thrillingly described as "fishing up the urethra."

That Connie has not yet been reduced to a boneless heap of quivering infective goo by all this, and has in fact raised two brilliant children, shows that her heart is made of strong elastic and her spine is cast from purest titanium. Her husband, meanwhile, has the loyalty of your average moon.

The first diagnosis came when Connie was in her early twenties and suddenly had an inexplicable series of red bumps on her shins. The doctor blinked at her, went away, then returned with a definitive diagnosis of erythema nodosum. This may sound impressive.

Erythema nodosum, if you have not spent months studying Latin roots in case Alex Trebek asks you about them, simply means, quite exactly, "red bumps." Which is what Connie came in complaining about. Gosh, thanks. As to what to *do* about the erythema nodosum, the doctor had absolutely no idea. It could have been associated with anything from tuberculosis to hepatitis to leprosy to, I kid you not, cat scratch fever. Ted Nugent, stay away from my sister.

The erythema nodosum could also have been, in the doctor's words, "idiopathic." "Idiopathic," when said by a doctor, means "we have absolutely no idea what the deal is," although the literal Latin translation would be closer to "one's own unique suffering." Both definitions are entirely too accurate.

Eventually the erythema nodosum went away on its own, although the doctor had to be paid to do the same.

This story repeats many times, changing only in what hurts for how long, and how much of my sister they surgically remove. The one thing

I can assure you Connie does *not* have: hypochondria. I have been present for many of the various innard rebellions, and can certify that there are days when her vital organs seem likely to fly out of any orifice at any moment. I would suggest an exorcism, but once confronted with some of the doctors Connie has had, any demon would long ago have retreated to Hell.

She will in any case be diagnosed with many other things, if only out of habit. Some doctors send Christmas cards with fresh diagnoses every holiday season. As I've said, if *Jeopardy!* ever has a category on AUTOIMMUNE DISORDERS, stand the bloody hell back.

Meanwhile, my PWW status during the Tournament of Champions is above question.

Double Jeopardy begins with these categories:

WANDERERS *(What is this? Explorers, maybe? Hmm.)*
VIVE LA DIFFERENCE! *(And what the heck is this? Some gender thing?)*
EXCHANGES *(What? Like needle exchanges? The barter system? I'm really lost.)*
NAME THE MUSICAL *(Great. I know what this is, and I'm not good at it.)*
AN "I" *(Things that start with an I. That's kind of a long list, but I've got a prayer.)*
FOREIGN EYE *(And, once again, what the heck is this?)*

It is the first time in eight games that I have looked at a set of categories with such confusion and fear.

My head's central heating system kicks up one degree.

Kim begins, playing from the top of the board, eschewing any hint of the Forrest Bounce or Daily Double hunting. It's a cordial, we're-all-friends sort of move. It doesn't feel like a surprise.

FOREIGN EYE turns out to be about fictional non-American detectives. I manage
*Who is Sherlock Holmes?* and
*Who is Hercule Poirot?*
while Dan reels off
"Who is Dick Francis?"
"Who is Father Brown?" and

"Who is Lord Peter Wimsey?"

—which are three more responses I've as yet never heard of. And I know that Dan has heard of Holmes and Poirot. This is not encouraging.

We wander to WANDERERS, which turns out to be about gypsies, bedouins, and other nomads. Kim gets the first clue, and then I reel off three in a row to jump back in the lead. My timing is finally perfect again—five for five in this round when I try to buzz in—but I think the Ivy League Serial Killer can smell my fear.

I call for the $1000 clue in WANDERERS. It turns out to be a Daily Double:

> THE MEANDER, A RIVER IN PHRYGIA, IS SAID TO BE THE INSPIRATION FOR THIS MYTHICAL STRUCTURE

As with the *Compleat Angler* clue, I have no idea. None. I never learned this in school, and I have no mnemonics in my notebooks. This is nothing I have ever heard of. However, there are almost always hints in the clues. Here, again, my frantic internal dialogue:

*OK, don't give up. Mythical structures. Whose name means the same as "Meander." Mazes? Mythical mazes? Maybe. OK, what else . . . Phrygia was a Greek term for someplace or other. So this is a Greek mythical maze. Wait! Icarus's dad was in a maze of some kind. Was that the "labyrinth"? I think so. Sounds kinda Greek, rhymes with "Corinth," at least. Yeah, there was a bull and some girl who rescued him, I must have read that somewhere. OK, all I got, give it a shot . . .*

*What is the Labyrinth?* I ask, and I am genuinely asking.

And this is actually correct.

In memory, the thought process takes several minutes. On the tape, it lasts just six seconds. However, as the adrenaline screws with my body chemistry, my timing begins to falter. As Jane will notice later, in watching my games on tape shortly after we meet, I always lose my timing and train of thought after any Daily Double, right or wrong.

Perceptive woman, that Jane.

Five clues later, I find the final Daily Double. I have a $1400 lead, and we are late in the game. Dan and Kim are starting to grow a little frustrated; I've gotten all three Daily Doubles, have not made a single mistake, and am in position to start taking command of the match.

What they don't know is that my fever is returning.

This is the Daily Double clue that comes up:

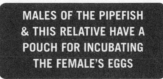

> MALES OF THE PIPEFISH
> & THIS RELATIVE HAVE A
> POUCH FOR INCUBATING
> THE FEMALE'S EGGS

Once again—as seemingly always now—I have no idea. None. I've never heard of the Pipefish. I have no idea what its relatives are. I am surprised to learn that fish with pouches even exist. So here again, I try to work with what's there:

*Pipefish . . . what does that free-associate to? Um . . . Tubefish? Plumberfish? Drainfish? Toiletfish? Monkeywrenchfish? Crap. God, I can't think. Pouch. Try pouch. Maybe that goes somewhere. Kangaroos? Mail pouch tobacco? Diplomatic pouches? Crap. Incubating . . . birth, pregnancy . . . heat lamps . . . fine, I've got kangaroofish with little diplomatic pouches under goddam heat lamps. I can't think. I just can't think all of a sudden.*

"Aw, I know this one, too," I say out loud, trying to convince myself while I'm thinking. It is not actually true. I just want it to be. I am helpless.

Even if given several weeks, the correct response—*What is a seahorse?*—would never fall from my lips. I just don't know, and I don't see any hints.

Thanks to this sudden case of actual ignorance, I blow this Daily Double. I fall back into a tie with Dan, whose over-my-head responses continue to punch holes in my confidence. Moments later, Dan whips this one out:

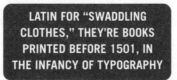

> LATIN FOR "SWADDLING
> CLOTHES," THEY'RE BOOKS
> PRINTED BEFORE 1501, IN
> THE INFANCY OF TYPOGRAPHY

"What are incunabula?" Dan says, with a maddening matter-of-factness. He gains $1000 and my growing panic as a bonus.

By the end of the round, Dan has only won on the buzzer seven times in twenty-eight chances, but frequently on the most valuable, bottom-row clues, the ones you'd expect a professor to get. He has just a $600 monetary lead, but as my fever rises, his psychological advantage is becoming enormous.

(Again: my physical stress is merely a symptom of PWW status. Dan and I have talked about it many times, and he knows I believe the outcome would be the same in any circumstance, including the disconnection of his buzzer. In which case he would have managed to ring in with his mind.)

The scores from the two Final games will be combined, with the highest total score winning the $100,000 grand prize. As Double Jeopardy concludes, I know that my concentration will fade in the second game. So I will need a big first-game score in order to win. If there's any opening at all, it's now or never.

As Alex steps toward the section of the board where the Final Jeopardy category will be revealed, I remember the broadcast date of this particular game: February 12. *Lincoln's birthday.* On Halloween, there had been Halloween clues. On Thanksgiving, there had been Thanksgiving clues. On Lincoln's birthday, however, there have not been any Lincoln's birthday clues. At least not *yet.*

And the Final Jeopardy category is—*p-TING!*

**U.S. STATESMEN**

My throat tightens. I swallow hard, knowing what I have to do. I write down my bet—every dollar I have—and start snapping my fingers, *snappity-snappity-snappity-snappity*, trying now to find calmness for just one more minute.

Brian Sipe slings the ball heavenward . . .

■ ■ ■

In 1981, the Cleveland Browns made the NFL playoffs, where they were big underdogs to the Oakland Raiders.

On an icy field, playing with a frozen ball in a bitter wind, they held their ground. As the clock wound down to the final seconds, they were just short of the Raiders' goal line, preparing to score the winning points.

Brian Sipe dropped back to pass, scanned the defense as usual by peeking between his own linemen, and flung the ball as he had so many times before into the end zone. Dad and I watched, thinking this time we'd win.

When the ball fluttered down, there was an Oakland Raider beneath it. The play Sipe had called was technically named Red Right 88. In the Snow Belt, however, this play will forever be known as The Pass.

In 1987, the Cleveland Browns made the NFL playoffs, where they were big underdogs to the Denver Broncos.

Facing a team full of All-Pros and fighting a series of injuries, they held their ground. As the clock ticked down toward the end of the fourth quarter, the Browns scored what appeared to be the winning touchdown. As a finishing touch, they managed to down the kickoff on the Denver two-yard line. Hall of Fame quarterback John Elway was faced with the nearly impossible task of leading his team 98 yards with no time-outs left. Dad and I watched, thinking this time we'd win.

In the Snow Belt, the inexorable Denver victory that followed will forever be known as The Drive.

In 1988, the Cleveland Browns made the NFL playoffs, where they were again big underdogs to the Denver Broncos.

With a team reaching its prime and in near-perfect health, the Browns fell behind by three touchdowns and still clawed their way back. Denver scored what seemed to be the winning touchdown with just a few minutes to play, This time, it was Cleveland's turn to rally dramatically. The Browns' offense drove the length of the field, reaching the Denver goal line as the clock neared zero. On Cleveland's final offensive play, running back Earnest Byner broke into the clear on the left side of scrimmage, chugging into the end zone to score a glorious, game-saving touchdown. Dad and I watched, thinking this time we had finally won.

But Byner had dropped the ball an instant before crossing the goal line. In the Snow Belt, this play will forever be known as The Fumble.

In future years, Cleveland Browns fans will surely endure other, similar shorthands. There will be The Blocked Field Goal, The Sack, and The

Tackle Eligible. Browns fans will curse these, and still they will look forward to next year. There will be The Sneak and The Statue of Liberty, The Blitz and The Safety, The Punt into That Freak Gust of Wind, The Onside Kick Taken Thirty Yards in the Wrong Direction, and The Ball Just Damn Exploding, and Browns fans will keep faith.

Finally, at last, there will simply be no more ways to lose a championship, heartbreakingly, in the final seconds.

And on that day, the Browns will leave town.

They will move to Baltimore. Again. And they will immediately win their first Super Bowl. Again. They will, in fact, defeat the *other* former Cleveland Browns team, which has already moved to Baltimore and immediately won a Super Bowl.

And—this is the essential part, if you want to understand life in the Snow Belt—Clevelanders will be genuinely sad to see them go.

I will wish Dad could have seen every play.

■ ■ ■

*p-TING!*

> **BETWEEN 1803 & 1848, HE SERVED**
> **AS A U.S. SENATOR, SECRETARY OF STATE,**
> **PRESIDENT, AND CONGRESSMAN,**
> **IN THAT ORDER**

If I can get this, I'll probably have a massive lead entering the second game, and possibly a psychological advantage. If not, I'm done. In this moment—right now—I seem to have $100,000 riding on this one clue.

As always, I have thirty seconds to think. Here's what comes next:

*Lincoln was never a senator. Lincoln was never secretary of state. Oh, man. OK. So. What president went to Congress after his term? Crap. I know that's in my notebooks. There were, what, four secretaries of state who became president? Or was it six? Shit. I just need one. OK. Think of a president somewhere around 1830, 1840ish. Lincoln is 1860, and he's number sixteen. So this is, what, twelvish, right? Zachary Taylor was twelve, Fillmore was thirteen. That's not ringing any bells. Polk was eleven. And wait, he was somewhere in one of my only-president-who lists. Crap, I'm running out of time . . . Polk . . . ? Polk . . . ?*

■ ■ ■

When my games first began, I called your attention to an Anthony Hopkins film called *Amistad.* You will also recall that I later blew off my buddy David, who wanted me to see the film *Amistad*, because I was too busy studying to take even one break to participate in real life. Here's what I missed out on seeing:

In *Amistad*, Anthony Hopkins portrayed the one U.S. president who, after serving out his term, was elected to the House of Representatives. It's a brain-sticky tidbit, too, since before long this president proceeded to drop dead in the halls of Congress.

This was not James Knox Polk, who was the eleventh president. I was not even close. The man played by Anthony Hopkins, a certain sixth U.S. president, *was* the correct response to the Final Jeopardy clue above. If I had simply stepped out of the house one day to see a movie with a friend, I would have responded correctly and easily.

Perhaps someday Cleveland Browns fans will call this The Polk.

Theoretically, I could still score more in the second game than Dan or Kim might total in two games combined. And theoretically, your subatomic particles could undergo a random series of quantum fluctuations, transforming you into Alex himself.

In which case, you'd know that I was done, although you'd be too kind to let on at the time. Instead, you would utter the Oooh.

As my response was revealed, a murmur of disappointment washed across the studio audience. A few seconds later, a hidden technician, somewhere amid all the humming doojobbies, pushed a button, revealing that I had wagered everything.

My score rolled over to zero.

"And I'll be going now . . ." I said to Alex. Wishing it were true.

My score at the end of the first game in our two-day final: the same as when we started.

Now all I had to do was figure out how to spend thirty more minutes on national TV with no chance to win, while somehow not completely humiliating myself and everyone I loved.

It was not exactly the subject I'd studied for.

CHAPTER

# 16

## THINGS TO DO ON JEOPARDY! WHEN YOU'RE DEAD

### Also, Private Moments with Mrs. Butterworth

I don't remember watching the second game of the two-day final when it first aired. Or, more accurately: I do remember *not* watching it.

It's not that I remember what I did instead that night. I don't. But I am sure it specifically involved not watching the second game.

Perhaps I did not watch the second game the night that it aired because I was rearranging my furniture, making my apartment look more like an apartment. Annika had moved into another place. We were still seeing each other, still trying to believe we might work things out, and still not going to.

The low bookcase became, once again, a low bookcase. The pedestal lamps found a closet. An entire living room full of books—almanacs and readers, *Norton Anthologies, This-That for Idiots* and *The Other for Dummies* by the score, a sheer 100-foot face of Cliffs Notes—went into a dozen cardboard boxes.

My notebooks went onto a shelf, next to

a ballpoint pen wrapped with masking tape. Certainly never to be used again.

The clutter and lights removed, the living room became large and empty and silent and dark.

There was room once again for Annika. Not that it mattered anymore.

Perhaps I did not watch the second game while trying to get reacquainted with my acquaintances, treating my friends once again like friends.

Most forgave me the distance, happy for my opportunity and looking forward to seeing the shows. Soon, however, the conversations inevitably came around again to the *Jeopardy!* FAQ, always asked with nothing but kindness. This had been fun after the initial five victories (and is obviously fun again, since this book exists), but for a time it was a constant reminder of failure.

More, since I couldn't discuss the results until the shows aired, I couldn't even say I didn't want to talk about it. That by itself would give the outcome away. And you do not talk about Fight Club.

So I said as little as possible and kept a big hard smile on my face, and soon enough the conversation would transition into trained-monkey displays. "Hey, Bob—what's the capital of South Africa?" I'd stifle and smile and just eat the banana. I was now compelled to be a good sport the next day, and the next, and the next, losing again privately every single time.

My friend David, the one so often blood-splattered on TV, the first to start introducing me this way, was also the first to stop introducing me this way, the moment he sensed I didn't want to talk about it. But such questions still came from most people I knew, and "Cape Town" I'd faithfully answer. This would be leaving aside South Africa's judicial and administrative capitals at Bloemfontein and Pretoria. Winston Churchill was once imprisoned in Pretoria. He and FDR came up with the term "United Nations" while Churchill was in a bathtub. President Taft got stuck in bathtubs a lot. Taft was from Ohio. I don't want to go back. I had one chance, and turned it into a full half hour with no chance at all.

Sometimes I would just wander off into Trebekistan. It was quieter there.

Bloemfontein, after all, is where the Truth and Reconciliation Commission held hearings in the wake of apartheid. These were mostly in English and Afrikaans, but the country has eleven official languages and its people speak about thirty. Afrikaans is derived from the Dutch spoken by colonists who first settled the cape. They kidnapped people from Asia as slaves, so to this day there is a large Cape Malay population of Muslims who shun depictive art, expressing themselves with details and color. Their homes are brilliant, reds and yellows and blues next to each other, like a giant roll of Life Savers candy. Life Savers were originally marketed to help "stormy breath." Wait—that was one of my Final Jeopardy clues. One I got. Unlike that last game. I might have embarrassed my whole family.

None of these threads ever seemed likely to fascinate the person I was speaking with. So I'd try to steer the conversation into something of mutual interest: *I hear Cape Town is gorgeous. Have you ever thought of visiting Africa?*

But usually the encounter would hold course. "Do the Czech Republic now. And Egypt. What's the capital of Estonia?"

Sometimes I just didn't go out.

I missed the quiet of study, the simple routine, and the structure of a single objective.

So I just kept reading. Occasionally I would try again to find some detail that would help heal Connie of Marvin. But mostly I let the subject wander. The joy of learning can be as addictive as any drug, it turns out. It was almost impossible to stop. South Africa's symbolic flower is the Protea, you know, which covers much of the Cape of Good Hope like a blanket. These are often trampled by wild baboons. If you disturb a sleeping baboon, it may shower you with excrement. This still sounds better than facing the Snow Belt right now.

I didn't imagine that someday I would visit the Cape of Good Hope, or that several of these very baboons would chase me, every one of us screaming, after one of the larger males had climbed into my rental car and decided to get all territorial about it.

I had never been chased by wild baboons before. I can't really recommend it. I did not react with dignity. I believe my cries of (and this is exactly what I said) "oh shit oh shit oh shit *oh shit oh shit!*" are still wafting in the Antarctic breeze.

I did things like that a lot, later. While I was coming to terms with how things turned out with Jane.

Perhaps I did not watch the second game on the night it was broadcast because I was in the company of some young lady who I hoped might take Annika's place.

The 200-unit apartment building I called home was around the corner from the three-block-long actual Melrose Place, which gives you lay of the land, and vice versa. Since Annika and I had moved in, we had passed many dozens of heart-stoppingly gorgeous young Hollywood hopefuls in the mailroom and elevators and stairwells, unavoidably bumping and brushing against them in passing. Half of these were female. Male baboons can frequently mate with any female, who signifies interest by presenting her swollen buttocks.

Few women looked my way, however. I was in my thirties, after all, which in Hollywood is legally dead. I was balding and nail-bitten, with chrome-colored skin. So headfuls of thick and fragrant hair were tossed to the other side. Skirts of remarkable contour walked off.

For a while I didn't mind. Annika was beautiful, smart, and kind. I rarely noticed other women for more than a fleeting few seconds. But now I was single. And I had just won a pair of sports cars. *His & hers* sports cars, in fact. Older males often lure younger females through displays of ability to obtain food.

So one day I arrived home in a cherry-red convertible, one of my two new Camaros. And I watched closely for any reaction. I was scientifically curious, you understand, about what effect this might have. After years of TV ads equating new cars with sex, I was interested to see if there was, in fact, any response from the opposite gender. Of course, it would be truly appalling if things changed, I thought. Bonobo chimpanzees use sexual intercourse as a form of greeting.

And ultimately, yes, there *was* this one defibrillating young lady who had never spoken to me before. She was a Hollywood attraction of unlikely curvature, fluffed and cantilevered and balanced on stilts, a display of primary colors (red lips, white teeth, blue eyes, black hair) kept in constant and eye-catching motion, less dressed than *presented*, all shimmering sweet-smelling gloss. I will leave her unnamed and little-described because I am sure by now she is married to either a studio chief, a powerful drug lord, or an entire platoon of marines.

"Nice car," she said—she *actually* said, like the most fictional ad—her flowing dark mane barely covering her pendulous stereotypes. Her voice was like wind chimes and talc.

My disbelief and delight were tempered with a certain disgust at us both. Still, this did not end the conversation, which continued all the way upstairs and lasted in brief spasms for weeks. I do not believe WORLD CAPITALS ever came up.

I never even tried to touch her, actually, although it was fun to let you think I did for a paragraph. I was just curious to spend time with someone who so clearly should have been dating the car.

I sold the Camaros not long after that.

Cars weren't the only prizes that arrived.

You remember Johnny Gilbert, at the end of each taped episode, zipping through a long list of sponsors and names. "Some contestants receive," Johnny would say in the broadcasts, and then he'd elaborate liniments, ointments, unguents, and balms, plus chocolates and cookware and home games and creams, noun after noun, as if chosen at random.

It took a few months to begin. But then: boxes and envelopes flooded into my living room, month after month, a dam overflowing, lifetime supplies of products I wasn't sure what to do with.

The sensual hands that made love to a Butterball never arrived in the mail, but Mrs. Butterworth's syrup arrived by the case, joined soon by Mrs. Butterworth's Lite. I arranged her kind faces in amusing long grids, a syrupy gauntlet running the length of my dining room table.

Next came multiple toasters, for multiple toasting. I held toast races for a while, with Mrs. Butterworth's judges.

Bon Ami cleanser came, case after case, enough to scrub California. There was Tiger Balm liniment for giving Asia a back rub, enough Ex-Lax to poop a new island. Robitussin arrived in emergency quantities, relief for some mass coughing disaster. There was Advil to soothe any armed insurrection, and ChapStick for nuclear holocaust.

This Berlin Random Noun Airlift was bewildering. I had almost enough medicine to open a pharmacy. I stopped playing with the new arrivals as toys and began to wonder how to respond.

It was Kim Worth who suggested I donate the whole pile to shelters.

It wasn't the last thing I donated.

Even after taxes, my pile of cash plus the sale of the sports cars meant that for the first time I wasn't broke, nearly broke, recently un-broke, or hoping just to get back even with broke. I had at least six months of not-broke in my future, possibly more. It wasn't enough to retire on or support anyone else long-term, but I was in a position to give something away. And this, too, came with unexpected puzzles.

All my life, I had thought myself generous. I hadn't realized how much easier this is when you don't have much in the first place. You share or you don't, and your reasons are clear and justifiable.

Now, for the first time, I would walk down La Cienega or La Brea or any prosperous boulevard nonetheless trafficked by people in need—elderly, ill, communing with private deities, or worse—and I would feel weirdly stripped of my usual certainty. How much to give, and to whom, and how often? I suddenly had choices. I could help very few people a lot, or lots of people a little, or lots and lots of people not very much at all, becoming anything from miserly to bankrupt in the process. This was confusing. Whom do you even ask for advice?

My Baptist minister grandfather was long gone, but I remembered the collection plate he passed after terrifying us. I liked the idea, if not the execution. After all, the word *kindness* appears exactly thirteen times in the New Testament, but *greedy* only five. (Then again, *ointment* shows up fourteen times. So live your life accordingly.)

And so eventually I sought wisdom in some of the older volumes I had bought for my studies. I can't reliably spell some of their names, but one is called the *Tao Te Ching*, another is the Bible, and still another is called the *Dhammapada*. There's a whole box of such books in Jane's spare bedroom, amid the giant dusty pile of my still-packed-up stuff.

I don't pretend to understand more than a fraction of it all, but on the point of charity there seems to be broad agreement: just break off a chunk between 2.5 percent and 20 percent (depending on whose version of the infinite you ask) and pass it around.

Fair enough, then. This was a real relief. I picked a number I could live with and got on with life.

By the way, and granting that I'm a foolish novice, these books really *do* all seem to agree on some stuff. You have to get past tongue-busting names, ripping creation tales, pre-refrigeration dietary laws, and miscellaneous amulets, but most of the remaining ruckus seems to agree on two basic ideas:

1. play nice, and
2. don't stab.

I admit this may be a slight oversimplification.

Then again, true words are not always fancy. The Golden Rule we learn as kids—"do unto others as you'd have them do unto you"— seems to be taught to pretty much *all* children, everywhere, and probably always has been. This "ethic of reciprocity," a handy survival tool for any troop of humans, appears somewhere in any major tradition you can think of, from the Confucian *Analects* to the Christian Gospels to the Taoist *T'ai Shang Kan-Ying P'ien* (whose spelling I had to check, but many of whose injunctions are so familiar you'd think Gandhi and Jesus were chatting on *Oprah*).

Maybe our disagreements, then, are just over definitions. Does "nice" require, for example, one set of dress codes and dietary laws? Is wearing the proper holy headgear so important that it's OK to stab someone if they don't? It kinda depends who you ask, and what they're eating, and what clothes they're wearing that day.

Meanwhile, all of our kids are on the back porch having cake together, wondering why the adults are all yelling about their hats.

Kids can be pretty holy that way, if you ask me.

I'm not saying that we shouldn't attempt to comprehend the infinite. We probably couldn't stop if we tried. It seems to be hardwired, possibly as a way to survive. A toddler shocked by a two-prong outlet might decide that *all* outlets have a *zzzap*. This assumes structure and rules and invisible connections, even though the toddler can barely imagine the other side of the wall.

This innate, constant sense that there *is* a fabric to things is so instinctive we don't even question it. We can scarcely imagine a universe without rules we can rely on. And since our brains are connection machines, we can't help but try out some cool explanations about why. And the longer we believe our favorites, the more hardwired they get.

And we're also wired to defend our beliefs, always, whatever they are. (Family reunions are so delightful this way.) Our brains actually give themselves neurochemical rewards for defending existing pathways from contradiction. (This makes perfect sense for survival: *You're alive? Keep doing the same thing*, your body says. *Here's a yummy.*) This explains why so much "thinking" is only the pursuit of reinforcement, and why disagreement involves trying to "win."

So even if all gods were wiped from human memory—and most of them, over the ages, probably have been—we'd probably start finding new ones tomorrow, and fighting over them not long after. Which would feel like exactly the right thing to do.

Meanwhile, science—a simple framework, bringing discipline to our fallible search for connections—has explained so much, so fast, that we can now, all of us, either feed all of humankind and/or kill every living thing, and possibly both in the same week.

Well, if *that's* not exciting, I don't know what is.

Maybe my God is the right one. Or maybe yours. Or maybe both. And if this isn't the time to start getting to know each other's gods, and saying hi, and making peace, I don't know when it will be.

I'll say this for the *Concordance:* nobody ever started a war over it.

Sorry to rant. Let's play some more. If it sounds like I'm down on the whole god thing, quite the opposite. In fact, near the end, I'll be reading from the Book of Common Prayer, presiding over Dan Melia's marriage.

So you never know.


Speaking of Dan, he spent most of the second game of our two-day final beating me about the face and neck with his buzzer. I was not particularly fond of him, at that moment.

Until I saw the tape, later on in the Snow Belt, I didn't remember much about that game. Or rather I *did*, but I didn't want to.

I remembered walking onstage. My head felt like it was being cracked open from the inside, as if all of the crap I had shoved in, realizing it was no longer needed, was now clawing its way out.

There was a big throbbing zero on my scoreboard. That's not something you forget.

But still, I resolved, I would fight with my best. I would smile and make light where I could. I would never give up until the absolute end, no matter how embarrassing the loss became. This was, after all, the Snow Belt way.

I got in on the first clue—*What is a rolling pin?*—and didn't win on the buzzer again until after the first commercial. My Weapon shot blanks. The first round was already halfway gone.

Kim made a good run, blocking my own for a while. This was an extra frustration.

In the Double Jeopardy round, I again got the first clue, but was shut out of the buzzer for the next two entire categories. Even so, at one point, I had about $3000 and both Daily Doubles in play. With a hot streak I could still conceivably win.

After that, I was beaten on about a dozen straight clues. If my buzzer arm had suddenly detached from my body and crawled away to a corner in shame, the results would not have been any different.

When Kim hit the first of the last two Daily Doubles, this signaled the end of my chances.

Still, I had one last opportunity to take second place. The last Daily Double. But I had to bet everything again.

You can probably guess how that worked out. A few more minutes of flailing, and it was over.

I smiled where necessary, clinked complimentary champagne with Dan and Kim, and walked the long march through the hard Sony lot. I was leaving for what had to be the last time.

Max drove me home to an empty apartment.

I wanted more. But my chances were gone.

And this really was, at last, the end of my *Jeopardy!* career.

What I had now was some money, a lot of friends I'd neglected, and an empty apartment. I also had a family in Ohio whom I felt I'd let down.

They'd be disappointed, and they would try not to show it. I was certain. And it would be so obvious it would hurt.

All kinds of kind people would try to make me feel better, and of course that would only feel worse.

Even Mrs. Butterworth was running out of reassuring things to say.

I was tempted to hide, stay home, and take long luxurious baths in her syrup. But there was not, unfortunately, enough Bon Ami cleanser to wash off the strong scent of failure.

There was only one way to do that, much as I dreaded it.

I bought a plane ticket to Ohio. It was time to face down the Snow Belt.

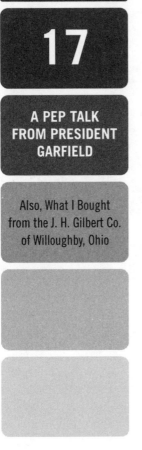

CHAPTER

17

A PEP TALK
FROM PRESIDENT
GARFIELD

Also, What I Bought
from the J. H. Gilbert Co.
of Willoughby, Ohio

On the drive from Hopkins airport in Cleveland, I passed through downtown for the first time since my retreat into Trebekistan.

My body felt surprisingly calm. This place was familiar. My stress was fighting against reassurance. This generated a great deal of noise.

Cleveland was bluer and brighter in spring than I'd remembered. The next long, gray winter was still at least weeks away. The roads were far less crowded than in California. This was physically relaxing, at least. I exhaled and stretched out for the ride through Cleveland's heart. The town was actually named for Moses Cleaveland, a surveyor sent by Connecticut. Cleveland was the home of Alan Freed's first rock-and-roll concert, which was called the Moondog Coronation Ball. No one ever specifies exactly when the previous Moondog died in office. Connecticut is the Nutmeg State. Man, that was fun.

The Cuyahoga River rolled up, cleaner and clearer than I'd remembered. But it didn't quite match what I expected to see, so it just looked confusing. I was having trouble enough staying focused. My mind was racing even as my body unwound from the flight. Cuyahoga comes from the Mohawk word for "crooked river." Curiously, what we call the Mohawk language does not contain an m. I'm not sure what noise the Mohawks made when something smelled good. I wonder what Mom's cooking right now.

To my left lay Lake Erie, glittering in the sun. There were shore birds at play on the horizon. Oliver Hazard Perry fought here in the War of 1812. An important expedition to Japan was led by his brother, Matthew Perry. One working title for the sitcom *Friends* was *Six of One*. This is also the name of a fan club for the TV series *The Prisoner*, about a man who didn't know where he was or why, and didn't know how to get out. I know the feeling sometimes.

Jacobs Field leapt into frame, a new stadium where the Indians could break people's hearts. I flipped on the radio and searched out the score, trying to distract my head.

They were winning, even leading their division, in fact.

I wondered if I was in the right city.

A half hour to the east, I crossed into the Snow Belt. I think I was expecting a snowy white curtain. But the sky stayed blue with defiance.

Soon I passed Lawnfield, President James Garfield's home, with its maple trees overlooking a park. Red-haired children played with a shiny blue ball. Twenty years in this neighborhood, and I had never once been to this park. I suppose it had always been there. I turned off the boulevard and pulled to a stop, watching the ball and a big fluffy dog and two families not worried about time.

I looked over at Garfield's house. Thirty years in Ohio, and I'd never once visited. I'd passed by here hundreds of times. He was dead; it was old. That was all I had ever seen.

But James Garfield was cool, I had learned in my studies. A Civil War general who fought against slavery. Classically educated, ambidextrous, and verbally fluent. He could write Greek with one hand and Latin with the other, both at the same time. He once found a new proof for the Pythagorean theorem. He did this for the sheer joy of learning. Our most intelligent president.

He didn't even try to be president. He was nominated against his will, and campaigned without leaving his porch. Such talent and modesty. He was unashamed of his abilities and succeeded through kindness and work.

Now here was a man to believe in. I nominate Garfield for president of Trebekistan.

Except he was shot just four months into office and died two months later. His doctors soon killed him from gross inability, infecting him, ripping him, bursting open his liver, and calling it medical care.

I believe Connie would vote for him, too.

The president died despite Alexander Graham Bell's best attempts. The good inventor showed up with a newfangled metal detector, hoping to track down the bullet. But the bed's metallic frame, a rarity then, kept the metal detector from working. No one in the room understood *both* how the bedframe and the detector were constructed.

Our smartest president died, ironically, from a lack of general knowledge.

I watched the children's red hair as they bolted toward their parents and bounded away with the bouncing blue ball. I listened hard at the *gleeeeek!* of their laughter. It was louder, I think, than my own ever was.

The Snow Belt itself held a world full of wonders. Somehow I'd just never noticed.

I was an hour late home to my mom.

Mom hugged me and laughed just to see me again.

It was nice to see all of her frogs.

There was starch on the table and starch in the freezer and starch in the fridge and the cupboard. I found pasta with beans, ravioli with crackers, and a three-layer cold gnocchi sandwich, plus pretzels and bagels and breaded fried nuggets of whatever was breaded.

I was home. It was good.

Mom never once mentioned *Jeopardy!* Never once. Not protectively. She just didn't care. She was proud of me for reasons only mothers must know. We walked through the yard and watched bunnies at play. She asked about my health, and my work, and my love life.

And when I finally dredged up the subject of *Jeopardy!*, she was proud of how I'd won, and prouder still of how I'd lost, that I'd hugged Grace and shaken hands with Dan.

*Am I yet just a child*, I thought to myself, *that I need my mother to tell me these things?*

Yes I was. Yes I am.

I ate pizza with dumplings, drank a gallon of eggnog, and fell asleep, back on Mom and Dad's couch.

When I awoke, Mom was sleeping in exactly the spot where she'd dozed after meals long before. Her cooking is strong anesthetic.

Dad would rest on the loveseat when spring nights were cool, on those nights when we'd all watched TV. He was gone now, but when I was asleep he was still there. I stared for a long time at the spot as if I could make him come back.

The TV was the same. So little had changed. Perhaps if I looked closely at the screen, Chuck Forrest would still be on *Jeopardy!*, winning and bouncing with ease. Maybe baby-faced Chuck would still trounce his opponents or towering Frank with his long walrus mustache would still gently murmur through clues.

I could almost imagine that no time had passed.

I was sitting in the very spot where I'd once been so sure I would never build any real life. Where I'd never find work I could do with real pride. Where I'd never move out, much less travel the world. Where for fun I'd watch people much smarter than I was.

And I realized that all those times Mom and Dad had watched *Jeopardy!*, they were watching it only for me.

In the morning the maple trees *whissshed* in the breeze. The backyard was alive like a zoo. Robins and cardinals and blue jays flew by. Squirrels were cavorting with glee back and forth, their tails flicking and curling as if just for show. The word *squirrel* comes from the Greek for "shadowtail," *skia oura*, which descends to our very own word.

*Wait*, I thought. *Hold on.* I'd seen Mom's backyard before, once or twice. *Was the connection to classical Greece always here?* That seemed new.

There were wind chimes from a box store, a distant echo of ancient China. And the cheap plastic birdbath had a vaguely Roman design.

There were ancient empires all over the backyard. *Quick, come look.*

I skipped lunch, not wishing to be rendered unconscious again, and headed out to see where else Trebekistan might lead.

■ ■ ■

The print of the new sign that read **Welcome To Mentor** was in "furniture font," Caslon Antique. It's made to resemble weathered type from old presses, now consciously chosen to evoke rural pasts, frequently after commercial rezoning that knocks down heirloom trees. *Aha!* I could see. And I smiled. This was fun.

The lawn of the church where I'd gone as a boy was enormous, the better to evoke a most powerful god. It's an architectural cliché all over the world, as common as the Golden Rule itself. Somehow I'd never noticed it here.

This was a town I had never seen before. It was almost the same. It was where I grew up. But the scale and the meaning had changed. The marsh was miles away, much farther than I'd always sensed as a child. The mosquitoes, for their part, were only the size of insects. How strange.

History now shook the ground. Economics and politics flew in on each breeze. Art and religion were painted on street signs.

Had this always been here on display?

In Willoughby, just across the Chagrin River, still the small town of my birth, I stood speechless beside the town square. Monuments spoke of the dead who had fought in great Wars of the Civil and both World varieties. These battles and places were *places* and *battles* now, actual cities and beaches where the flesh of men bred from this very ground bled.

The park has a captured enemy cannon I would climb as a boy, unable to imagine its meaning. It's there to mark men who were neighbors and friends before they were names on a plaque. The places and times of their last days on earth had been distant and meaningless. Not anymore, although there are no markers for the price paid by the living, left behind to carry on. Soldiers died. Loved ones faded away.

Children like me sometimes play the same way here, straddling the cannon and yelling "boom," with no sense of the horror and loss. I stood for a moment in silence and wonder. Would it be solace to the grieving to know they, too, would be forgotten? Or would it have made everything worse?

I didn't think I'd ever know the answer.

On the corner of Erie and Vine in the town of my birth once stood the first three-color traffic light in America. The original is in a museum somewhere, but I turned and watched the new one in its place, *click-clack-clack*-ing back and forth. Green yellow red. Green yellow red. Clockwork since before I was born. I'd passed through here hundreds of times, thousands, never knowing the history of even the tiniest thing. So I stood in the sunlight and gazed into Trebekistan, watching cars pass for a century, green yellow red, green yellow red, green yellow red. Studebakers, Corvairs, and Edsels rolled by.

A woman pushing a stroller saw me watching the stoplight, and stopped to watch me watching it. We stood for a moment that may still be continuing. When I noticed and smiled, she averted her eyes, pushing her baby away from the strange man.

Finally, I believe I must have passed the J. H. Gilbert Company of Willoughby, Ohio, the receipt from which we've considered in detail.

I promise you I didn't know what the receipt was for when I wrote chapter seven. But state-dependent retrieval has unusual power, and coincidence is much of reality. Remembering home, as I've written these words, has brought back memories I didn't expect.

I stopped on that day at a cemetery at Mentor's far end.

The cemetery is where Dad taught me to drive.

"There's no traffic," Dad said, "and everyone's dead, so at least you can't kill anyone here."

I was creeping a blue Malibu along a narrow road between headstones, doing 5 mph, nervous, embarrassed, and trying too hard. Dad was outstanding. His teeth had gone bad, so he was shy about smiling, but he could be wicked and kind all at once. He was both on this day. This was great. We had fun.

"Just go slow, be respectful, and get good with the brakes. If you don't, you could wind up right back here."

I could see in his eyes he was kidding. And not.

So in my teens I was taught about danger in a place built on death, and I've been careful as hell ever since. Dad had a way of his own with these things.

Dad beat me back to the spot, returning too soon. He's under the shade of a tree near my first shift of gears. There's a marker that came from the army.

I go there sometimes without telling my family. I don't want to remind them of loss. So I go there and walk, or I sit, or just leave. It's a place Dad and I can still talk.

On one particular visit, perhaps this one, it was raining real hard.

I think it *was* rubber galoshes.

I drove Mom down to Connie's house, completing my trip. Carefully. Good with the brakes.

We sat in the dining room, Mom, Connie, the kids, and her faithful-as-tides husband, Rich. Quilted place mats for plates, quilted squares to keep food warm, quilted cushions on wood for our butts. Connie served protein, with proteins for sides. We were cutting and shoveling, knives and forks, *clickety-clackity*, stray bits flying onto the carpeted floor, devoured by two quilted dogs.

"Well, what, *exactly*, did you plan on spending the $100,000 *on*?" Connie asked. With a dozen things hurting her body at any given time, my sister can cut right through crap.

My mouth was too full to reply.

"Then you don't even know what you lost," Connie concluded. "And you've won several good friends."

This was true. Kim and Dan and I got together a few times after our two-day final. We had dinner and went to movies and sat around exploring Trebekistan with each other. Dan, since he'd won the $100,000, would usually pick up the check. In a way, I was becoming glad he had won. It turned out his financial situation was even more dire than mine, and with a son to raise in the balance.

And the conversations were a great prize on their own. Kim might relate something I was eating to a bit of French history. Dan would pick up the thread and hold forth on the Celtic influence across the west coast of Europe. Kim would respond by noting a similarity in linguistic patterns in Arabic. Dan would then relate a recent archaeological anomaly which might explain the relationship.

I would nod a whole lot.

I did the same to Connie, nodding and chewing.

"I *know* you, Bob. The money wouldn't have made you happy. You just would have wanted more money." This was also true. I chewed faster. Too much truth makes you want to respond, if only to stem the flow. "The biggest win in the world wouldn't have made you happy. You just would have wanted to win more."

Large amounts of truth can cause gastric discomfort. I was almost angry, for no valid reason, which is how my anger is usually served.

"Nothing that could have possibly happened on that stage would have done you a damn bit of more good. You won lots of games. You've made everyone proud. The only one who expected more, or who is remotely upset, is *you*."

I swallowed.

Connie, I should add, is reasonably happy, despite never once being able to afford a single fine luxury, and despite never getting the education she deserved. Despite physical pain for most of her life. Despite so many surgeries that her anesthesiologist gives frequent-flyer miles. Despite being abandoned by too many doctors and even friends whose compassion ran out.

Connie is able to be happy.

Here I had spent all this time feeling guilty. She'd just gotten on with her life, forgiving and surviving and raising her kids, and even making time to teach other kids how to blow flutes.

Now she was giving me the education *I* didn't get.

Later on, alone after everyone else was in bed, I let myself watch myself lose. Connie and Rich had taped all the shows. I watched with the same sneaky shame that most people reserve for their porn, but with much less excitement.

It wasn't as bad as I'd thought.

Alex was kind as he opened the show: "Bob Harris may have outsmarted himself yesterday . . . but I would like to point out that many, many times in our tournaments in the past, the player who was a distant third after our first day wound up winning."

"I don't need your pity," I replied with a grin. The audience and Alex laughed. We were on our way to surviving the half hour. Much of what followed was similar.

All those years on the road—biker bars, strip clubs, prom nights, bachelor parties, the Giggle Ditch in Knoxville and the Comedy Yurt in Dubuque—seemed to kick in when I needed them most. A comedian is always of low social status, begging for your amusement, re-earning his place, and so losing was not really new. Pain channels to laughter, frustration is jubilance, anger just sets up the joke.

If you ever see the show, you will probably believe I'm enjoying it. And I *was*, in a way. I was enjoying Dan and Kim. I was enjoying the inevitable Clevelandness of my loss. I was mostly enjoying the whoosh of the air in my ears during the long fall.

But my timing, on the tape, was almost like in a nightclub. I got maybe six answers but made jokes all game long.

Kim joked the same way in the end.

Unlike me, he still had a decent chance. Near the finish, in fact, on a Daily Double, he briefly had a realistic shot at winning. However, Kim had to bet everything.

"Let's see," he said. "If I'm gonna get back in this game . . ." Kim paused, considering the math. "Y'know, I've always wanted to say this, Alex: let's make it a true Daily Double."

The audience cheered. So did I. And then he was faced with the following:

> IN 1 KINGS 10, GOD TELLS HIM "ANOINT HAZAEL," BUT HE DOESN'T TELL HIM TO VISIT HOMES DURING THE SEDER

Kim's face was an expression of puzzlement, concentration, and chagrin. I knew that look well. I had worn it myself. Seconds later, Kim exhaled audibly, not a sigh, but the sound of releasing a heavy burden. He knew he would soon hear the Oooh.

Next to me, I could feel Dan's shoulders unclench. Relaxing. He could already sense he had won. And we both knew that the correct response—"Who is Elijah?"—would become to Kim what John Quincy Adams was to me.

Kim had lost. But he was still the same man I had met in Wisconsin, the comedian trapped in the cold of an unwilling tavern, the one telling his own jokes anyway, still cheerful, still smiling despite it all.

"What the heck, I'll come back," Kim said. And when he won $200 on the next clue, he deadpanned, "See?" The audience laughed with appreciation. He deserved it and smiled back, enjoying the moment as best he could.

I had a similar rueful smile of my own. My two-day total: $1.

One. Single. Dollar.

I jokingly reached for my wallet as Alex announced my total. "I figure you've got it on you," I said.

"I've got a buck, yes," Alex replied, grinning back.

To my knowledge, my $1 remains the worst two-day final score in any *Jeopardy!* tournament in history.

*At least I made some kind of mark*, I said to myself, still not thrilled, but with a touch of increasing amusement. I'd made the best of it, anyway. It wasn't so bad after all.

In fact, I'd like to add that after this moment, I didn't care one bit.

I'd also like to go on to say I stopped being embarrassed on that very night, when I first saw the tape. And that I learned great lessons about losing, and the value of friendship, and the things to cherish in life, and how much one single dollar can actually mean.

Yes, that would all be very nice to say indeed.

I did feel better, though, learning that my family didn't care. No one did, in fact. In fact, it was oddly liberating to screw up so utterly in front of everyone I cared about on earth.

Maybe my brain or success didn't matter nearly as much as I thought. How odd.

"You've learned enough and won enough for a dozen people," Connie said once, during dinner. "Try figuring out how to be content enough for just one. Win *that*."

I told her I would, and I meant it.

So I would return to Hollywood and try to seek a more genuine kind of happiness.

You might want to guess just how well that worked out.

GREED, A QUICK
SMUSH, AND
A SHAMEFUL
LITTLE BOOBY

Also, I Help
with Another
Howard's End

Flying back to Hollywood, I convinced myself that if I only saw the place with better eyes, I might find contentment, as Connie had suggested. I had some real hope that this might work.

Apparently I must have forgotten exactly what town I was coming home to.

In Hollywood, even driving home from the airport can present frustrating challenges. Street closures, parking rules, and traffic laws are dictated by studio production schedules, which are determined by the availability of makeup trailers, which in turn are dictated by the normal bodily functions of celebrities. As a result, the 405 freeway can be tied up simply because (for example) Patrick Stewart has a difficult zit, Heather Graham needs to floss, or Mandy Patinkin isn't getting enough fiber. If Lindsay Lohan eats that shrimp, no one's getting home for hours.

Somewhere in the middle of all that, people

think there's happiness here. Some folks move here from thousands of miles away. I certainly did.

Los Angeles, on the other hand, is not Hollywood. And Trebekistan is everywhere you turn.

After years living here I still had never quite seen the city. The guidebook I'd used on my very first visit had remained the extent of my knowledge: only Melrose, only Beverly Hills, only Venice, the Strip, and always, always the ocean.

I looked for the history and the art now, cultivating the past as a habit. My apartment, just off Melrose, became a beanfield not far from an oil well. In the far distance, Chumash Indians built homes out of willow and whalebone.

Los Angeles is actually an incredible world. Within twenty minutes you can visit enclaves from Russia, Korea, China, Iran, Ethiopia, or almost anywhere else. In every new neighborhood, you'll find no shortage of people eager and flattered and glad to share their own ways.

*Had I really not noticed? Had this always been here? Has the backyard always been filled with hundreds of civilizations?*

I hadn't. And yes, it had been.

Max and I drove down to Sony again before long.

A year after our tournament, Dan had a whim to watch the next Tournament championship in person. He called Kim and me, and we drove in as a group, watching from the studio bleachers with the rest of the crowd.

I played along silently, again over my head. It had been months since I'd studied. Categories flew by. I was stunned by the speed and unsure of my footing. For a moment I was Charly from *Flowers for Algernon*, the mentally challenged young man whose miracle treatment wore off. I was a half-step behind, lots of almosts and not-quites, Cliff Robertson trapped on the film-version downslope. The knowledge was there, but the practice was not.

Now that I knew just how much was required, the podiums looked more distant and unlikely than ever before.

Three excellent players battled their final, standing where we'd recently stood. *Was that really us? Did we really do that?* I wondered. I tried to picture it, slipping the timeline, closing my eyes, conjuring up a real but distant image, bringing Trebekistan into the *Jeopardy!* set. But I couldn't quite do it.

I wasn't sure it had all actually happened.

There were eventually plenty of reminders.

Two major U.S. airlines actually played the last episode with Dan, Kim, and me as in-flight entertainment.

Later, on cable TV, the Game Show Network began rebroadcasting the entire season in which we played. I do not know why, but they continued repeating this one season for four solid years.

Soon, some of the Small Midwestern Colleges at which I'd performed invited me back to give lectures on memory and test-taking skills.

This was an incredible prize, a chance to relive my wins while helping students do much better in school. Maybe my own college years, which had long seemed so wasted, were what compelled me to study in newfangled ways. My mistakes and bad choices had finally paid off, in a sense, now that I was helping other kids do what they loved even better.

Speaking at colleges about memory made my own memories feel much better. Granted, I didn't spend a lot of time talking about losing at the very end.

I tried other quiz shows eventually, picking up cash on the side.

There was an Internet thing run by a company called GoldPocket, in which people played in real time all over the world. There were thousands of contestants at once, with eventually just one final winner.

But few of these people had spent months filling notebooks with cartoons of great artists and writers.

So that was an extra thousand bucks on a Thursday.

There was a cable game show on the USA Network called *Smush*. The host was Ken Ober, who had done MTV's *Remote Control*, which I'd also

watched long ago in the Snow Belt. The hostess of *Smush* was a Playmate named Lisa who said "Whoo" a lot when the camera was on.

But "Whoo" is not "Oooh." I was worshipping false idols.

On *Jeopardy!* there's a category called BEFORE AND AFTER, which is
two clues in one, smushed together. So:

"GOOD GOLLY MISS MOLLY"
SINGER WHO RESIGNED THE
AMERICAN PRESIDENCY

would be *Who is Little Richard Nixon?* These are no more difficult than
an ordinary clue and can often be easier, since if you know either response, you have two-thirds of the answer and half of what's left.

*Smush* was played the same way, only pushing the words themselves
closer together. So the answer to:

BARBARIC TRIBE RULED BY ALARIC PLUS SHAKESPEARE'S MURDEROUS MOOR

would be *Visigothello*, although the questions were never remotely that
highbrow. (*Jeopardy!* has tried something similar recently, in a category
called OVERLAPS. The only difference: *Jeopardy!* would not consider Visigothello much of a challenge.)

While providing simple answers like "Momen-to-talrecall" and
"CN Tower of Bab-yl-on Five," I'm visibly embarrassed on the tape,
much more than I realized. After losing to Dan, this felt like being made
to sit in a high chair.

Fortunately, the clues got longer as the game progressed. I finally
won in the end with the six-bagger "Born in East-L.A. Sto-Rita More-
Nova Sco-shalom-ega." (Say it aloud and you'll hear a song, a movie, an
actress, a province, a Hebrew word, and a Greek letter.) For a moment I
had escaped the kids' table.

For the final lightning round, hostess Lisa the Playmate wrote a
key word in lipstick on a mirror, from which I'd construct five other
words.

The key word was "Booby."

The Playmate posed inches away. This was supposed to provide
humor or tension or possibly amusement for the ghost of Fellini. I just

hoped no one at *Jeopardy!* watched. It felt almost shameful to reach for such low-hanging fruit. I had forty-five seconds and finished in thirty, accepted the prop money for coming up with "Malibu-by" and "Boo-beeper" and "Boo-beef" and the like with some visible embarrassment, and skulked away out the nearest door.

That was eight thousand bucks on a Monday.

There was *Greed* on the Fox network, taped at Television City. When I was a boy, this was where Carol Burnett was from. I wore the same sport jacket I'd worn for my first *Jeopardy!* game. This seemed respectful.

Chuck Woolery hosted, and the game play was not *quite* as simple as *Smush*. I swear these were really the rules:

Six contestants (or sometimes five) would answer questions whose answers sometimes depended on what year the data came from. After each answer, another contestant would have the chance to change the answer; later on in the game, after each answer Chuck would offer this person money to chicken out. If they didn't chicken out, and the answer was right, then two contestants (including the one with the option to change the answer) would face off for one separate question, with the winner getting the loser's share of the pot. Then the remaining contestants would play another round, unless everyone decided to quit, which was not a group decision. If the game continued, then another question would be asked, but this time with even more possible answers, although one of the options could be eliminated, but only once. In which case Chuck would offer another chance to chicken out, and so on, until Chuck Woolery himself would start hollering at the producers, WILL SOMEONE PLEASE TELL ME WHERE WE ARE AGAIN? EVEN *I* DON'T KNOW WHAT THE RULES ARE! *I HAVE NO IDEA WHAT I'M EVEN SAYING UP HERE!*

This was even more fun than it sounds.

Part of the rules involved players fighting each other for shares of the growing pot—if that wasn't manifestly clear—but anyone who had multiple shares became an immediate and constant target. It was obvious from studying the rules that the most likely way to win was to avoid being challenged, thus sneaking through the rounds until the pot was large enough that it was time to quit.

If that didn't make a whole lot of sense, don't worry. Judging by ratings, a quantum mechanics seminar would have been simpler and gotten a bigger audience. Bottom line: I needed people not to challenge me.

So I spent virtually every minute in the green room working the phrase "five-time *Jeopardy!* champion" into ordinary conversation. As in: "Yes, I've been on other game shows, I'm a five-time *Jeopardy!* champion," and "Gosh, this is a good sandwich, and I am a five-time *Jeopardy!* champion," and "Excuse me, can you tell me where to find the bathroom? I need to wipe the backside of a five-time *Jeopardy!* champion."

Needless to say, nobody challenged me. In fact, they barely even spoke to me.

The taping took under two hours. I answered all of three questions on a team that collectively won a million dollars.

That was $200,000 on a Saturday.

The money, it turned out, was actually an annuity, payable in tiny bits spread out over a decade. The immediate cash value was thus substantially less. Once the taxes were paid, I'd won only a third of the money they flashed on the screen. Still, it was more cash in one day than I'd won in whole weeks of *Jeopardy!* For three total questions. If *Jeopardy!* was a relationship, *Greed* was a tawdry affair: quick, flashy, loud, and kind of confusing.

Some time after *Greed* was canceled, I ran into Chuck Woolery in an LAX terminal. We were both walking toward baggage claim. I introduced myself, and he remembered our game, and he didn't mind passing time with a stranger. He was exactly the same as he is on the air: just-folks, easy smile, no pretense at all.

"*Man*, that was a complicated show," he volunteered with a laugh.

*Who Wants to Be a Millionaire* has never asked me to appear on their show. I don't know why this is. I've passed their test several times. Perhaps I'm not playful or friendly or animated enough. In any case, the Hot Seat seems safe from the cool of my keister.

But I've been on the show, or my voice has, at least. My friend Howard chose me as his Phone-a-Friend Lifeline. I was more nervous about this than I'd ever been for my own games, because I had a friend's life in my hands.

So one day I was home by the phone when it rang. This was a producer, telling me Howard was playing. Soon it rang again. This was Meredith Vieira.

Howard was playing for $250,000. With one answer, I could help pay off his mortgage, get braces for his kids, and send him and his wife on a new honeymoon . . .

Or not.

My chest started to clench. I could just barely breathe. Howard began reading his question:

> Which of the following writers stabbed his wife Adele with a
> penknife in 1960?

*Norman Mailer!* I blurted.

Howard hadn't even given the choices.

The studio audience laughed and applauded. I didn't know at the time, and it was edited from the show, but Howard had mentioned that I was a *Jeopardy!* champ. So my instant response was like the punchline to a great joke.

I was not showing off. I just didn't want to risk not getting it out of my mouth. I knew that I knew, and I wanted to breathe again.

That was $250,000 on a Wednesday.

Thanks to this lengthening list of quiz show successes, I've been invited for years to the annual Game Show Congress, a convention where fans mingle in hotel ballrooms with players, producers, and hosts. It's like any smallish convention of TV fanatics. There are keynotes and souvenirs and the trading of bootlegs. People split off into small rooms to discuss exotic passions. Everyone knows just a little too much.

I was reluctant to go at first. I like meeting new people who enjoy the same things that I do, but being a part of any convention always makes me feel like a total geek. (This includes political gatherings most of all, and I've attended Democratic, Republican, and Green national conventions. These are much like *Battlestar Galactica* gatherings, only with sillier costumes and much less believable dialogue.)

But the GSC had two things in its favor: it's always somewhere not very far from Los Angeles, and there's always an exhibition game between former champs, hosted by a Canadian (of course) named Paul Paquet.

So I went, and we played, just for fun.

I first met Jerome Vered this way. Jerome held the one-day *Jeopardy!* winnings record for a decade. He lives up in the Valley, knows every good place to eat in the northern hemisphere, and will share every ounce of his knowledge so eagerly that he may still be talking to me, right this minute. Jerome was the first person to win Ben Stein's money, so impressively that he became Ben's sparring partner in warm-ups for years. On *Jeopardy!*, Jerome's a fabulous Jedi who never looks at the lights. He will wear the same shoes and trousers throughout an entire tournament. You already know why.

I also met Leszek Pawlowicz, once called the "Michael Jordan of game shows" by the *New York Times*, a Tournament of Champions winner who can spell his name without looking it up, which is more than I can do after knowing him for years. (He's also the sort of guy who will smile gamely at that joke, even though it must have been made a thousand times.) Leszek won Ben Stein's money by a score of 7 to 4, and is four-for-four as a *Millionaire* lifeline. Perhaps we should start up a service.

In front of maybe a hundred fervent Trebekkies, the three of us and several other good players wrestled in a simple buzz-when-you-know-it contest. I didn't win. Neither did Jerome. Neither did Leszek.

Ed Toutant, a tall Texan who works for IBM, possibly as a supercomputer, beat all three of us. I played Ed again the next year, and I even led for a while, but he made a spectacular comeback before buying the beer.

Ed was one of *Millionaire*'s biggest winners. But when Ed was on *Jeopardy!*, he won just one single game. The correct millisecond escaped him.

Still, I often walked home to an empty apartment.

There was a serious girlfriend at the time I won *Greed*, my last One-True-Eternal-Soulmate™, but she wasn't there for the taping. I think she was doing something terribly important, which I cannot remember at all. This particular woman was deep into showbiz. Tall and glamorous, stunningly beautiful, and well connected in Hollywood: everything I thought I wanted when I first moved to L.A. She's a fine person, I truly believe. I still like her enormously, and I wish her much good. But we went to lots of big parties and I shook many big hands and I wondered why I still felt so lonely.

And then I wondered why I still didn't know how to be happy.

A few months later, I met someone who did.

It was a blind date, actually.

My blood-spattered friend David and I often hang out with a fellow named Danny, another actor whose work you might have seen. For several years, Danny had a recurring part on a well-known TV series, a sensitive and realistic portrayal of a teenage girl fighting vampires. Really. So this meant I now had a second friend who got splattered with blood on TV. Perhaps Andy Warhol was nearly correct: in the future, everyone will be famous for fifteen minutes, and splattered with blood at the time.

Danny was once in an episode that was centered entirely on his minor character. It was his chance to shine, so he threw a big party with all of his friends. I knew he was talented but I had seen little of the show, so I went to his house prepared to enjoy the evening in portions.

I shouldn't have worried. It was one of the funniest hours I'd ever seen, even though I knew few of the characters. Danny rose to the occasion with a cocksure performance. I was also impressed with how clever and honest and surprising the writing was. I envied Danny the chance to spend time with such talent.

Months later, on our way to a ballgame, I was grumbling to David and Danny about how things had ended with the tall glamorous woman. They both had an idea for a fix-up: the woman who'd written the all-Danny episode. Jane.

I was feeling down and reluctant, but I agreed to meet her as friends, just because I admired her writing. Danny called her on his cell phone, and David introduced me—for I believe the final time—as a five-time *Jeopardy!* champion.

I could hear Jane was reluctant as well. I respected that. I couldn't speak to her myself because I was driving on the 101 freeway, and earlier in the day John Stamos had eaten a bad piece of fish, so traffic was monstrous. Through David and Danny, Jane and I picked out a restaurant in an undistinguished shopping mall, thinking only of convenience and getting it over with.

So one cloudy afternoon of no symbolic significance, I didn't dress up and arrived a few minutes late to meet Jane by a decaying brick wall in a dusty construction site at the edge of an unromantic mall. The restaurant, I discovered, had been closed and torn down, leaving only the nondescript bricks.

Jane hadn't dressed up either, and was only seconds less late than I was.

*So far, so good*, we both thought.

It wasn't love at first sight for either one of us. I had described myself to her as "balding and nailbitten." She called herself a "tiny nerd with delicate hands." These were both pretty accurate, but we had fun right away.

We traded our flashiest conversational thumbnails—my game shows, her rhymes-with-Squeema—and laughed without force. We were friends by the time we found a place to eat, completing each other's sentences by the time dessert came, and officially dating by the time I called David and she called Danny.

In fact, I'm not sure I ever actually fell in love with Jane. It was more that I liked her so much that it crossed into passion. I mean, Jane's explanation of linguistic morphology involved the "Manamana" song from *The Muppets*.

This was someone to spend serious time with.

There was one thing about Jane that bugged me, however. I couldn't quite put my finger on it for a few weeks. Just something that made me edgy around her.

And then I realized: she was in a good mood almost all of the time.

Jane didn't speak harshly when she was upset. She'd just be upset, and speak plainly, and try to solve the problem. And then she'd go back to being in a good mood.

I mean, come on. How creepy is that?

This was a woman who could throw sharp verbal knives. In a script, her characters could wield words as edged weapons, slashing and dicing and wounding precisely. But in life Jane would throw only cotton balls filled with chocolate. Even anger came wrapped in cushioning Styrofoam.

How long could you stand to be around that?

Plus, she would sometimes start to sing and dance for no reason. We'd be walking down the street, perhaps discussing ancient writing systems (Jane was learning to read many Egyptian hieroglyphs), and then she'd suddenly break into a semi-related song, dance an impossibly silly new dance, and—worse—implore me to join right in.

How disconcerting. Obviously, this would have to stop.

Either that, or I'd have to learn how to calm down and dance.

People who really are happy, it turns out, usually don't go around wearing billboards announcing it, handing out fliers, or evangelizing other people to be exactly the same. At least Jane didn't.

She was just happy. Glad for every day.

We talked about it a little at first. And then we talked about it a lot.

I took the position that being happy required some definite knowledge that there was something to be happy *about*—that choosing to be happy for no particular reason was not only slightly unhinged, but possibly counterproductive. There are grave problems that must be addressed in the world, you know.

Jane would usually get up and start dancing.

And as she danced, I'd hold still in my seat, while we'd talk about the overuse of antibiotics or coastal populations threatened by rising sea levels, in all seriousness, while she was shaking her hips to the rhythm of something by Cher.

Jane almost always knew something I didn't about the subject. Jane almost always had more fun in the process.

Eventually, she got me to stand up in these talks.

Sometimes I'd even let my hips move a little.

One day we're curled up in a bed, and Jane finds a lump in one breast.

Of course, we'll just go get it checked out, and it'll soon be forgotten, we think.

Jane's too young for this to be anything much, and there's no environmental or dietary or other risk we can think of. So we'll go, and they'll say it's nothing, and we'll get on with our lives.

I think of my sister and missed diagnoses.

I think of my father at the end in the hospital. The doctors were *sure* he was cured.

I am secretly terrified, right there in that bed.

If Jane is, she doesn't let on.

We go in. They do tests. And it's something.

It's something that has to come out.

So they cut.

They got it all, they say.

They didn't get it all.

We go back. They cut some more.

This time they say that they're sure.

They didn't get everything. And there's a chance it might have spread.

The doctor speaks in lots of technical terms. Jane asks him to fax all the test results to me. I volunteer to sort through it and translate. We both want to know every detail. It's in our nature to know.

Jane sleeps in the bed in my book-cramped apartment while I sit up at my desk and read, looking up unfamiliar words. Cramming like *Jeopardy!* for a quiz we don't want. If we win, the only prize for Jane is survival.

I learn about *ploidy*, which is the number of copies of DNA. In a tumor, you get extra sets. Hypertetraploidy is bad.

Jane's lump has hypertetraploidy.

I learn about hormone receptors, indicating a tumor has integrated with the body. Having lots of receptors is bad.

Jane's lump has lots of receptors.

I go through category after category, and Jane runs the table. Maximum bad. Maximum bad. Maximum bad.

I stop panicking halfway and notice fascination growing alongside my sadness. Grief, fully felt, can give way to sheer wonder as you realize how much you can lose.

I fall asleep at my desk, too tired to cry, just wishing I didn't know.

How would I tell her?

How would you?

So one morning we're driving and singing the tune of "Sing Hallelujah, Come On Get Happy":

> *It's a Giant Drug Store*
> *But they don't sell Giant Drugs.*
> *They don't sell drugs to giants,*
> *So what the hell kind of drug store is it anyway?*

The melody always sort of peters out at the end, incidentally. That's the part where we'd trail off into laughter.

We're going for another round of cutting, and this time they'll look at her sentinel cells, which are camped out at lymph nodes not far from the breast. If the sentinel cells are still normal, the disease hasn't spread.

If not, then things can get very bad.

The doctors have promised that Jane will be fine.

Doctors said exactly the same things, in exactly the same tones, about Dad.

■ ■ ■

Part of me will forever be in that waiting room. I have never left, even now, as I write this. It's the biggest Hiroshima flash of my life. You know how memory kicks in.

At the other end of a very long hallway, too far even to shout or cry out, is a pair of double doors. Through these will soon come a doctor.

And then comes the rest.

The Cleveland Browns, you should know, aren't the only losing team I've cheered on.

The Cleveland Indians haven't won a World Series since fifteen years before I was born. In 1994 they had their best season in forty years, but there was no World Series to go to. It had been called off because of a strike.

The Cleveland Cavaliers have never won an NBA title. In the year still most cherished by fans, they heroically managed to make the playoffs and not immediately lose. This is still called "The Miracle of Richfield," named for the remote village where the now-abandoned arena was built. The Cleveland Barons hockey team folded, was reborn, and then folded again. The Cleveland Crusaders just folded.

Losing is what Clevelanders learn to do well to survive. Losing, in truth, is something we're good at. Tomorrow, next year. We tried, we played well, we go on. This, too, is an essential survival skill. Understood, it should be a source of great pride.

When the Cuyahoga River caught fire when I was a boy, it made the national news. What the world didn't know was that the river burned often. The fire chief called it "routine" the next day. Not very long later, the mayor himself caught fire. A forgettable fellow named Ralph Perk went *whoooom*, or at least his hair did.

I got used to the idea that anything could suddenly go up in flames.

Not just in Cleveland, of course. It's just life itself, really. Losing is what we do in this world.

Two out of three *Jeopardy!* players lose, game in and game out. More than that, even, since winners return and keep hogging the wins. And by the standards of life, *Jeopardy!* is actually kind.

One-third of humanity doesn't even have clean water, the single most basic necessity. Nearly half of our kind will be born randomly into war or famine or poverty or some other great ill. This is rarely the fault of the infant.

Most people are good, with a deep need for fairness. So the world and the present can be painful to look at directly, assuming you're lucky and aren't forced to notice every day. We can hide, we can rationalize, we can look away and go on with whatever. We can scream our denials with anger or smiles, with whispers or cries. We can build complex ideas to create explanations and demand our own permanence. This is a good deal of work, but it gives us a past we can live with and a future to live in.

And even so: We didn't ask to be here, and we don't ask to leave. While we're here no one shows us the controls. We don't stay very long in the end.

Heaven and Earth are not humane. Life is terminal, whatever we do.

But newborns don't ask why they're laughing or crying. A newborn just *is*.

And when they're happy, that's *it*. They're alive, glad for the moment, glad for air or the hug or the glimmer of light. Glad for the warm human heartbeat nearby.

Joy is in every moment of waking in life. So is grief. We can embrace both and still choose well.

Jane was awake on this morning. She was *alive*. So she sang.

She was glad for the day.

This is still my one favorite moment on Earth.

I am still awake in the waiting room. Right this minute.

I will never again hope for any One-True-Eternal-Soulmate™. I don't want more anymore. I don't want plans for the future. I swear off false permanence. I only want to see my best friend well. I want her to live a long time before we die. I will trade everything I've ever learned, had, or done, just for one extra day for Jane.

I am trying to find joy. Even now.

In this very moment, even now as I write this, I believe I will fail.

■ ■ ■

On the day that it happens, I glance up. In the distance, the double doors move. I stop breathing.

Jane's surgeon emerges slowly, taking a breath. *He looks tired,* I think.

He sees me now, standing to meet him.

But I'm too far away to address in hushed tones and kind calmness. I am too far away to console.

So instead he just stops.

He *stops.*

*Is he afraid to face me?* I think. *How would I give someone the news?*

He stops in the spot where he's standing. A tenth of a second. A *Jeopardy!* buzzer fraction. Considering his expression. Choosing his words and his posture.

He stops, and his arms start to rise.

*Oh, no,* I think. *Here comes consolation.*

He stops, and his arms start to rise.

*Here come soft murmurs. Here comes grief counseling. Here comes empty space.*

He stops, and his arms keep on rising.

*What's that?* I wonder. *That's not a hug. It's not solace. What is it?*

His arms start to rise, and keep rising, until they're straight up in the air.

It takes me a moment to understand what I'm seeing.

A touchdown.

It's a *touchdown.*

He's signaling. A touchdown.

A winning touchdown. Like a victory.

Like we've finally won at the end.

He's sharing the good news, down the hall, right this instant. From a distance. Not wasting a second.

Jane's doctor is signaling victory. His arms are rising up in the air.

We won.

And now I'm running, excited. I am running to hug him. I need to hear words. I need to see eyes and smiles. I need to see Jane. I can scarcely believe it.

Jane's doctor is standing, his arms going straight up in the air.

I shake his hand and I grab him and hug him and I think pretty soon I am crying.

No galoshes.

I am dancing.

Days later, I'm driving home from the hospital. Rainy and gray, water stacked at the curbside going *whisssssh* in my wheels. Smell of ozone and sound of windshield wipers *wubbity-wubbity-wubbity.*

Jane's half-asleep, leaning back, at my side.

She has fragile bits still that can't be jostled, so I'm focused, alive in this moment. Careful with the brake, just as Dad taught me once. Avoiding every bump in the road.

We pass a certain drugstore. I start to sing, quietly to myself:

> *It's a Giant Drug Store*
> *But they don't sell Giant Drugs . . .*

I glance over. And Jane is smiling.

> *Sing Hallelujah, come on, get happy . . .*

CHAPTER

20

THE IMPORTANCE
OF MEMORY
IN RECOVERY

Also, A Brief Look at
Estonian Revolutionary
Movements

The next several months involved doctors, procedures, exams, and much indiscreet poking and probing. There were tubes that took draining and drains that took tapping and taps with new tubing. Fluids and goos went inside and out at all hours. I'd give lots more details, but you would remember them, and you'd probably rather not know.

But Jane was alive every day and still is. She is fine. She is *great*.

She had long days in bed and long nights uncomfortably not, in such number that they blurred even at the time.

But these were not difficult days. Only long ones. There was no chemo and no radiation. There were no experimental drugs, harsh side effects, or recurrences. Jane was lucky as hell.

Jane's tumor was a type that can look truly horrible in all the tests but that turns out to be no big deal after all.

It was small. They got it all. They really did.

All we needed now was time.

When Jane was back on her feet, we went out to a park by the beach for a walk. And without meaning to consciously, we found ourselves approaching a fifteen-foot religious statue, meant to honor Saint Monica. Instead it looks more like an erect human penis.

This was not far from the spot where I'd once said the wedding vows, the spot that fell over the cliff. Jane knew how much this patch of dirt (or at least its vicinity) had once meant.

This wasn't planned. We were just walking, and arrived at this spot, which we noticed. So for a moment we weren't quite sure what to do or to say.

So we just did a happy little not-dead-yet dance—which in this case looked like a little sidestepping Bob Fosse sort of thing, as if performed by arthritic pandas who'd just had their first beer.

And then we walked away, holding hands.

Incidentally, if you were surprised by the end of the previous chapter, well, good. I was pretty thrown by it myself when it happened. I wanted you to feel it exactly as I did, so I kept the verb tenses ambiguous about Jane's future existence (life does that to all of us, anyway), and implied doom (which we all face) through other means. I wanted you to feel every ounce of joy and surprise when that touchdown thing happened. It was just a small gesture from the doctor, but it's my favorite slow-motion highlight ever, better than anything I ever saw with Dad. So I hope you'll forgive me. And maybe even cheer like something's unspooling.

Either way, there are some pretty cool twists still coming, and nobody else gets cancer that I know of. Honest.

Plus, I hid a dollar between pages 320 and 321. But you have to read straight through. It's only there if you don't flip ahead.

OK. Now, that was a complete lie. I thought I'd write something *actually* deceptive, so the difference was clear.

Still, I bet you still have a slight urge to flip ahead, looking for the dollar.

It would be really cool if completely impossible things happened like that.

"Hi, is this Bob? This is Susanne from *Jeopardy!*"

I had overslept and was still lying in bed, half-groggy, not familiar with sleeping in my own apartment of late. I looked at the clock radio, which had arrived years earlier as one of the Johnny Gilbert some-contestants-receive prizes during the Berlin Random Noun Airlift. It was just after 10:00 a.m. on some December weekday.

"Hi, Susanne! How are you?" I replied cheerily. I sat up, squinting and sniffing and squirming awake. I was trying not to let on I was only half-conscious.

I had no idea why Susanne was calling. It had been years, after all. But the day before, a new contestant wrangler named Tony had called, telling me Susanne would be calling me at home. This was puzzling. My only theory was that they were looking for new players and might ask if I knew anyone who would be good for the show.

This theory was not even close.

The actual reason was memorable enough that the following is very near, I promise, to Susanne's exact words:

"Fine. Listen—we're having a special tournament in a few months. We're inviting fifteen of the best players from the show's history to compete at Radio City Music Hall. We'll fly everybody in, first class, and put you up at the Waldorf-Astoria hotel. We're calling it the Masters Tournament. Oh—and the grand prize is a million dollars."

She said this with excitement and friendliness, but also a bit crisply, as if she had said precisely this a dozen times in the last hour. Which, I imagine, she had.

I still wasn't sure that I was included. Maybe I was supposed to carry Frank Spangenberg's bags or something. And then she actually said:

"So what are you doing in February?"

*This doesn't make sense,* I thought. My mind was suddenly running at full pace. *Dan Melia has already beaten me. Twice. Kim beat me, too. So did Grace. And those were just players from my year. There must be dozens of players more deserving. I wonder who else is involved.*

I wanted to ask, but there was a speed to Susanne's phrasing, as if she was working down a list and had more calls to make.

*Maybe Dan will be there, and I'll get a new crack at him. Or maybe he can't make it. Maybe lots of better players just can't make it. They're like Wes, curing people and stuff, too brilliant to take time for a game. Or maybe the show is planning multiple tournaments, and this is just one that I'm in.*

I also had the feeling that if I wasn't quite sure, I could be replaced. *This could be humiliating. You'll be way out of your league. Another good game for the airlines.* "Would you like to play?" Susanne asked, waiting, as *Jeopardy!* instants ticked by.

I thought it over for about four or five tenths of a second. An eternity. *Someone else could ring in.*

"Are you kidding? Of course!" I heard myself say. Then I thanked her, she promised more details, and we hung up the phone.

I took a few breaths and stared at the wall, straining hard for old memories. *Who came first again?* I asked myself, scared.

*Buchanan or Pierce? Or Millard goddam again Fillmore?*


I called Mom right away. I was already worried again about letting her down. It's amazing how old habits die hard.

She was excited and proud I was even invited. She couldn't care less if I won.

I was worried I might not deserve even to go.

"But they *invited* you, son," she said. "It's their show, after all."

Sometimes I need my mom to point out the obvious.


I called my sister a few minutes later. I was still afraid that saying yes had been a mistake.

Connie picked up the phone, but her voice sounded weak. Marvin was having a very good day.

At the time we believed Marvin might have been lupus, an often-tragic autoimmune disease with a scary-bad future. She had symptoms so constant and yet changing and frustrating that you could almost lose track and forget. But there were other symptoms that didn't align with lupus, so we couldn't be sure what the hell Marvin was.

And here I was calling with my vanity troubles. After everything that happened with Jane. I was ashamed of myself in an instant, before I even said hello.

"That's fantastic!" was Connie's only real thought at the news. It was a show to look forward to, something the kids could brag about in school. No envy, no concern for results.

I wished she could go in my place.

I thanked her and promised to have fun enough to share.

Jane squealed when I told her the news. An actual squeal. *GWEEEEP!* would be a decent transcription (although the laugh that can be spelled is not a genuine laugh).

I was sitting on the edge of her bed, actually worried I'd have to choose between spending time studying and spending time helping her heal. Previous relationships had taught me to think that such choices were necessary, that my own life and any partner's would overlap only slightly. There still was so little I knew.

"We have a project!" was the next thing she said.

*We.*

And then followed more *GWEEEEP*ing and giggles.

Shortly thereafter, I saw the list of my Masters opponents. Two names leapt right out:

*Frank Spangenberg,* the highest-scoring five-time champion ever
*Chuck Forrest,* Chuck, actual Chuck, the real Chuck guy

I went down the list. It was an amazing array.

*Rachael Schwarz,* first woman to win a Tournament of Champions
*Brad Rutter,* the reigning Tournament of Champions winner
*Robin Carroll,* winner of both a Tournament of Champions and an International
  Tournament of Champions

And so on. Players I'd seen and admired, all much stronger than I'd been.

My eyes scanned on down and finally found:

No Dan or Kim.
No Grace.
Nobody who'd beaten me.

I did not quite understand. I wondered if I was only chosen to be the funny guy. It's a *show*, after all, entertainment, and I can't help but be playful while we're on stage. After so many years on stages where laughs meant survival, it's probably as built-in as my name.

I did know for sure that if I lost, that's why people would *think* I was there.

I called Dan. I called Kim. They were both graceful about it. Via e-mail, so was Grace, but you'd figure on that. They were friends, and they were kind in a way I suppose I would muster, but I still felt bad they were mustering now. All anyone said was they hoped that I'd win.

Besides, it would look better for them if I did.

Jane hurled herself into prepping and coaching and quizzing and teaching. Seeing her brighten this way was the best prize the show ever gave me.

Keep in mind that Jane's love of learning at least equals mine. She's a writer with a vast knowledge of literature, a linguist from Berkeley whose education far outpaces my own. So like a mother beast pre-chewing the kill for her beasties, Jane prepped me on things even Chuck never listed. We knew the clues would be the toughest *Jeopardy!* had ever dared ask. So we couldn't rule anything out.

Jane's strengths were many of my weaknesses, so those were a main focus: Greek and Latin roots. Archaeological sites. Great poets and prophets. The lives of great writers and artists.

Even for subjects she knew nothing about, Jane would spend every spare minute poring through books, preparing me lists of things I might need. Fashion design, flowers, and fabrics. Ethnic cuisines. Tallest trees. Deepest geologic depressions. Explorers and songwriters. Dancers and theme parks. Airports and boy bands. Her dancing enthusiasm was startling and joyous. It made me want to win just for her.

And Jane wanted *me* healthy, just as I did her. She made me jog and take breaks and eat vitamins. I wouldn't be sick, not on her watch. I got all of my rest every night.

Every evening before sleeping she'd grill me on basics. Every world capital, no matter how obscure, in every nation of Asia and Africa. Every world currency. Presidents, vice presidents, and first ladies. Greek and Latin roots.

Most nights, we'd run one-to-ones.

"One-to-one" is Jane's term for unique *Jeopardy!* identifiers, words in a clue that often provide instant answers. Here are a few that most fans of the show already know:

Bog fruit = Cranberry
Belgian + surrealist = René Magritte
Danish + philosopher = Søren Kierkegaard
Grand duchy = Luxembourg
Finland + composer = Jean Sibelius

There are hundreds of these, if not thousands. And even if *Jeopardy!* someday has a clue written something like

> IF A FINNISH COMPOSER AND
> A DANISH PHILOSOPHER WENT
> INTO A BAR IN THIS GRAND DUCHY,
> A BELGIAN SURREALIST AND A FINNISH
> COMPOSER MIGHT HAND THEM
> A BOG FRUIT

you'd only have to scan for the word "this" to sort out which one mattered.

Compiling a list of one-to-ones is itself a fine exercise. You have to check to make sure they're truly exclusive, and that means looking deeper into each subject and name.

Take Jean Sibelius. Please. (Buh-*dum*-bum! Thank you, I'm here all book. I write this with a plunger on my head.) What, pray tell, would make this particular guy the composer identified with the nation of Finland?

Turns out he wrote a courageous piece called the *Karelia Suite*, standing up to Russian domination of his country. Imagine Thomas Jefferson singing, and you've got the right idea. (And now we're back to the musical *1776* again.) I found myself wondering how patriotic Finnish music might sound, and how the Finns would then honor the man, and what his Helsinki monument would look like.

Music and revolution mix potently in that part of the world, especially in anger at Russians. Not long ago, tens of thousands of people stood in Tallinn, Estonia's capital, in what became known as the Singing Revolution, playing forbidden songs night after night.

Soon, tens of thousands became hundreds of thousands. Eventually, two million people formed a line across three countries, joining hands in protest through Latvia and Lithuania, a human chain literally crying out for freedom, extending hundreds of miles, made from millions of hands holding hands holding hands.

Everything connects to everything else.

This must have been something to see.

Potent Potables, however, was still a hard subject. Neither Jane nor I drink much. Since Dad liked his beer, I avoided it for years, even when working in bars every night.

Fortunately, I had just the instructor to call on. One weekend I drove up to Berkeley to receive specialized coaching from a certain professor I knew.

Dan Melia, my friend, now becoming my old friend, invited me in. An evening of hard work awaited. His girlfriend Dara, a college English instructor with graduate degrees in Advanced This and Comparative That, came to join us with a hug and a smile. We had dinner and played with the dog.

Dan, you understand, is an esteemed professor of Celtic Studies. If it's Irish, has been mistaken for Irish, or once touched a green surface, he knows all about it. Perhaps this is a complete coincidence—and I write this as an Irish-American writer who grew up around alcohol—but Dan also knows much about Potables of every conceivable Potency.

Dan knows exactly what you distill or ferment. He knows what you brew and he knows what you decant. He knows just which wine goes in which glass and why, which grapes grow in which ground from which vine, what the hops do with barley or malt for how long.

Dara went to bed early and left the two of us to our studies. There were many lessons to come, with many tastes, smells, and colors. It was a long night of work in the lab. A few hours later, we discovered that Dan reads Old Norse more easily after a few rounds of aquavit.

So did I.

If livers ever stage their own *Jeopardy!* tournament, mine will know every response.

As the weeks passed, Jane's recovery sped along. We did learning dances in great number. We were closer than ever, joined by what felt like our own private language: Sinhala and Sotho; Arbuthnot and Achebe; Celebes, Lombok, and Komodo.

Whole worlds I wanted to see opened up.

This was much as before, only more so: the more that I learned, the less I realized I knew. Entire lifetimes can be spent learning to marvel in humility at all the diversity.

Lifetimes like *mine*, I was beginning to realize.

Many miles from here (although not far away really) is a country called Bhutan with a capital of Thimphu. It is here you can spend the ngultrum. (The ngultrum, so you know, is worth 100 chertrums. You can buy five of the latter for two U.S. cents.)

Bhutan lies high between China and India, not far from Himalayan Tibet. Kathmandu is not far, nor is Kolkata, nor Dhaka. The kingdom is explicitly Buddhist, the only such state in this world. It was closed off to us, mostly, until very recently. It's the place fiction calls Shangri-La.

The main thing to know is how little we know. One of their mountains is the highest one left that has never been climbed. No one even quite knows where the name *Bhutan* comes from.

But the king once announced, with the pomp of such things, that "Gross National Happiness" was more vital than Gross National Product. This is the kind of a king I could vote for.

They eat yak meat and drink butter tea and sometimes wear large red hats. Their big sports are archery and shot put. There is no word in their language for "traffic jam," although elephants frequently migrate. Cigarettes are an illegal drug.

They just got their first traffic light. Then they took it back out. It was too much, too soon. People just stopped and stared.

I'm not saying Bhutan is paradise or ever was. Nowhere is paradise. But Bhutan seems as close to nowhere as the world may have left.

Someday I'd like to visit, and sip butter tea in a large red hat under a Bhutanese sun, eating yak meat and watching young shot putters. But I'm oddly afraid I might spoil it all. Perhaps the remnants of cola still deep in my bloodstream would contaminate something and all of the elephants would die.

Then again, something like this is happening already. Seven years ago, Bhutan got TV. There now are five satellite dishes, in a field filled with pink flowers. And so Bhutanese schoolchildren in flowing ceremonial robes can be seen acting out *Wrestlemania* moves.

Timelines and cultures converge in an uncontrolled Bhutanese swirl. Centuries mix.

So perhaps I will go. Perhaps I *must* go, and soon. It's mutating anyway. That's what human cultures do. But for me and for now, Bhutan remains just a place in my head, another small part of Trebekistan.

There's so much more to the world than I ever dreamed in the Snow Belt.


The notebooks filled quickly, although not quite as fast as Jane's hopes for my performance. She was smiling and healing. The days ticked away. We were running out of time faster than things left to study.

I just wanted to win once. Just once.

For myself, I wanted to prove I belonged on that stage. But for Jane, and more than anything else, I wanted to see the smile one win would bring, what the excitement would look like as it played on her face. This was *our* project, after all, and with time feeling so precious, every day a prayer answered, I wanted every minute she invested to pay off. I didn't know what a we-won-at-Radio-City dance could look like, but I could imagine nothing more wonderful to see.

This was my old lifelong racket, of course, performing for others' happiness and approval. But I understood why, in this case. Jane's laugh was good reason. The best reason of all.

One game. Just one game would be enough.

**CHAPTER**

**21**

**MY LIFE AS A ROCKETTE**

Also, Why I Have an Ancient Civilization in My Pants

Newark was dark and freezing when I landed.

In the car, my nose kept fogging the window. It was the first time I'd seen New York without two of its towers. Six months after the unspeakable happened. Now there were empty shafts of light, a glowing memorial, rising in the twin towers' place.

I stared from the car all the way through New Jersey. Trying to comprehend. Fogging and wiping. And trying to comprehend once again.

Grief, fully felt, can give way to sheer wonder as you realize the size of a loss.

I arose at 7:00 a.m., which was four in the morning on my body clock. The producers wanted us all downstairs and ready at 7:30.

As you may have guessed, I had been rising at 4:00 a.m. in preparation back home. At 4:00 a.m., every day, in Los Angeles. For a month, I arose at 4:00 a.m. so my body would be ready.

Jane woke up with me. Every morning.

She loves me, you know. I am grateful. Although I question her sanity.

My own you've already assessed.

I hurried downstairs, hoping to spot the *Jeopardy!* group in the Waldorf-Astoria lobby. I was wondering whom I would recognize in the tumult.

In the distance stood a man who looked just like Frank Spangenberg, only larger than any human being I may have ever laid eyes on.

I'd seen Frank on the show, so many years earlier, oozing the quiet assurance of a spaceship computer, all whispering menace and walrus mustache. But nobody had warned me that Frank might not be human. But here he was, almost seven feet tall.

He was so big I was slightly frightened even to say hello. He could crush me or stomp me or just gently crinkle my neck in one giant paw, all possibly by accident, not even noticing until the *thwump* of my limp body hitting the ground. I felt like a pudu approaching a moose.

(The pudu mentioned here is the world's smallest deer, native to the mountains of Chile. They come up to your shins when they're full-grown adults. As babies they fit in your hand like a prize. Their full Latin species name is just *Pudu pudu*—scientifically extra silly—and they look like furry Vienna sausages with large worried eyes. Their only defense is to run up a log, but only if there's a log nearby. Sometimes they bark when they're scared. Overall they're endangered and look like they know it.)

Frank couldn't have been nicer, as he shook my arm in his hand. He was as excited and nervous as I was. This was no HAL computer, just a big friendly guy with a big eager brain.

And then I noticed, around him, all the human-sized players. So many I liked. So many so good. Tournament of Champions winner Bob Verini was there. Eric "Powerhouse" Newhouse, winner of both a Teen and a Teen Reunion tournament. Kate Waits, Claudia Perry, Leslie Frates, Leslie Shannon, India Cooper, Babu Srinivasan, accomplished champions all. Jeremy Bate, the alternate, in case one of us dropped dead from nerves. Every name I recognized, every player was good.

To my left stood Chuck Forrest, winner of a Tournament of Champions, laughing with Robin Carroll, winner of a Tournament of Champions and an International Tournament. Behind them were Tournament of Champions winners Rachael Schwartz and Brad Rutter. In one glance, I could see more tournament wins than people.

The last player I glimpsed was perhaps the most skillful: Eddie Timanus, the show's only blind five-time champion. The greatest Jedi of all. Anyone who doubts you can win without looking at the Go Lights needs only to have seen Eddie's first five games.

The show gave him a braille card with the names of the categories. After that, he was flying solo. And Eddie soared, timing the Go Lights exquisitely. Which is all the more amazing, because he had no way to read ahead in the clue, so he couldn't anticipate which word was the end. Alex would stop, and he'd just hear it and feel it and still beat his opponents and then out came the answers. His thumb seemed to work on its own.

He's the Yoda of timing, the Obi-Wan of the buzzer. Watching him play is pure joy.

Also, I'm told, he will crush you in poker.

*I don't belong here*, I thought to myself. But Jane had given me one last extra present.

She couldn't make the trip, but I wanted something small to hang on to, something to remind me of what really matters.

Jane had an old $1 token from the Luxor casino from some Vegas trip of many years earlier. (The Luxor delighted her because her knowledge of hieroglyphs meant she could fact-check the walls. She was pleased with the glyphs they got right—the headboard proclaimed "Cleopatra," in fact—but more amused by complete random nonsense. The Luxor, seen clearly, is a transcendent work of art, a compendium of ultimate Dada poetry, unknowingly composed across entire continents and ages.) The coin was a worthless old token, in a box on a shelf in the back of a closet, but it seemed exactly right for the need.

It was just a token, not wealth. Just like excess money itself.

All its symbols were of civilizations long gone. So our time here is borrowed. It's each moment that counts.

And as she gave it, she kissed me, with a promise to kiss me again on its return. So what mattered was already in my life, no matter what.

**Just play each moment. Let go of outcome.**

Jane and her token told me this three different ways.

*I don't belong here*, I thought several times. And then I'd turn the coin in my hand, quietly, and relax, and stop worrying, and remember what mattered.

We were alive. This was a very good day.

Susanne, the head wrangler, and old compadre Glenn were grinning at our group, all twitchy and eager and already buzzing like kids on their first day at camp. So were two fellows named Tony and Bob, whom I hadn't yet met, and a sweet, smiling woman named Maggie. (Wrangler Grant was still with the show, but in some other capacity. I think he's the guy who says *p-TING!* now.)

We were all joined together, all twenty of us, in something so novel we knew we'd remember it as long as we lived. The only question now was what those memories would be.

So we packed into a shuttle bus and rode across town. The bus itself trembled with nervous delight. There was no competition, no battle of egos, no staking of territory. Just smiles and introductions and sporting mutual encouragement. And then we all filed through the stage entrance to Radio City Music Hall. The birthplace of *Jeopardy!* 340itself.

In all the years I was a comedian, I never got near this. *How do you get to Broadway?* I mused to myself. *Practice Jeopardy!*

We wound through the hallways and climbed up back stairwells. The walls were all covered in photos of singers and dancers and Rockettes, decades of glorious kick-lines. Each step cast an echo of footfalls in spangles, the excitement of youth and the knowledge of age, seeking fulfillment on a stage before thousands.

Every atom here bounced with excitement.

The green room was strangely familiar, even routine. We'd all done tournaments like this before. Next would come waiting and listening for our names to be called, small talk and nerves and a tick-tocking clock, a day passing too quickly and too slowly at once.

Alex came by and said encouraging words to the group. He looked eager and nervous himself, and why not? A big Broadway debut, his face on the cover of *Playbill*. (The rest of us were all listed inside, like a cast.) I was proud for him. This was a long way from Sudbury.

Harry Friedman, the boss, and others popped in. They'd invested millions in this. Not just in prizes, but special lighting and cameras, transport and housing, the design and creation of an entire grand stage. Every player could see in the producers' wide eyes that the games to be played meant as much to the show as to us.

I thought many times about Dan and Kim and Grace and the others. I wanted to make them look good by extension.

And then came the thought: *I could let the show itself down. I could make them look foolish for choosing me.*

I knew this was almost pathologically extra, a burden no one else would have put on me. It wouldn't help me. It wouldn't help Jane. But there it was. I felt what I felt. I didn't know why I was there, but I wanted dearly to live up to the honor.

I sank into a cushion and wondered whom I would play, or whom I would even want to. A wild card slot was the only real target.

The format was exactly like the earlier tournament. Five games in the first round, with five winners and four wild cards advancing. The rest I would worry about later.

After squeaking through against Grace and Wes, I'd researched other tournaments, curious what my odds with $3200 had been. Virtually zero, I learned. So my presence in New York was miraculous.

I had hoped for a miracle on the day I was sick backstage. Fair enough.

The show had doubled the value of each clue, so any score below $10000 would have almost no shot. A $20000 score virtually assured one of seeing the semis, unless something truly odd happened again. So I aimed for $20000 and hoped for the best.

The math of the situation was hardly encouraging. A miracle wasn't necessary now. Near-perfection was.

As you already know, there are sixty clues in a game. With three Daily Doubles on which nobody buzzes, there are fifty-seven buzzer decisions to make. With difficult clues, I'd be lucky to know two-thirds of the responses. That would be thirty-eight clues. But everyone here had the skills of a Jedi, so I could only expect to win on the buzzer one time in three.

This meant in a game I'd get perhaps thirteen responses. Thirteen times Alex would say "Bob!" and I'd speak.

If I was right every time—every single time—with an average clue value of $900, my projected score entering Final Jeopardy would be $11700. Still in the game. All I'd need after that would be a big bet in the Final.

A small slip on a cheap clue might be tolerable, but that's all. Just one mistake on a high-dollar clue—just one—could be crippling. (An incorrect $2000 response would knock the projected score down to $7700. Even an all-in bet in the final would still leave less than a fifty-fifty chance of survival.)

So I'd focus instead not on responses, but on making fifty-seven good buzzer decisions. No mistakes. Ring only when certain. Just playing each moment. This was the way to survive.

One perfect game. Just one. And then Harry would smile, Dan would be proud, my family would clap, and Jane would make up a dozen new dances.

Just one perfect game.

And then the waiting began. I was prepared for a long day.

Susanne entered, calling out the first round of names:

"Frank Spangenberg! Rachael Schwartz! Bob Harris!"

Oh. OK. Well. *That* was certainly fast.

If I lost, I'd be out in the very first game. The whole trip would be over already.

*Frank Spangenberg*, I thought. In almost twenty years and four thousand shows, no one had ever broken his five-day record for winnings. He was still considered possibly the best player ever to pick up a buzzer. *I'm playing Frank Spangenberg.*

As we stood, my eyes came up to Frank's armpit. *Just don't eat me,* I thought, feeling ever more like a pudu.

And then: *I'm playing Frank Spangenberg at Radio City Music Hall.* Facing him. As equals, almost, at least for this moment backstage. I could scarcely believe I was here.

I looked at Rachael, remembering her defeating all contenders in her year. Her smile was genuine, but her eyes were busy with thought. She was focusing, readying, already playing ahead in the pre-game game.

The wranglers led us downstairs through an electrical labyrinth, where we meandered until reaching the stage. Taking our places, we were wired for sound. My forehead was de-chromed by courageous professionals. This last touch was familiar, an odd little comfort amid so much excited strangeness. I had been placed, I should add, at the champion's podium, the one nearest center stage. I do not know why.

Rachael and I were given small boxes to stand on, to raise our heads level with Frank's. Somebody checked how this looked, and they gave us both a few more. I was teetering higher than ever before.

To my right was the opening through which Alex would enter. Perhaps there were technical people making last-minute fixes, but it sounded like someone tall from a snowy working-class town in Ontario was pacing back there.

I placed Jane's Luxor token on the podium near the buzzer. I didn't want it out of my sight.

We were still behind Radio City's grand curtain, still safe in our glamorous cave. Beyond, there was hubbub from great pregnant masses. All around us, dashing bodies made last-minute adjustments, calling urgent instructions in hushed rapid tones. The electronical doojobbies all gossiped and thrummed. The air itself glowed.

I had to close my eyes and shut out the murmur of six thousand people, hidden just beyond the large fabric mountain. Snapping my fingers, again, *snappity-snappity-snappity-snappity,* like a member of a dancing gang in New York. Which, in a sense, I had finally become.

*This is not a podium. It's a low bookshelf. This is not a buzzer. It is a roll of masking tape wrapped around an old ballpoint pen, the one Jane recognized in exactly one glance . . .*

■ ■ ■

I can hear, in the distance, the floor director, John Lauderdale.

"Quiet, please," he says quietly. And the mass starts to settle.

"Quiet, please," John repeats softly. Bringing Middle East peace. But it's not quite silence enough.

"Quiet . . . *please*," John says a third time, a tiny edge in his usual hush.

And then molecules stop.

Music plays. Johnny Gilbert's voice booms through the cavern.

The multi-ton curtain slowly starts rising. I smile at Rachael. She's edgy, but beaming. Frank glances our way, just as excited. We are in this together, all together, for one bewildering moment.

And revealed to us now, throbbing and golden and sparkling in light, are nearly six thousand people, bodies and motion to the very last balcony, applause coming so hard that it makes the stage throb, cheers echoing off the back walls.

I've been on stages for most of my career. This is the biggest and best. The greatest one I might see.

But this is only a stage. One, in a sense, I've been on all my life.

This is Wisconsin. This is Ohio. This is a strip joint in Arkansas, a Mexican biker bar. This is the place where I've worked many years.

It is actually calming to be here at last.

And in this moment, surprised, *I understand why I'm here.*

I will give the producers their show.

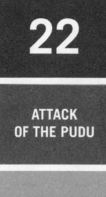

Alex strides out, all smooth reassurance, commanding the room just by projecting a sense of comfort. But I know his voice by now. There's a tremor, barely present. I've never before seen Alex even mildly ruffled. But he's smart enough to acknowledge the fact.

"Understandably, we're all very nervous. Myself included," he says. The four of us, dwarfed, take a tiny deep breath. "But I think the best way to break the tension is to play the game."

We turn to the board. The crowd disappears.

I brace myself, remembering the clues will be a bit esoteric. And so we begin, as the six categories for the first round are revealed.

LATIN AMERICAN HISTORY *(OK. Not a strength. But OK.)*

WATER TRANSPORTS *(Hmm. How many of those are there?)*

WAX MUSEUMS *(Hmm again. And how many of THOSE are there?)*
AUTOIMMUNE DISORDERS

Wait. Hold on. You're kidding me.

AUTOIMMUNE DISORDERS

is an actual *Jeopardy!* category? Be serious. But there it is:

AUTOIMMUNE DISORDERS

it says. I'm standing here with six thousand people in the audience, play-ing the biggest game of my life. And Alex says

AUTOIMMUNE DISORDERS

is one of the categories.

Connie, I love you, and I am so sorry for your years of great pain. But, just this once, I am almost glad to know Marvin so well.

Now everybody just stand the hell back. Pudu coming through.

The other two categories,

LET THEM EAT CAKE
AW, SO YOU'RE THE "SMART" ONE, EH?

barely even register. But I'm at the champion's podium, so Alex will give me first choice. I'll want to think ahead in the first three categories if possible, and I'd like to save my tribute to Connie. But with my years of performing, I finally realize, I'm probably the least nervous of the three of us. I might have an early timing advantage. I choose the SMART cate-gory—general knowledge, relatively easy, since half of the answer is al-ready provided—as a simple buzzer contest. This will be the best time to try it.

Naturally, Frank wins on the buzzer on the first clue. I'm a hair early. (Reviewing the tape, this hair is exactly three frames wide. A tenth of a second.)

I take another deep breath and go back to my apartment. *Not a podium. Not a buzzer. Radio City Music Living Room.*

My timing kicks in, hitting three straight clues under SMART:

*What is* Get Smart?

*What's the "smart money"?*

And this, still stuck in my head twenty years after I first read about it in college, thanks to the dark irony of calling a solid ton of explosive "smart":

ONE EXAMPLE IS THE
2000-POUND GBU-24

*What's a "smart bomb"?* I ask, and I jump out to an early advantage. The $1000 clue, however, I know nothing about.

FROM 1914 TO 1923
H. L. MENCKEN CO-EDITED
THIS SATIRIC MONTHLY WITH
GEORGE JEAN NATHAN

I stand down, doing Jeopardy Zen. Rachael grabs the clue immediately. "What is 'Smart Set'?" she asks. She's good. I remember just who the hell I'm playing.

Rachael then takes a breath, and takes us straight into AUTOIMMUNE DISORDERS.

OK, Connie. This is for you.

ON "THE WEST WING"
JED BARTLET HAS A
RELAPSING-REMITTING COURSE
OF THIS AUTOIMMUNE DISORDER

When Connie was thought to have this disease, "relapsing-remitting" was the term doctors used to describe the random timing of Marvin's strange visitations.

*What's multiple sclerosis?* I practically shout.

BOTH GRAVES' DISEASE &
HASHIMOTO'S DISEASE
ATTACK THIS GLAND

Connie doesn't have either of these. But she has been diagnosed with hypothyroidism, which I then looked into as a possible co-factor in her symptoms. *What's the thyroid gland?* comes out without blinking.

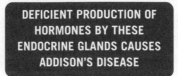

DEFICIENT PRODUCTION OF
HORMONES BY THESE
ENDOCRINE GLANDS CAUSES
ADDISON'S DISEASE

Lupus, Connie's then-current diagnosis, is often treated with a synthetic version of a steroid produced by these very glands. Their eventual fatigue and failure, known as Addison's disease, sometimes accompanies lupus.

*What are the adrenals?* flows out so fast I almost feel like I'm cheating. But another part of me is thrilled at the chance to say this on national TV: *See, only sister? I've been paying attention. I think of your health every day of my life.*

Incidentally, the adrenals also pump out the stress-related glucocorticoids that can impair memory function. So in this moment, I'm trying to keep my own glands from getting too thrilled. I'm not exactly succeeding. Once the category begins, in fact, I know I should bounce out and save my strongest subject for later. But I am too excited by my growing momentum to change the subject.

But the fourth clue, surprisingly, is a disorder I don't know. I thought Connie and Marvin had encompassed them all.

AKA REGIONAL ENTERITIS,
THIS DISEASE, A CHRONIC
INFLAMMATION OF THE INTESTINES,
BEARS THE NAME OF A U.S. DOCTOR

Frank buzzes in: "What is Crohn's disease?" he responds.

Twenty years after the red bumps on her legs were first certified as "erythema nodosum," no one has ever suggested Crohn's as the major part of her illness.

It's the disease, we will learn a year later, that she probably actually has.

Please throw this book across the room in frustration.

■ ■ ■

Frank jumps us to LATIN AMERICAN HISTORY. His tone of voice says he considers it a strength.

It is. He reels off three quick responses, including the nation once ruled by Pedro II ("What is Brazil?") and the first democratically elected Marxist in the western hemisphere ("Who was Salvador Allende?").

The guy's good. But I'm not giving in. The next two clues ask for the South American country once ruled by Alfredo Stroessner and the capital of the Aztec empire.

*What's Paraguay?*

*What's Tenochtitlán?*

I'm beating Frank on the buzzer, I am sure, by fractions of fractions. (On the tape it looks like only one frame.) I still want to think ahead in the remaining full categories, and there's a good chance of a Daily Double at the bottom of AUTOIMMUNE DISORDERS. So I dive for the last clue in that category. There's no Daily Double, but there's this:

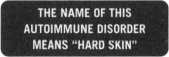

THE NAME OF THIS
AUTOIMMUNE DISORDER
MEANS "HARD SKIN"

Jane has grilled me on classic roots every night. "Hard" and "skin," translated into Greek roots, would be *sclero* and *derma*. Without even thinking I blurt out:

*What's scleroderma?*

The audience, strangely unaccustomed to hearing people blurt "Paraguay," "Tenochtitlán" and "scleroderma" *bang-bang-bang* like this, audibly gasps.

I will tell Jane about this later, doing an audible-gasp dance. She will then gasp audibly in quotes.

But I also know Frank and Rachael will get their own gasps and applause by the end.

Alex takes us into the first commercial. I look up at the scoreboard. I'm up to $5800, more than twice the score of Frank and Rachael combined. I've made fifteen good buzzer decisions and—as always—let a third of the game go by without playing.

So far, so good. One quarter of the way home.

The only surprise is that I'm winning on the buzzer. And I've been lucky to land on a tailor-made category. The latter is over. And the former can't last.

As the commercial begins, I look out at the theater, where the audience is still applauding on cue. Radio City is a stage like no other. I am seeing the obvious, detaching from outcome, enjoying the moment.

This lasts for perhaps five seconds. I let the sensation soak in.

Years later, here in Los Angeles, the walls of this coffee shop shake with the sound.

I start playing ahead in the categories left, pondering cakes, wax, and watercraft with all my might. Nothing comes whatsoever. Not one thought. I have nothing inside me but air. So I just try to relax as the chats start with Alex.

Frank is soft-spoken as always, self-deprecating, shy with his eyes. For the first time I see that what I'd always read as ferocity was just nerves and focus, perhaps magnified by sheer physical size.

Rachael seems playful and funny and bright, with the demure body language of someone too internally busy to notice how attractive she is. She's here to win, after all, as she has done many times.

When my turn comes with Alex, I'm already thinking of the buzzer, trying to feel the rhythm in my body, hoping not to lose my timing. I burble out words that I hope will sound grateful.

That's what I am most of all.

The second half of the first round begins.

Frank!
Rachael!
Rachael!
Rachael!
Frank!
Rachael!
Bob!
Rachael!
Rachael!

Rachael!

Bob!

Rachael!

Rachael!

Frank!

Frank!

Rachael and Frank get their own gasps now, too. So goes the rest of this round. I know as little in real time as I did playing ahead, letting half of the clues go untried.

Rachael is flawless. I can see how she won a Tournament of Champions. Not a single wrong guess. Not a single wrong buzz. When a difficult clue has a lateral hint, she's the one who will think it through first.

Frank also makes not a single mistake. In the last clue of the round, the monitors display a black-and-white photo of a nondescript steamship. No markings, no flags, not one visual hint.

SEEN HERE, IT SHARES ITS NAME WITH A FRENCH REGION, AND BROKE THE TRANSATLANTIC SPEED RECORD IN 1935

There are a dozen French regions we'd all probably recognize—Brittany, Burgundy, Picardy, Champagne, all the other popular children's names in Hollywood—so the only real hint is the query itself: What boat held one specific speed record seventy years ago?

"What's the *Normandy*?" Frank replies nonchalantly. That's not almanac data—and I'd know by now—and not a thing on a list in a textbook. Frank actually walks around *knowing* this stuff.

At the break, I'm still clinging to my pudu-sized lead, $7000 to $6000 to $4800. But Frank and Rachael are charging.

The token from Jane is still right by my buzzer. I remember the plan. Fifty-seven good decisions and just one Final Jeopardy. Just detach and relax, and fire the Weapon with care.

I have twenty-nine done. Not a single mistake. In the lead by $1000.

Just one round to go.

■ ■ ■

The Double Jeopardy categories are

THE NEW YORK TIMES ARTS & LEISURE *(Hmm . . . that's pretty general.)*
FROM THE GREEK *(Yes! Thank you, Jane!)*
THE RENAISSANCE *(Not my best; I hope we get through this one early.)*
MIDDLE NAMES *(This could be anyone, ever. Oh, dear.)*
HOPE YOU LEARNED YOUR AFRICAN CAPITALS

Again, I say: *really?*

HOPE YOU LEARNED YOUR AFRICAN CAPITALS

it says. And, um, yes. Yes I did. Every night, as a matter of fact. And finally:

PLACES TO PUT YOUR BIG WINNINGS

is the last category.

Frank jumps directly into the heart of THE RENAISSANCE, preferring to push his own strengths, hunting for a quick Daily Double.

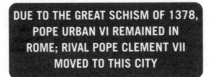

DUE TO THE GREAT SCHISM OF 1378,
POPE URBAN VI REMAINED IN
ROME; RIVAL POPE CLEMENT VII
MOVED TO THIS CITY

Of course Frank would know. "What's Avignon?" he replies for $1200. But what he doesn't know is that I know it, too. I'm *not* out of my league, I am starting to realize.

I belong here.

But Frank also gets Cesare Borgia and Jan Hus, the reformer, and Brunelleschi the Florentine architect. Passing Rachael in second place and me for the lead, he's ahead by $3000 in seconds.

The audience cheers, which Frank fully deserves. He seems to be pulling away.

We dive into Greek. Pudu fights back against moose.

Bob!

Frank!

Rachael!

Frank!

Bob!

The $2000 clue here you've already seen. You may know it from just reading this book.

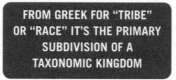

> FROM GREEK FOR "TRIBE"
> OR "RACE" IT'S THE PRIMARY
> SUBDIVISION OF A
> TAXONOMIC KINGDOM

Remember "King Philip Glass Ordering his Family a Generous Special"? So what comes after "kingdom"? That's all that this clue really asks.

If you remember "Philip," then "phylum," you'd have gotten it, too.

*What's a phylum?* I respond.

I am back in the game.

The AFRICAN CAPITALS come up next. I make a mistake on the first, confusing Kigali, Rwanda, with Kampala, Uganda.

*That's my one small mistake,* I think to myself. *Be glad it was small. Just relax.*

But still distracted, I blank on Niamey, the capital of Niger, one gaffe living on in my head to make two. I am forced not to fire my Weapon.

Rachael and Frank, however, are not touching their buzzers. Neither of them, on the two easiest clues in the column. *They don't know Africa,* I realize. So I relax and let the next three just come, as if sitting up late with Jane in Los Angeles. For perhaps the only time in any game I've ever played, the buzzer simply may not matter for the next three clues. *Slow down,* I tell myself. Ignoring the blah-blah, I see the following capitals:

N'Djamena. *What's Chad?*

Bujumbura. *What's Burundi?*

Bamako. *What's Mali?*

And I'm back in the lead. Six thousand people applaud.

Just three categories left.

MIDDLE NAMES. I grab one. So does Frank. And then *Bweedwoo, Bweedwoo, Bweedwoo-dwoo-dwoo-dwah*. Frank gets the first Daily Double.

He goes big, betting $4000, which would give him a $3000 lead.

I hold my breath, helpless and hoping. He can still lose with a single mistake now, just like me. But I'm just watching and waiting, like you are right now.

> THIS MIDDLE NAME OF SUPREME COURT JUSTICE WILLIAM DOUGLAS REMINDS US OF AN EARLY AVIATOR

It's a lay-up. He'll nail it. But Frank pauses to ponder. *Come on, you can do this*, I think. *The "O" was for Orville. I know that you know this.* And then I think, *What the hell, why am I cheering him on?* Like he can hear my thoughts from two podiums away.

"What is Orville?" Frank says, like he hears me, leaping far in the lead. I feel twenty-eight things, but there's no time to sort them. In seconds:

> BECAUSE THIS IS A MILLION-DOLLAR TOURNAMENT, YOU HAVE TO SPELL THIS MIDDLE NAME OF PRESIDENT WARREN HARDING

*What's G-A-M-A-L-I-E-L?* I blurt, no hesitation. Another small gasp from the crowd. I'm still trailing, but charging. A pudu, now ferocious himself.

*I belong here*, I think. *I may not win or go on. But I've earned this now. I belong.*

In the first clue in WINNINGS, I pick up $400. Frank's lead has been cut to $1000.

The second WINNINGS clue is worth $800 more. Frank is now up by only $200.

Eight clues left. Closing in.

But I am thinking too much. I am forced to let the $1200 clue go by:

> **USE YOUR GENERAL FUNDS
> IN THESE TWO "GENERAL"
> COMPANIES IN THE TOP
> 5 FIRMS IN THE FORTUNE 500**

Asked for two giant "General" companies, I think quickly of three: General Foods, General Electric, General Motors, in that order. I cannot aim my Weapon and hesitate. Frank instantly buzzes in, and chooses Electric and Motors correctly. I have truly forgotten my engineering degree.

His lead is $1400. Seven clues left. For $1600 and the lead:

> **ON THE CHICAGO MERCANTILE
> EXCHANGE, THIS INVESTMENT
> OPPORTUNITY IS ABBREVIATED
> "PB"**

I think quickly: *PB is a chemical symbol for a traded commodity . . . What is lead?* I blurt out.

This is wrong. Very wrong. A klutzy high-dollar mistake.

"What are Pork Bellies?" Frank says, picking up the rebound and jumping far in the lead with just six clues remaining.

Six thousand people suddenly chortle and giggle. It is a moment of choking stupidity.

The Merc, as I know, because I once lived in Chicago, is a place where you trade cattle and lumber and livestock. It's the *Commodities* Exchange where you trade metals. And lead is so cheap, of course, it even *means* "worthless," although they trade it in London and elsewhere. It's no "opportunity." Pb, yes, of course, is the symbol for lead. But my answer is still almost as dumb as it looks.

All of Radio City Music Hall begins laughing. Six thousand people. More in-flight entertainment. Just like *that.* It took less than ten seconds.

But this time, I don't care. I'm not thrilled, but it doesn't hurt. Kinda cool. I'm still playing and glad. I think I might laugh, too, given time.

Rachael soon finds the last Daily Double, so I can't catch Frank before the Final. I breathe and refocus and remember the plan.

A wild card is still possible with a correct Final response. So I let most of what follows go by unplayed, never guessing, barely touching the buzzer. At the end of this round, Frank has $19200. I have $15800, and Rachael has $10100.

My goal was $20000 when I walked on the stage. I can still pull it off.

It comes down to just one clue again.

I bet $4200 for an even $20000. A wild card spot, if I respond correctly. A small present for Jane I can take home.

The Final Jeopardy category—*p-TING!*

**ESPIONAGE**

**HE WAS BORN IN INDIA; HIS FATHER WORKED FOR THE BRITISH GOVERNMENT, & HE WAS NICKNAMED FOR A KIPLING CHARACTER**

*OK. We need an overlap between Kipling characters and spies in Great Britain . . . Jungle Book . . . Mowgli . . . Gunga Din and Kim . . . Kim . . . Kim Philby, the Third Man case, MI6 in the sixties.*

Before Alex has even finished reading the clue, I begin. *Clackity-click-whap-clackity.* Electronic pen on hard glass.

I finish exactly three seconds into the Think Music, dropping the pen with a certainty I once couldn't have imagined: *Who is Kim Philby?* and done. I check my spelling and reasoning, and find no cause for worry. This is an unusual feeling for me, as you certainly know.

As the Think Music enters its second chorus, I have fifteen full seconds to relish the scenery. I am standing near center stage of Radio City Music Hall before a packed and excited house, near the climax of a show they've enjoyed.

Some contestants also receive memories they will cherish.

I catch Alex's eye with an accidental glance. He's smiling in the half-light, possibly taking it all in for himself. I suppose he might feel something similar here. But I look away quickly. These moments are private. And the Think Music is ending at last.

Rachael has written down "Who is Kim Philby?"

She's *right.* So I know I've advanced.

Frank will respond correctly, of course. This is why his name has become such a gold standard. But Frank, to my shock, is just shaking his head.

Frank has written "Who is John le Carré?"

This is a very good guess at first glance. This is the pen name of David Cornwell, who is British and writes novels about espionage. This fits most of the clue.

It's an even better guess at second glance. Before writing novels, Cornwell himself was a spy, working for the British Foreign Service during the Cold War. He was betrayed in West Germany, however, by a Soviet mole.

And which spy betrayed Cornwell? You guessed it: *Kim Philby.*

It gets even wilder at third glance.

As this very clue is asked on that *Jeopardy!* stage, David Cornwell is about to begin writing a novel called *Absolute Friends.* In this book, Cornwell mentions Kim Philby. Not as a double agent. Not as a mole. Not as the man who betrayed him.

Cornwell describes Kim Philby, of all possible things, as someone with the same name as a Kipling character.

Trebekistan is everywhere.

I have *won.*

*What the hell?*

I have actually won. I've defeated Frank Spangenberg, whom I watched long ago from a world far away, who ranks with the best who ever played.

It's an upset, of course. Douglas clocks Tyson, Flutie passes to Whelan, *How Green Was My Valley* beats *Citizen Kane.* A pudu outrunning a moose, just this once.

I cannot wait to see Jane. We did this. *We* did this.

Standing with Alex, center stage. I look up from Frank's armpit. He is pleasant and sincere with congrats. Since he'd bet large for a win, not simply to advance as a wild card, he was now out, eliminated, just like that, falling not to my skill but to having thought about outcome.

Still, Frank is a New York City cop. We are playing this game only months after September 11. I believe Frank knows far better than I how little this game really matters.

If we play twenty times, I think Frank wins a dozen. Or twenty. Or quite possibly thirty. And this would be fine. I have one. It's enough.

So we stand there with Rachael, herself a Tournament of Champions winner. Six thousand people applaud. Years later in Los Angeles, the windows of this coffee shop might break any second.

In a moment we're off, ushered down into the front row, to watch the remaining four games. I sit between Rachael and Frank, making friends, spending the day watching a parade of great players displaying their skill.

Each group descends from the green room and plays. Each trio soon joins us and asks how the first game turned out. I take secret delight watching each group try to mask their surprise. I could let their shock tell me there's still much left to prove, so much that I still need to show. But there isn't.

Nine of us will play again tomorrow. In two days, one of us will be a million dollars richer.

But the token from the Luxor is worth more.

It was strange that two such great champs were already out of the field, but of course, that was the point of the tournament. More shocks followed in the other games, too. Soon, Robin was gone, our international champ, felled partly by *bioluminescence* in the category 15-LETTER WORDS. (Glowing meat is a thing best not trifled with.) Eddie, Kate, and Babu also fell by the end of the day.

But Chuck Forrest played like Chuck Forrest, of course, overcoming Leslie Frates and Eric Newhouse in one of the finest games I've ever watched. Between them, they responded correctly fifty-six times:

"Who is Gaudí?"

"What is Bayreuth?"

"Who is Aaron Burr Tillstrom?"

At the end, Leslie and Eric advanced as wild cards, and Chuck had the highest score of the day.

Returning to the hotel, all fifteen of us agreed that the matches were all fairly even. It was obvious there was little between us. One clue here, a Daily Double there, one lucky category, a millisecond of a blink on the buzzer. (My math, incidentally, had been surprisingly decent. If Frank had won our game, my $20000 score would been enough for the last wild card spot, advancing in a tie. My guess was correct to the dollar.)

Robin Carroll and I wound up talking about Jane. Robin is a fan of Jane's writing, and Jane's a fan of Robin's games. I promised to say hello in each direction. Robin is a tech writer and full-on triple-kid mom, one of the few players I've met who won with almost no study, in her case because there was simply no time. She plays Jedi, has trouble with the Forrest Bounce, loves the game win or lose, and I think she misses her dad as much as I miss mine, appreciating her parents even when she's onstage.

Brad Rutter had been briefly thrown by one clue about the Icelandic Parliament. Which by now I thought *everyone* knew was the Althing. But to be fair, Brad knew his African capitals, and the difference between Kigali and Kampala. He probably also knew the distance between them, the train schedules and fares, which window to sit at to get the best view, the name of the woman who had installed the new safety glass, and the man who had broken her heart. Brad played football in high school, one of the popular kids, and had a squadron of friends in the crowd. He worked in a record store until his big wins, and always laughs when he says he might still be working there otherwise.

The afternoon and the evening went on like this, all comparing of clues and exchanges of phone numbers and e-mails, less a competition than a well-informed party.

That first moment, when the curtain rose, and it felt almost as though Frank and Rachael and I were briefly on the same team, became more the rule than the exception. These were just hardworking people with great curiosity, all willing to try interesting things. One of which was *Jeopardy!*

Knowledge and creativity and a sense of community wove through all of their stories. Eric worked for the Alzheimer's Association. Leslie

Frates and Babu taught Spanish and history. Kate was a law school professor. Claudia and Eddie were newspaper writers. Rachael was an attorney getting a degree in biotechnology. Bob Verini and India both worked in theater. Leslie Shannon ran a technology research lab after living on four continents. Jeremy was an EMT who had saved numerous lives.

The conversation hopscotched far corners of Trebekistan.

Chuck, whom I sought out to thank for his book, was glad to chat for a while, hanging out in a hallway of the Waldorf-Astoria. We were both playing the next day, so we had to be brief. There was much sleep to gather, and I still wanted to review a list of foreign phrases that Jane had faxed to my room.

As we chatted, I learned that Chuck lived in London, where he'd founded a group that worked to prosecute war criminals. Well, of course. No surprise. *Of course* Chuck fought ultra-evil. I was finally able to hang almost even with the guy, and it turned out his day job was Superhero. Me, I told jokes to alcoholics and complained on the radio. Chuck was bopping around Eastern Europe and the Middle East, helping governments figure out the whole justice thing. Me? I said "boo-beef" for eight thousand dollars.

But Chuck was humble. (Of course he's good at *that*, too.) Years later, he would tell me he was a little surprised at his own success the first time on the show, and about a clue ("What was *The Sotweed Factor*?") that was as big a surprise to him as "Who are the fishmongers?" was to me.

I started at last to express thanks for the book, but somehow it sounded kinda dumb. But Chuck was delighted to hear that someone could put it to as much use as I did. "I always wondered," he said. "That's cool, and you're welcome. Thanks for telling me. Maybe we'll play each other tomorrow."

I hoped so. But I wasn't here to compete anymore, at least not like before. It was enough to keep learning how much I can still learn.

The next morning, the nine remaining contestants rehearsed on the Radio City stage, warming up both ourselves and the crew. We rotated in and out, playing all sorts of match-ups for a minute or two.

For a moment, for the first time, I was playing against Chuck.
We went about fifty-fifty before he was rotated out.
He smiled as he stepped down. I grinned.
Good enough.

Rachael was the alternate for the second round of play, the highest-scoring player who didn't quite make the wild card.

*That's got to be frustrating*, I thought, watching her go through all the makeup and rituals, knowing she wouldn't get to play. Like Jeremy the day before, stuck just outside the clubhouse, even though the kids would have happily shared.

Clanging backstairs above the Radio City stage entrance. Green room and couches. Not quite so crowded as yesterday. Strangely, not quite so exciting.

Hours, again, as six thousand more people gather.

Susanne, the head wrangler, reminisces about Broadway and her younger days in New York, years filled with song and dance and magnificent drama. It's a thrill for her, too, sitting backstage in this hall.

As Susanne speaks, time flattens, and you can see younger dreams poking up through its fabric. Many of these dreams are satisfied now. Enough that Susanne is only pleased to remember them.

Her contentment is a lovely sight. I am grateful she once called out my name.

A few hours later, "Eric Newhouse! Leslie Shannon! Bob Harris!" Susanne calls out my name yet once more.

First game again. Nothing new, really. Already becoming a familiar experience.

Leslie giggles excitedly. But of course, this is Leslie. I've learned that she laughs almost constantly. It's not fake, not even slightly. Her laugh simply lives near the surface. The slightest amusement produces shorts bursts of *giggigggiggigg*, a bit like Jane's noise but smaller, more rapid, and thus even harder to transcribe. (Of course, as we've seen, the laugh that can be spelled is not a genuine laugh.) If an encyclopedia could look like Barbara Feldon from *Get Smart* and speak with a slight

Australian accent while thriving in a bath of pure nitrous oxide, that's Leslie. I adore her immediately.

Buried in the back of the *Jeopardy!* website, there's a snapshot of Leslie and me. We are laughing, mock-wrestling for control of a buzzer, playing like children on the Radio City stage. This photo was taken literally seconds after our very first real conversation. This tells you a lot about Leslie.

In a back hall by a bathroom, Eric stubs out a last furtive cigarette, vowing to quit, waving the last remnants of smoke out the window. He works for a health-care organization, and he smokes. Eric has a fierceness of gaze, as if he could outstare the eye of a needle. He's quiet in the green room. This could be intimidating. I will later learn, however, that he's simply interested in listening to everyone else. The fidgety secret smoking means he's as vulnerable as you and I are. I enjoy him immensely. He puts on a game face and wishes me luck, meaning it more than his grimace lets on.

Down the stairs to the stage. Winding through hallways and power cords and large men in thick gloves, little flashes of light from above and ahead filtering through.

The Radio City curtain has remained up since I watched it raised yesterday, at the moment the tournament began. I was lucky to have been on the stage for the view. The audience peers in as we're wired for sound and I'm daubed freshly again with humanoid-colored powder.

I'm at the champion's podium again for some reason. To my right, Alex is peeking through the set, relaxed now and joking.

Even Radio City Music Hall can start to seem familiar. Newness of experience can command your attention almost as strongly as danger. But once the newness wears off, even playing *Jeopardy!*, live, at its highest level, on Broadway no less, can start to slip into routine.

In truth, I don't remember much of this game. I believe this is because I've quite carefully not tried to. But Eric played so well he deserves a full list of memories.

Eric's Weapon was smoking. He seemed to black out the Go Lights for much of the match, repeating the nameless induction of buzzerly darkness I had only previously experienced against Dan and Kim.

He had $5500 at the first commercial. I had zero. And I was in second place. Leslie was momentarily no longer *giggiggiggigg*ing. Eric "Powerhouse" Newhouse was earning his affectionate nickname from Alex. All Leslie and I could do was applaud.

I'd rarely even glanced at the Go Lights in ten prior games. But this time I looked—there was time to, since I wasn't getting in a lot anyway—and the lights often just winked when they came on at all. *If I ever learn how to adjust to the lights mid-game, that's when I'll really know what I'm doing,* I thought silently. Eric gave me time to consider many such thoughts.

Still, I'd learned much about patience and biding my time. I would try to fight back like a pudu enraged.

If you haven't noticed, pudus are really quite small.

In a new category called BEFORE, DURING, AND AFTER, a triple Smush requiring three responses at once:

"Who is Steve Martin Luther Vandross?" Eric asks, correctly.

*What is Gulf Stream of consciousness raising?* I reply.

"Who is Sitting Bull in a china shop master?" he counters, making one tiny slip.

*Who is Sitting Bull in a china shop steward?* I retort, correcting him. Aha.

"What is Sudden Death in the *Afternoon of a Faun*?" Eric finally adds, getting the last word here, and most of the money, again.

By the time we reach a category on Shakespeare, now one of my strengths, Eric has over three times my score and over fifteen times Leslie's: $18700 to $6000 to $1200. But the first clue, at $400, is unusually hard for that level, and Eric, for once, doesn't buzz.

> LAVINIA HAS HER TONGUE CUT
> OUT & TAMORA IS SERVED HER
> OWN SONS BAKED IN A PIE
> IN THIS FAR-FROM-TASTEFUL TRAGEDY

This early play is notorious as one of Shakespeare's least brilliant efforts, a splatterfest so sticky that his authorship is often questioned. Trebekistanily enough, Anthony Hopkins, who played the drop-dead guy in *Amistad*, played this title role shortly thereafter.

*What is* Titus Andronicus?

I have control of the board, late in the game, in a category I like. There are still two Daily Doubles in play. Beaten badly all day, I suddenly have a real chance.

I call the next clue in the category and hear a delightful sound: *Bweedwooo, Bweedwooo, Bweedwooo-dwoo-dwoo-dwah.*

A Daily Double in SHAKESPEARE. It is my chance to risk everything, attempting another Brian Sipe comeback, going deep as the last seconds tick down, and before a large cheering crowd on Broadway. This is a prize in itself. I make it a true Daily Double. The crowd cheers. I bow, with a silly grin. I am grateful for this moment, but still trying to win.

> HE HAS THE NERVE TO WOO
> A WIDOW BESIDE HER
> FATHER-IN-LAW'S COFFIN, BUT
> SHE MARRIES HIM ANYWAY

After all these years, now, no mnemonics are needed. It's a scene I know well. My favorite performance on film is by Ian McKellen, who looks remarkably like my own father. I think Dad would have loved seeing himself seduce Lady Anne.

*Who is Richard III?!* I exclaim, giving battle in vain. The crowd cheers again. One more Daily Double and I could still steal this away, just as Lyn almost did to me once years before.

But in less than ten seconds, as my blood floods with glucocorticoids, I make two small but lethal mistakes. I choose poorly, remaining in SHAKESPEARE, the only category where the second Daily Double cannot possibly be. While realizing this one error, I let one become two, screwing up an easy response while distracted. Eric seizes the rebound, chooses well, and takes away the last Daily Double. My chance at grabbing the lead is gone.

This takes less than ten seconds. That's what a good game is like.

Eric now controls the game. There are still ten clues on the board, but the only question remaining is how the betting will shape at the end.

It comes down to the Final once more.

The category—*p-TING!*

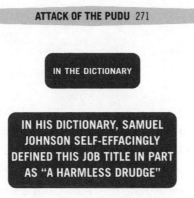

IN THE DICTIONARY

IN HIS DICTIONARY, SAMUEL JOHNSON SELF-EFFACINGLY DEFINED THIS JOB TITLE IN PART AS "A HARMLESS DRUDGE"

*"Self-effacingly." So Johnson is calling himself a drudge. While he's making a dictionary. So they must want the word for the person who makes dictionaries.*

*What's a lexicographer?* I whap with my light pen on glass. This seems far too easy, I fear.

I am correct on both counts.

Eric has bet the minimum necessary, like the good sport that he is, and defeats me, in the end, by one dollar.

This is precisely the value of the token from the Luxor and Jane, which I hold in my left hand throughout.

We all join, center stage, and I take one long last look at what Radio City looks like with that great throbbing mass of applause. Eric is cheered loudly. Leslie and I cheer him, too. We thank Alex, who goes off to prepare the next game.

After a moment or two, the three of us realize we're still up on stage. In the emotion and commotion and congratulations to Eric, we've simply forgotten to leave. It's an odd little moment. What to do? Unprepared, with six thousand watching. Fortunately, I am holding a token from someone who knows the correct Final Jeopardy response.

So as we exit, stage left, I start to dance. Just a few seconds, a dumb hammy thing, a little mocking soft-shoe, all pumping of arms, with accomplished unskill. But it's good for a long, rolling laugh. Leslie joins in at the end, and *giggiggiggiggs* all the way off the stage. Eric smiles and bows slightly, which I count as enough.

Imagine a chance for one moment of dancing, on Broadway, before a full happy house. With new friends you will know for a lifetime.

This game, in which I lost my chance at a million dollars, was a spectacular win.

The rest of the Masters games were a breathtaking show, fireworks I could barely believe I'd been part of. Answers were pulled from the remotest of orifices. The betting was daring as hell. We were all here to win and believed in ourselves. True Daily Doubles were common.

Here's a typical Final Jeopardy clue from the rest of the games:

> NUMBER OF MALES WHO SERVED AS
> BRITISH PM IN THE 1990S PLUS
> OSCARS WON BY TOM HANKS PLUS
> PROTONS IN A HELIUM NUCLEUS

Take thirty seconds and mull that one over.

Chuck, unsurprisingly, got the correct response easily.

But like me, Chuck had been only in second place entering the Final. Bob Verini, the leader, also responded correctly, and so Chuck lost by the exact same one dollar. In a sense, Chuck and I had finished dead even. "What is six?" was not enough to advance at this level.

My score was the highest that didn't quite reach the Finals. So on day three I took Rachael's and Jeremy's place as the alternate. Groomed for a million bucks, primped, pruned, and powdered. And then doomed to look on, watching others compete.

This was fun, in a way. It was my most Cleveland result yet.

Life is too strange to believe much in destiny. But our subconscious habits are real, and they're powerful, and in effect would look exactly like destiny's hand. Standing to one side while three others played for the grand prize, I wondered if deep down I would ever completely leave the Snow Belt behind.

Brad Rutter, age twenty-four, defeated Bob Verini and Eric, winning the show's first million dollars. Alex handed him a check the size of Bhutan itself. We were all glad for Brad's win. He deserved it.

Brad's buzzer timing was so machine-like precise that a term finally existed for someone snuffing the Go Lights: "getting Ruttered." The phrase has been used ever since.

That night, Brad (aka the Master from Lancaster, the Ruttweiler, the Eviscerutter) took the entire group out for dinner. Most of us had changed into new shirts or blouses, relaxing offstage like any gang after work. Rotating ourselves as in a pre-game rehearsal, we matched up with new friends all night long. Pictures and a sense of fraternity grew. Beer happened. We promised we'd stay in good touch. Most of us do to this day. In this very hour as I write this, I swear, I've received e-mail from Robin and Leslie Frates. Dan Melia hasn't met them all yet, but he will someday, I am sure.

As parting gifts, some contestants will receive friendship in Mrs. Butterworth quantity.

And this, finally, definitely, at last, for certain this time, was the end of my *Jeopardy!* career. Had to be.

You'd know I was lying if I said I wasn't disappointed. Of course. A million bucks would be nice.

But it didn't matter. It couldn't matter. I had more than great memories; I had new friends on three continents, a head full of curiosity from months buried in notebooks, a girlfriend returning to health glad for every new day, and a token of love to take along on my travels.

This was hardly an end. It was a beginning.

It was time to explore Trebekistan with my own eyes.

I didn't realize baboons would be waiting, or that lost in Malaysia would be a fine place to be, or that slinging bricks in a cave could be a source of such joy.

CHAPTER

23

LOVE, KINDNESS,
AND AN OLD
CHICKEN
SANDWICH

Also, Why Penguins
Throw Up Down Under

After the Masters, and some sleep, I came back to Jane.

The *we won!* dance was everything you'd hope. A lot of arm movement involved in this one, with a Rockette-kicking thing going on. Very aerobic. The kind of thing you do when you've fully returned to health.

I'm afraid, however, that I must confess something that I didn't like any more than you will.

Jane and I didn't quite manage to get married.

Or move in.

Or even keep dating for long.

I warned you of many surprises to come.

In fact, we even broke up, then stayed best friends anyway.

We dated other good people, whom we drove up the wall by talking about our best friend. This was a cruelty to all concerned: to the people we dated, and to each other, and most of all to the smooth resolution of this book.

Why did this happen? I do not know. But I think it is this:

Survival's not scary. But deciding what you do with it can be. Forever, in all its forms, can be frightening. Jane and I simply saw it and barked and ran away up a log.

This was confusing as hell. It took a while to sort out that was what had happened. I wound up dating an actress, took a job on a certain TV show about crime scene investigators in Las Vegas, and went about getting on with a normal Hollywood life.

I pushed Trebekistan aside, ignoring the lessons and the fun sharp turns life had already taken. I showed just the right amount of forearm for a while, or at least that's what I tried.

You can guess just how well that worked out.

Once Jane and I were good and miserable, just enough, we agreed to start dating again. But this time, only on one condition, for us both: we were alive, after all. So we'd best start behaving that way.

For Jane and for me, part of recovery meant thinking about what to do with our time still on the planet, challenging each other to follow interests that grew in the months that we crammed for the Masters. Call us eclectic, or dilettantes, or just eager students. All I know is it's brain-fizzy fun.

Jane paints now, in fact, splashy abstracts and dazzling surrealist still lifes. These are bold and colorful and gorgeous, although my retinas often need to lie down. One day she will have a grand museum debut. I will print warning labels and alert paramedics. Eyeballs could burst from seeing colors that sharp.

Her study of languages continues to grow. Mayan hieroglyphs are Jane's most recent challenge. She points and explains and I nod like a dog. There are theories and questions and great urgent ideas, and nobody really knows much at all. But sometimes I bark to show interest.

Jane has taken to cooking the same way that she paints. Which is to say: everything, all at once, vivid colors and styles. Taking the fine-dining "fusion" trend to a new level entirely, Jane has pioneered *confu*sion cuisine. It's fragrant and vibrant and intensely tasty. You might have smelled some of Jane's food, if you've ever flown over California.

I think that the paintings and cooking are Jane's secret plan to re-animate Mayans to explain what she's reading.

My *Jeopardy!* cramming left me with unsolved clues about the world. They are many and ridiculously far-flung. As a writer, I can work any-where there is paper, so it's easy to go looking for answers and hints. This is what I've done often since, traveling to places I never would have imagined except for my notebooks, getting as lost as I can, and not al-ways intentionally.

Jane drove me to the airport and kissed me good-bye for a while, although we'd talk when we could on the phone. I was headed east and then south and then north and I would return from the west, carrying only what would go over one shoulder, on a half-aimed safari in the wilds of Trebekistan.

Soon, baboons seized my rental car at the Cape of Good Hope. You may remember my one-word response, repeated many times, still waft-ing in the cold, salty air.

I now know how it feels to believe you are about to be savagely killed by wild animals. It is not a good feeling. But I swear this is true: the adrenaline rush really *did* feel much like the *Jeopardy!* green room, amped by a factor of lots. This was a difference of degree, not of kind.

Leaving my car to walk toward the lighthouse on the Cape's south-ernmost point, I left a small bag of tzatziki-flavored chips on the floor of the passenger side. I didn't realize I'd left the window open a few inches. That was all it took. On return, I soon learned just how clever a hungry baboon can be.

The baboon, for his part, discovered he didn't much like tzatziki. Neither of us was pleased with these particular lessons. Another baboon chased me off. I ran. One repeated word has floated in the air ever after.

It was evening, darkening, with an Antarctic breeze. Few people were left, and other baboons were emerging to scavenge food. I was in little real danger, but I didn't know that quite yet. I was afraid that they might scavenge me.

Another tourist passed by. She was amused and concerned, and gave me an old chicken sandwich as a lure. Five minutes of planning and screwing up courage. Then *sprint, toss, evade, dash, slam! Roll the window!* and suddenly I was safe in the car.

So now I know something else, if it ever comes up:

> **WHEN TRAPPED BY HUNGRY BABOONS WHO HAVE SEIZED YOUR RENTAL CAR JUST BEFORE NIGHTFALL IN AFRICA, THIS IS WHAT GETS YOU TO SAFETY**

*What is charity?*
An old chicken sandwich can be spectacular wealth.

In Malaysia I got trapped in a sudden dark cloudburst.

I was looking at chevrotains, tiny snaggletoothed creatures, even smaller than pudus. (They're also called "mouse deer," despite being neither deer nor mouse. If that sounds confusing, consider the woodpecker.) I was in a park with a garden by a lake, and I had lost track of the time and the sky.

The downpour was almost blinding. As the rain soaked my clothes, a few minutes of walking brought me within sight of a highway. I wasn't sure which way I was headed, but at least now I had a road. So I anticipated a long trudge, a hike that was becoming a swim.

Within moments, a guy pulled his car off the road to help out. This wasn't a cab. I wasn't trying for a ride yet. Before I had a chance, someone stopped. Just a guy with a heart, making room in his car.

A Proton Saga car, in fact. Malaysia's national vehicle.

In the side window was a prayer cloth lined with Islamic verses. There was also a stuffed Pink Panther doll, hanging by four suction cups, in the rear.

For the next forty-five minutes, I sat with Faraad, a construction worker from Melaka, as he drove through a sky-opening torrent. His English was only slightly better than my Bahasa Malaysia, which is little more than "thanks" and "hello." But still we talked about the rain and movies and music, using names and hand gestures. The conversation gradually warmed as we helped each other find words.

Faraad was about a hundred miles from home, it turned out. He had a job on a building site nearby, and was making enough money to send home to his kids, whom he loved the way he loved breathing, even though he couldn't see them often now. His jaw clenched at this thought. I didn't know what to say in my own language, much less his. But I understood, just like you do. So he saw that on my face, as he would have on yours.

He didn't mind for a moment that I was dripping all over his new national car. He smiled and waved once he got me back into the city, then he drove back the way we had come. Faraad must have gone out of his way. How far I will never know.

Faraad was just glad for the company, happy to help, eager to help out a stranger.

> **WHEN YOU ARE STUCK IN A TORRENTIAL RAIN IN THE MIDDLE OF MALAYSIA, THIS IS WHAT GETS YOU SAFELY WARM AND DRY**

*What is kindness?*

Not far from that spot, there's a Hindu temple hundreds of feet in the air in a cave. You climb stairs lined with small monkeys who try to steal from your bags. Some people bring flowers that are scattered around. The cave ceiling is open, so light and vegetation descend in an ecstatic display.

It looks like a place where a god might hang out. Or Harrison Ford might get chased by a boulder. Or both.

In the distance, once you climb, are condos and industrial tracts, small explosions of squareness that block long horizons. So centuries merge, as they tend to in Trebekistan. But once you step inside the cave, all of that goes away. Light pours in from above. When I arrived, the raised temple was sun-flood-lit and glowing.

Tourists come, just as I did, so there's work to be done, keeping the walls and the statues intact. The work on this day involved the lifting of bricks up a steep twenty-foot stairwell inside the cave, reaching up to the shrine. There was a small hill's worth of bricks at the bottom to move. This was all done by hand in a bucket brigade: five men on the stairs, in a tireless line, hurling bricks up a slope all day long. Catch a brick, turn, and throw. Catch a brick, turn, and throw.

The bricks, I should add, were much bigger than bricks. Closer to truth: catch a cinder block, catch your balance, and heave.

These five men worked as hard as my own father did.

And they were *singing with joy.* All five. The whole time.

Not well, I would add, judging from how they laughed at their own sudden strange harmonies. But they were singing.

I stopped for a chat, which involved lots of hand-waving and pictures scribbled down on a small pad of paper. (It's a fine way of talking; when I don't know the words, I just draw, and then offer the pen. Most people will smile and engage in the game.) They were, after all, slinging heavy bricks in the air in a backbreaking fashion in the dark in the dank in the heat, already fatigued, with apparently days of the same to look forward to. I couldn't quite see how singing fit in.

Perhaps, near the temple, they were singing a hymn?

No, it turns out. It was just a truly happy song.

These men were from Bali. Their families were poor. They were a very long way from home. In Los Angeles they'd be the Mexican day-laborers lined up outside building-supply stores. They were singing because they were making what to them were great riches—enough that they could send home the extra, and make things better for their families.

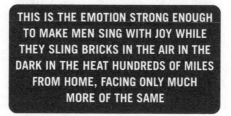

THIS IS THE EMOTION STRONG ENOUGH TO MAKE MEN SING WITH JOY WHILE THEY SLING BRICKS IN THE AIR IN THE DARK IN THE HEAT HUNDREDS OF MILES FROM HOME, FACING ONLY MUCH MORE OF THE SAME

*What is love?*

Fathers working too hard to spend time with their kids specifically *because* they love them.

Halfway around the world, in other cultures entirely. And still I had not left the Snow Belt.

I promised that next time I was back in Ohio I would return to the spot where I first learned to drive. I would visit my father and thank him again with new eyes.

I could give dozens of examples, but over and over, what I've found almost everywhere looks so much like home.

On a hillside in Thailand, a Theravada monk named Yut sat atop a golden-domed temple that looked like a big Hershey's kiss. This was high-test exoticism, as good as it gets. Yut and I sat with the Buddha nearby. There was much playing nice, and no stabbing at all.

Over the doorway to the stairwell, in British English and with no intentional sense of irony, a small sign said MIND YOUR HEAD.

So I try.

At a Ping-Pong table in a rural Indonesian village, where the only phrase I know is "thank you very much," which lasts all evening long.

In the ocean off Rarotonga, splashing with strangers in a night so dark we never even see one another's faces.

Lost in the streets of Cairo, suddenly surrounded by children who appear out of nowhere and even now are still helping me find my way while we imitate famous soccer players to pass the time.

> IT'S THE ONE COMMON COMMODITY
> YOU CAN TRADE IN EVERY CULTURE
> IN THE HISTORY OF HUMANKIND

*What is friendship?*

Not very far from those places, I once met a man who was an icon in his own wealthy country and yet has donated his time to assisting Christian humanitarians, visiting some of the world's poorest children, volunteering his time to their aid. There is no self-promotion, and he rarely discusses it. The only attention he calls to it is in promoting the charity when asked.

*Who is Alex Trebek?*

■ ■ ■

Even buildings start shouting long tales.

In my notebooks, in all of them, is a place called the Hagia Sophia. It's listed as a museum. And a church. And a state building. And a monument. It's in Istanbul, which before that was Constantinople, which before that was known as Byzantium. This is a hint of Trebekistan already.

The Hagia Sophia—"St. Sophie's" in English—is as high as a stadium, a football field squarish in size. In the year it was built, it was the greatest cathedral in Christendom, the St. Peter's Basilica of Byzantine Greece.

A few centuries later, it became Roman Catholic. Two hundred years more, and it was a mosque. One timeless tribute to holy ideals, its details rearranging with each shift in time.

As more lifetimes passed, things changed once again. Secular Turkey arose. The Hagia Sophia was declared a religious museum, with all traditions to be celebrated inside.

So you enter this football-field stadium of godness and see the names of Allah and Mary and Jesus all merging, as one holy place where peace is called many names. People are studying and learning and talking and listening. History matters. It teaches humility.

Trebekistan here smells of candles.


Not far down the road, near a town called Çanakkale, is another small hill called Hissarlik. This is where a man named Heinrich Schliemann invented the science of bad archaeology.

Schliemann was a head case of epic proportions, whose massive Athenian tomb portrays him as an Olympian demigod, all for his fine work at Hissarlik. In 1870 he came to believe that this hillside was once ancient Troy. Since that meant fantastic treasure and Schliemann loved wealth, he hired dozens of Turks to act as a massive nineteenth-century backhoe.

*CRUNCH* went Hissarlik, or at least a big chunk. And with it went priceless antiquities, shards of uncountable number, even more uncountable now that they were smashed down to fragments.

But Schliemann was right, at least in one sense. The Troy of the Iliad may or may not have been real; Homer wrote centuries later, at a time when fact-checking was impossible, unfashionable, and hardly the point. But sure enough, under the *CRUNCH*, in Schliemann's great trench, was a town, and a people, and a civilization long gone.

And another.

And another.

And another and another and another and another and another.

All stacked up like pancakes over several millennia.

More-responsible people with tiny fine brushes now clamber and crawl, armed with tweezers and trowels and small air-puffing syringes. Each fragment is indexed, the story unfolds, and Schliemann is praised and cursed in each audible breath.

So on the side of a hill in what was once Asia Minor (which, as it happens, is a fine place to vacation), if you stand on one spot and look down in the trench, you can see at least *nine* different histories, *nine* different places, *nine* different times, all cultures now gone, in one bewildering glance.

It's the hillside in Virginia, Bull Run and Manassas, transcendent Trebekistan, re-looping over thousands of years.

A people came. They grew. They had their own sports and their gods and their fashion designs. They were in charge. They loved their kids, ate their food, kicked somebody's ass, and curled up when they cried. And then they screwed up. They forgot to build walls or they ran out of fish or they didn't quite plant enough food. And poof. They were gone, with a *gone* kind of goneness that might terrify you to think hard about.

It couldn't happen to *them*, of course. This was fact. They knew how things worked. As they always had for as long as anyone really knew. And then.

Gone. Unremembered. Their gods are all dead, their dreams non-existent, as if they had never been born.

Then, a few centuries later, it happened again. The whole thing.

And again.

And again.

The end of the world isn't some distant supernova off far in the future or a strange philosophical construct.

It's in front of your face. It's as real as your eyes.

There's a spot on this Earth where it comes nine times at once.

I hope, for their sake, they had dances we've also lost. I hope they were glad for their time.

Maybe one day some grad student with an air-puffing syringe will discover they all died from *giggiggiggiggl*ing.

This would be a comfort to know.

In Finland you find a great tubular structure that sings Aeolian songs in the breeze. It's the monument to our old *Jeopardy!* friend Jean Sibelius, whose music helped his nation gain freedom. (He might not be pleased that the wind, in his monument, can sound more like *ah-ooh-gah* than anthems, but still, it's a singular sculpture.)

Across the Baltic, you'll find a spot up in Tallinn, Estonia, where 300,000 people sang away the Soviets. If you stand on the slope in this big concert area, their voices are almost but not quite still floating above you.

Robben Island, in Cape Town, is where Nelson Mandela was caged for much of his life. You know who won. But you can still visit the prison and see what he faced. You glimpse what each day he must have kept overcoming. Or you can still stand on the steps of the courthouse, as he did on his release, dreaming of a world of peace and equality, and try to barely imagine the people he saw. (It helps if you sit down then, and simply start asking. The folks are still there. The answers come flooding. So wear your galoshes.)

In Prague, there's a cell in an old secret prison, where Vaclav Havel, a playwright, was imprisoned as much for his thoughts as his actions. Havel eventually became the Czech president. The prison became a hotel. You can sleep in a cell down the hall, staring up at the bars that are still in the window, letting Trebekistan seep in.

> THIS IS THE ONE MOST IMPORTANT THING IN TREBEKISTAN; FORTUNATELY, IT'S ALSO THE EASIEST THING TO FIND

*What is hope?*

■ ■ ■

There's no shortage of horror and sadness on Earth, much of it our own bit of doing. I offer no wisdom. I know no solutions. I'm still trying to learn what questions are even worth asking.

But I do know that *them* is a flexible concept. It causes much trouble. It is very widespread. Play nice and don't stab—except for *them*, go the rules, if we're honest about it. And for *them*, we're soon *them*. And those other guys—*them*. And then all hell breaks loose.

Six billion of us, seeing *them*, not the mirror, not *us*, not six billion of *us*, can only give Troy one more layer for others to find.

It can't all be that simple, of course. Unless it is. And in practical terms what this means I don't know. Very smart people might have some ideas.

Very kind people will have better ones.

I do know, for certain, that some random guy right this second in Bhutan would be your best friend if you and he were both dropped in Bulgaria. And the Bulgarians, in general, would be happy to see you. Soccer would happen. (It usually does.) So would beer, or perhaps butter tea. Someone would think your shirt was cool. Something would taste like walnuts. There'd be nothing on TV, but you'd have it on anyway. Something good would come on. An old dog would fall asleep. Pretty soon you'd start feeling at home.

This, at least for me, is where Trebekistan leads.

Someday I will be old. I will have a poor memory.

This will be the one thing I have learned.

■ ■ ■

I was reminded of this, as a matter of fact, in a small hotel room in Hobart, Tasmania. I was reading about why blue fairy penguins barf.

Blue fairy penguins, it seems, spend their days out at sea, with their offspring all hidden in nests on a hill. The adults travel great distances in order to hunt and eat, all so they can bring home food to their young. (Not unlike my own father, omitting the beak-to-beak transfer of food. Even penguins, it seems, never quite leave the Snow Belt.)

But when returning to shore, waddling up onto the beach, fairy penguins are vulnerable to predators. They're only as tall as your forearm is long. They weigh about as much as your hand. So: safety in numbers. Every evening at dusk, hundreds of penguin parents stage a Normandy-style invasion, a sudden onrush of honking and waddling and climbing and panting and finally upchucking right into their off-spring. It's an ecstatic display of magnificent nonsense. Nature in her full psychotic glory.

I was there to take photos of this penguin invasion. I should add that the blue fairy penguin can sometimes attack. They don't do much damage. Still, one once took a chunk from a man named Linus Torvalds, which is why Linux has a penguin for a logo. The first popular version of Linux was known as "Red Hat," inspired by the co-founder's large red fedora. The world is a wondrously small place.

So I was about to head off to an even smaller island off the coast of the island of Tasmania, just to watch penguins go all *Saving Private Ryan* and then upchuck en masse. I had night-vision goggles at hand for the task, amplifying the nonsense by a factor of several.

And I was thinking of *Jeopardy!*, believe it or not.

I was appreciating how interesting things had gotten. How small the world seems and how much of it now feels familiar. I had first read about fairy penguins more than eight years before, in fact, in a tiny apartment in Hollywood, preparing for a televised pop quiz, not realizing I would one day learn so much fabulous crap I can't sit still in one life anymore.

For all that would not have happened otherwise, to *Jeopardy!* I am grateful.

Suddenly my laptop went *p-TING!* with an e-mail.

My friend Howard, the fellow I'd helped out on *Millionaire*, was asking if I was in the new tournament.

*WHAT new tournament?* I wondered.

## THE ULTIMATE TOURNAMENT

### Also, I Swear Off the Weapon

I still visited the small island with the beach with the fairy penguins—wouldn't you?—and stood shining red lights on birds to take green night-vision pictures. But my mind was already back in Los Angeles.

*I can't learn all the Vice Presidents again.*

As to Jane's response, you can say it out loud with me here, if you like. All together now: *GWEEEEP!* Jane replied right away. Jane also reassured me I *could* relearn Vice Presidents, not to mention First Ladies, Oscar Winners, Which Fork to Use with Yak Meat in Bhutan, and whatever else was in my stack of *Jeopardy!* notebooks. The books hadn't moved, after all.

Actually, they had. I had. I was living with Jane, sort of, at last. We had decided that forever was less terrifying, at least, than paying two monthly real estate checks. So I'd given away about two-thirds of my stuff, packed the rest into boxes, and moved in.

These are the boxes and bags that you

know as a familiar old pile. *I'll get around to unpacking.* Every day, as a matter of fact. I didn't. I often wondered if I ever could.

It takes one kind of trust to get into a strange car ten time zones from home, or to let a drenched stranger like me scramble in.

It seems to take another kind of trust entirely to climb into someone's entire life.

So we didn't marry, or get engaged, or even commit long-term. When you're committed to the present, that can be hard to do.

As you realize, I have much left to learn.

In the years since the Masters, *Jeopardy!* had changed one key rule: champions would no longer be marched off after only five wins.

Instead, they could play until they lost, racking up as many wins as they could. Six wins, as Sean Ryan soon managed. Seven wins, as Tom Walsh mustered soon after.

Or, finally, seventy-four.

Ken Jennings, a sweet-faced young feller with an open-eyed smile, a generous heart, and the instincts of a pissed wolverine, took over the show for months.

Something like this was almost inevitable, or so thought most players I knew. The advantages of incumbency grow greater with time. More time to study, more studio time building state-dependent retrieval advantages, growing skills with the buzzer, increased mastery of strategy.

So *something* like this, yes, but Ken's run was unique. No one has repeated his feat or come close. You remember my own shakiness in the first five games. Ken did five games, and five games, and five games again, day after day, over and over, more than a dozen times in a row.

And Ken did get better and better with time. He had a few struggles early on, but once Ken hit his stride, the game was transformed into a one-man Japanese monster movie. Players would scream, and one of them would point at the sky, and then Ken would breathe fire and crush them and eat them, stopping only to tithe and read from the Book of Moroni. After a few months it seemed Alex had a permanent co-host.

Even Ken's penmanship—his freaking *penmanship*—improved. He was signing his name in meticulous light-pen calligraphy. I can barely spell "Bob" with that thing. Ken's record may be broken someday, but his handwriting will stand forever.

Best of all, to his credit, Ken remained humble and kind. The show was lucky for his lighthearted presence. He could have turned into an attitude nightmare, the Shootah from Ootah, the Creature from the Great Salt Lake, the LDSOB. Instead, he's just Ken. We've exchanged a few e-mails, and he is funny and modest beyond all expectations. I believe if he ever used the word "booty" sincerely, he'd explode.

Ken's half-season-long run presented an unusual problem. The annual competition, if held, would be a Tournament of Champion.

The producers had a better idea.

People often wondered, when Ken Jennings was mentioned, if he was truly the best player ever. How many games would Frank Spangenberg have won? Or Chuck, or Dan, or a few dozen others, given the chance? Even *I* had four straight runaways; I might have won for weeks, given only my skills at the time. And as you know by now, there are dozens for whom that may well have been true.

So: dozens it would be, *Jeopardy!*'s producers decided. Bring 'em all back. Let's find out.

One hundred forty-five players would compete, a tournament ten times the size of anything the show had yet tried: the Ultimate Tournament of Champions, it was dubbed.

The world's most buzzer-skilled frat party is what it turned out to be.

Ken, since he'd earned it, was given a pass into the finals, which would take four rounds to reach. Nine other great players were given a bye in the first round. Why nine? To make the brackets work out, I suspect.

The Nifty Nine (as they were called, alliteration trumping all sense of gravitas), included six of the Masters: Brad, who had won, plus Bob Verini and Eric, the other two finalists. Robin Carroll, who'd won both a ToC and an International title. And of course Chuck and Frank. The others were Sean with his six wins, Tom with his seven, and Brian Weikle, who had won the most money in a single game until Ken came along.

You could quibble with some of this, and people did. Fans of the show debated these choices in earnest. And so what? It's a game, after all. Just a show. A game show, in fact. Who could be a big enough goofball to waste time on such things?

Or write 340 pages about it? Or read them, for that matter?

That cleared up now, let's move on.

The other 135 of us were thrown into 45 games to produce 45 winners.

Those 45 would be joined by the Nifties, in a group of 54. And 18 second-round games would produce 18 winners.

After the third round, there would be 6 winners.

The fourth round would narrow the field to 2. And these 2 would play Ken in a three-day final for two million dollars.

One champion would be left standing. Before collapsing from exhaustion.


I looked at the names in the list of 135. It felt like the end of *The Wizard of Oz*: "And you were there, and you, and you . . ." So many faces would be welcome sights if I were lucky enough to tape on their day.

From the Masters came India and Leslie Frates and Rachael and Babu and Eddie the Jedi. From my Tournament of Champions, Fred Ramen and Grace Veach, sweet people I was eager to see. There were others I'd met, whom I hadn't yet spent much time with, but I was sure it would be good to see them again.

There was Arthur Phillips, who you will recall had such backstage intensity that pages exploded in flame when held in front of his forehead. In the years since our first meeting, he'd become a best-selling novelist. This was hardly surprising. He seemed destined to do things to wood pulp.

There were dozens whose skills were of championship level. Michael Daunt, reigning International champ on the day I finally passed the entry exam. Tom Cubbage, who, like Eric Newhouse, had won two separate tournaments, in his case a college tournament and a ToC.

Mike Rooney, a philosophy professor I'd met at a party a year before he won his five games. He had picked my brain that night for a few details of strategy; I like to imagine it helped. Jerome Vered and Leszek Pawlowicz, whom we met at the Game Show Congress.

Dozens of others. On down the list. (If you're one of them and not listed here, you deserve to be.) Many were names I didn't recognize at all.

At last I saw Dan Melia. Perhaps I'd get one final crack. Either way, later on, there would be Potent Potables.

But any reunion would wait until the games were all over. As a matter of honor, not to mention contracts in Latin drafted on goatskins impressed with buzzer-finger blood oaths, all of the players broke contact, every one, suspending friendships until eliminated from play.

I said a temporary good-bye to several good friends. We knew we'd have a lot to talk about when it was over.

This was the only downside of the Ultimate Tournament.


With three single-elimination rounds against people this good just to get to the semis, I had as much chance as anyone, which is to say: not a lot.

Later on, everyone I spoke to—everyone—agreed this was much like a golf tournament. It wouldn't likely determine who was best, just who won. It would take dozens of tournaments over several years to truly answer the question of who's best. (I am not, incidentally, hinting to the producers right now that I think this would be an excellent idea, good for ratings, the spread of democracy, and the fate of the world's children. Although clearly it would be all of those things.)

So fun was in order. This would be uncompetitive. An excuse to play again in the sandbox. With this lighthearted intention, I sat at Jane's kitchen table and cracked open the notebooks.

An hour later, I realized how much I'd forgotten. Even more, I was enjoying decoding my strange old mnemonic cartoons.

A few hours after that, I was listing things I still needed to study. I was getting excited. This was familiar and fun and another excuse to make neurons leap high in the air.

Pavlov's contestant was hearing a bell.


With forty-five first-round games to play, taping just the initial round would take more than a month. Needing to study, I hoped for the latest date possible.

Instead, I was given the very first one. First, once again, while I'm still catching my breath. Perhaps it's just a coincidence. But it sure seems to happen a lot. I am sure I will never know why.

I hung up the phone knowing I wouldn't be ready for the first round. It wouldn't even be close. I wouldn't know what I knew at the Masters.

To a sane, healthy mind, this could be more reason to relax and have fun.

But you know me better than that. For all my talk of detaching from outcome and great lessons learned, as a student of wisdom I'm still just a freshman, stuck forever in remedial lab.

Jane always insists that I sleep for eight hours each night. I agree. But that leaves sixteen hours to cram.


"Bob Harris!"

I'm as startled as you are. *I'm not ready.*

Fortunately, I am still just on the roof of the Sony parking garage, on the morning of the first taping day. I am parking dear Max, my beloved rumbling old mule, in the same spot on the roof where I've parked for ten years. The Camaros, like most things, are now long forgotten, except sometimes when I'm hanging out with other *Jeopardy!* champs who still drive their own.

It's a voice I don't know. I turn, and Alan Bailey is smiling. He's a five-timer himself. I was out of the country when he played his games, but he forgives this, and we're friends by the time we're walking downstairs.

Alan's from Georgia, where the munch of chilled boiled peanuts helps cold beverages dilute any muggy old August. We share happy memories of insufferable days made pleasant by this cold soggy snack. Later on, he will surprise me with a homemade batch as a gift.

In the green room we find Leslie Frates, the Spanish teacher from the Masters. Her hug is like falling into a room full of bright-colored balls. There's Arthur, whose intensity has been channeled more carefully, now relaxed and amused and full of wry best-selling comments. There's Babu, whose wit is as warm as his East Texas home. There's Rachael, who has now taken a government gig, stopping impending Enrons. Another superhero like Chuck, doing good in a large way.

There are almost a dozen others there, people I don't yet know. Tom Cubbage stands out, a two-tournament champion. He has the square jaw, easy grooming, and massive confidence output of a kid who must have played quarterback from seventh grade on. *I do not want to play him. I'm not ready. Not yet.*

But everyone's able to beat everyone here, I remind myself. This is what I must believe.

I reach into my pocket and pull out a coin. It's an old token from the Luxor and Jane.

Johnny Gilbert's voice booms through the studio.

"This is a special *Jeopardy!* competition, bringing together the greatest *Jeopardy!* players of all time in the Ultimate Tournament of Champions!"

We begin.

Since it's single-elimination and no scores need to be kept secret, we can sit in the bleachers instead of the green room and watch, taking our turns.

Leslie Frates plays well, but goes out in the first game. This tournament is over for her way too soon. It's not well remembered, but in the Masters at Radio City she led Brad Rutter entering Final Jeopardy. And she answered correctly. She only lost from overthinking her bet.

There is much Cleveland in this. There is Snow Belt. There is work unrewarded. But Leslie has put her son through college with her game winnings over the years. She is happy just to be here. I may understand how she feels.

Of the people I know, Rachael is called on next. And she plays well, and loses. The next day we'll have coffee, and her competitive spirit will almost carry us both right back onto the stage to change the outcome. But not quite.

Alan is called on, and he plays well, and loses. We'll have lunch a few weeks later, and he'll laugh about it more easily, as Rachael surely would by now.

Babu and Arthur must play one another. I am torn over which one to cheer for. It's a close game. Arthur implodes on a Daily Double but still makes a stirring comeback. Then they both screw up on the Final.

Babu writes, "What is *All's Quiet on the Western Front*," which is a one-letter slip. Arthur writes, "What is *All Quiet on Western Front*," a one-word omission. Two brilliant people definitely know the correct response, but neither one can simply write *All Quiet on the Western Front*. (Look closely.) The pressure is lethal in those thirty seconds. Arthur wins on the fluke by just $100. But both frat brothers are laughing.

"Tom Cubbage! Bob Harris! Frank Epstein!"

*I am not ready.* Tom has won both a Teen Tournament and a Tournament of Champions. *Look at that suit. He's a lawyer. He's an adult.* Tom has a wife and kids and a happy family in Oklahoma. *He doesn't just run off to Tasmania to watch penguins throw up.*

I am psyched out completely by Tom's shiny Confidence Field. *He has great hair.*

Dead man walking again.

I am not ready. I know it. If you ever see the tape someday, you can see it in my face.

But there is a plan. A Path, actually. There are rules you must follow.

Tom's Confidence Field is as strong as Dan Melia's. I can't let it get to me and start thinking I'll lose.

*You can often see only what you think you'll see.*

I must anchor myself and relax. I must stop seeing Tom kicking my ass.

*See the obvious.*

Well, I'm not ready. That much is obvious. So I know the next step.

*Admit you don't know squat.*

OK. I'll aim my Weapon with care.

*Doing nothing is better than doing something stupid.*

OK, OK, *back off*, enlightenment. I'll keep my hand the hell off the buzzer. If I know, and I know that I know, I'll buzz. Otherwise, nothing. Just trust in the process.

This would be a test of pure Jeopardy Zen. *What is the sound of one hand not buzzing?* My only chance was to swear off the Weapon as never before.

Believe it or not (although you can really believe it), not far away, on a bench in the sun on a hillside in Thailand, I once mentioned this game to a saffron-robed monk.

Yut thought it was funny, the whole exercise.

Was he laughing with me or at me? I wonder.

### Let go of outcome.

Oh. Whichever. Right. Never mind.

Frank Epstein, I should add, is a Los Angeles police officer. He playacts stern gruffness, but he's kidding. I think. Al Pacino would play him. But only if Frank said it was OK.

If Frank is as controlled with the trigger as he is with a buzzer, there is one neighborhood that sleeps very safe.

This is the second straight tournament where I've played a local cop named Frank. I would say this is odd. But compared to everything else, it is not.

The first clue goes by. I'm not sure. I let it pass.

I do this over and over. More than my usual third, I am letting half—*half!*—of this entire game go by unplayed, unattempted. Surrender is my only chance to survive.

Tom and Frank are as careful as I am. They also know not to play with a Jeopardy Weapon. So they aim every shot. I stand down. Even when I try to ring in, they usually beat me on the buzzer, over and over and over. And then I stand down again, letting yet another clue pass. And another. And another.

It's nerve-wracking.

I'm in a distant third place at the first break.

Ken Jennings once responded correctly to twenty-five of the thirty clues in a single round. At the rate I'm going, I might not even attempt that many responses all game.

Before the first round is over, I have passed up at least a half-dozen clues on which I knew the right response but was not quite certain enough to ring in. I haven't brushed up enough yet. Here's an example:

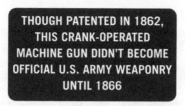

*That's the Gatling gun*, I think. And then: *Wait—what if it's the Maxim gun? No, it's Gatling. Maxim was something else. I think. Ahhhh! I better not buzz.*

"What's the Gatling gun?" Frank quickly responds. I suppose I should be glad that the cop knows his weapons.

With just one extra week to review my notebooks, I'd be playing a completely different game. *Maybe I shouldn't have stuck around in Tasmania, taking those night-vision photos of vomiting penguins.* I try to put this thought out of my mind. Besides, the clues and the competition are more than enough of a burden.

THE FOLLOWING IS A BOX CLUE:

> ST. AMBROSE CREDITS THIS
> MOTHER OF CONSTANTINE
> WITH FINDING THE TRUE
> CROSS OF JESUS

*Jesus*, I think. The writers have made the clues as difficult as in the Masters. *I'm not ready.* "Who is Helena?" Tom smoothly intones, pulling away in the distance. I have to squint just to see his shadow on the horizon, even though he's just two feet to my left. This guy is good.

So is Frank. Third place might be how this works out.

With five clues left in the first round, I get a clue and control of the board. The Daily Double still hasn't been played, so I hunt around the bottom, finally landing on it.

Choosing a wager is a challenge. My little spurt has taken me up to $3800. But Tom has $6600, not quite twice my score. The category is STONES, and I'm not that good at geology. Worse, the clue is in the very bottom row, so it might be one of the hardest on the board. I can't make my comeback, but a small wager would also tell the other players just how unready and unconfident I am. So I bet $1500, a least-bad compromise between unwise large and small wagers, and hope for the best.

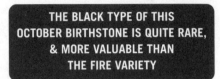

THE BLACK TYPE OF THIS
OCTOBER BIRTHSTONE IS QUITE RARE,
& MORE VALUABLE THAN
THE FIRE VARIETY

Jane had prepped me on birthstones for the Masters. Two years later, thanks to butt-oriented mnemonics, this one remained in my head:

In college, a friend and I used to salve our depression by making escape runs for pizza down an icy brick road that shook his tiny sports car so hard I could imagine my own butt falling off through the floorboards. Senior year, he took me out on my birthday. And thus my birth month—October—is connected (via my vibrating little bottom) to my friend Paul's rusting old Opel.

*What's an opal?* I reply, playing now by the seat of my pants.

The Double Jeopardy round:

OPERAS BY CHARACTER *(I need study time for this; now I might know one or two.)*
1970s TV *(Yes!)*
THE HUMAN BODY *(I haven't reviewed this yet, either.)*
EVERYTHING HAS A NAME *(Although this category name doesn't tell us much.)*
THE SECRETARY OF STATE WHO . . . *(Eek. I haven't studied enough.)*
DERIVED FROM ETRUSCAN *(You are kidding me . . . right?)*

DERIVED FROM ETRUSCAN turns out immediately to be simple wordplay, seeking out words that can be spelled from letters in the word *Etruscan*. So at least this is something mere humans can do.

Tom gets the first two in THE SECRETARY OF STATE WHO . . . right away, picking up Colin Powell and John Marshall in about twenty seconds combined. The third one I don't know right off and so, again, must let go.

THE SECRETARY OF STATE WHO
GAVE WAY TO EDMUND RANDOLPH
IN 1794

Frank guesses incorrectly, which gives my subconscious a few extra seconds. Suddenly I notice my finger is moving on the buzzer. It's involuntary. My hand seems convinced that my head knows the response. I have no idea why.

*Who was Thomas Jefferson?* my mouth says. I am both surprised to hear this and bizarrely certain of the reply.

*This would be some deep-seated thing*, I am thinking (although not in these words; there's not time), *some neural cluster stimulated by long-ago practice, state-dependent retrieval from a forgotten mental cranny, triggered now perhaps by the stage and by Alex.*

"Correct," Alex replies.

This must be how a high-school quarterback feels in his forties, his arm aching but still mustering one last perfect spiral, with no thought or planning but still marveling at the result, wondering just how his hand still knows what to do.

Speaking of quarterbacks and middle age: it occurs to me that Tom may be fighting the same rustiness that I am. He's a lawyer with a family to raise. He has a new baby. The only thing cramming in his house is diapers.

The next clue is a Daily Double. If I miss a big wager, still not ready for this level, there will be no chance to come back. I bet only to tie for the lead.

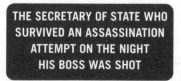

THE SECRETARY OF STATE WHO
SURVIVED AN ASSASSINATION
ATTEMPT ON THE NIGHT
HIS BOSS WAS SHOT

*I know this. I knew this. I know that I knew this. But I don't know if I know this. Brain, will you shut the hell up?*

*Hold on, I'll get it,* I tell Alex.

I bow my head and breathe. *This one should be easy. It's the guy who bought Alaska.* I think of an old cartoon mnemonic for the other targets on the night of Lincoln's assassination: *there's Alaska, and garbage, and a big Johnson named Andrew—wait, go back to garbage—it's sewage!*

*Who is Seward?* and I'm tied for the lead.

Tom and I bounce back and forth for a few clues, pushing each other into errors, scooping up rebounds, playing even. Frank charges back, so we wrestle with a cop for a while. But Tom's focus and discipline have never quite left him. He's as careful as I am, letting clues go by, aiming his Weapon.

The board starts to empty. The Final approaches. Whoever has the lead will probably win.

Tom hits the last Daily Double, bets large and confident, and jumps up by $3000 with just twelve clues in the game. I am once again fighting for my *Jeopardy!* life, and with time running out. There is no wild card.

The next clue I know—*What's the thyroid?*—but once again I don't *know* that I know. *I'm not ready.* I let it pass. The nine steps on the Eightfold Path can be pure torture to follow.

The next clue I *do* know, and I know that I know.

> IF THESE AIR SACS WERE
> FLATTENED OUT, THE LUNGS
> WOULD HAVE A SURFACE AREA
> OF UP TO 1,000 SQUARE FEET

You may remember that I worked for a while as a writer on a TV drama about crime scene investigators with formidable powers. My contributions were tiny, but it's the most brilliant show of its kind, perhaps the most popular program on earth, and certainly the brain-stickiest show ever devised.

As a junior writer often asked to do research, my job involved getting to know a few coroners, who are morbidly funny as a means of survival. I can die now in three states knowing I'll be dissected by people I like very much. So there's that to fall back on.

This is how I learned much about our lung-lining air sacs. If you drown, as it happens, which I hope that it doesn't, mineral traces will lodge in these sacs in your lungs. If you're found in the ocean but have sacs full of chlorine, you died in a friend's pool, and your body was dumped. So choose your friends wisely.

*What's the alveoli?* I reply.

Alex asks me to repeat this, which I do. But my speech is so slurry with the stress and the speed that it stops the game cold. It takes archaeological digging with air-puffing syringes to extract all of the sounds. With so much on the line, the producers try dearly to get everything right.

I am lucky again. Someone finds all seven letters, under nine separate layers of pottery shards and Brad Pitt's leather skirt. The game resumes.

Tom's lead is now only $1000. Ten clues left.

He gets the next one. He's up $1400.

The next one, we all let go by. One mistake and it's over. Just one mistake.

We're in DERIVED FROM ETRUSCAN. I grab *enact* for $1200. The lead falls to $200.

The next clue goes by. It's about a work by Tennyson. Which is forgotten, and by three *Jeopardy!* champs. Alfred Lord Tennyson, timeless poet, in this moment, is like the town in Wisconsin where Kim Worth and I met, or the guy with the plunger on his head. This is not reassuring.

Frank gets the next clue for $2000. He's closing in. Five clues left to go in one column. OPERA BY CHARACTER will determine our fate.

Frank starts at the bottom, with the $2000 clue. We all could probably guess. But we all let it pass. One mistake and it's over. Tom's lead is $200. Four clues left to go.

For $1600, the clue mentions a clown.

BEPPE, SILVIO, CANIO THE HEAD CLOWN

"Clown" is what matters. You need nothing else. This is a great *Jeopardy!* one-to-one. There is exactly one opera famous for its lead character clown. I am sure that everyone here must know this response. They must know that they know. The game hangs in the balance now, one hard plastic triple attack:

*Cliklikikkitylikkityclikit.*

My light, somehow, comes on.

*What's "I Pagliacci"?* and I'm up $1400.

There are only $1200, $800, and $400 clues left. To have the lead entering Final, Tom, the better player, who has deservedly led the whole game, suddenly must get the $1200 clue and one other. The only other way he can take the lead is if I ring in incorrectly. So I won't.

Frank rings in on $1200. Once he responds correctly, I let go of my buzzer.

You can win by not playing. But you know that by now.

The Final, in SHAKESPEAREAN CHARACTERS, has a familiar response.

> KINGS EDWARD IV &
> EDWARD V, THE FUTURE
> HENRY VII & THE CORPSE
> OF HENRY VI APPEAR IN
> THE PLAY NAMED FOR HIM

For the second time in my *Jeopardy!* career, I am thinking of Ian McKellen, and how much my father would have loved watching his doppelgänger seizing and seducing and chewing on everything in his path.

*Who was Richard III?* I reply. Just as in Radio City.

It's the first time I've ever given the same response twice, and it occurs while playing against my second local cop named Frank.

There is a kink in the Matrix. A black cat walks by.

This feels weird, as if the world has just run out of all information. *Jeopardy!* will never exhaust its material, of course; the world is too large, and the writers too observant. This is just a coincidence.

Still, there are many things that defy explanation.

I've answered exactly sixteen clues all game, and just six in the entire Double Jeopardy round. *Six.* I have let fully half of the game go by. And somehow, unprepared, I've defeated another Tournament of Champions winner.

I say this not out of modesty: there is much luck in this outcome. All I have done is helped my luck do its best.

There is much we don't know. It is useful to know this.

Not far away, on a hillside, I can still hear Yut laughing.

■ ■ ■

After defeating two ToC champions and the winner of the 10th Anniversary Tournament, I no longer, at last, feel a debt for being asked to the Masters.

I've now also defeated members of both the NYPD and LAPD.

Let me add, then: I always obey traffic laws. Always.

Speaking of which, when the taping is over, I give Tom and Arthur a lift back to their hotel. We climb into old Max and rumble off through Culver City. There's no competition, just a bunch of guys with a common interest in everything. They have families with kids. Stable lives. I feel envy. They're the real winners at the end of this day.

I haven't read Arthur's novels, I confess on the ride, but I genuinely mean to. (And I have, finally, as you read this. There is much light on each page.) Arthur asks what I'm writing. I mention, perhaps, someday, an article about *Jeopardy!* Or a book, maybe.

You can guess just what came out of that.


I'm still studying for the second round when the month of first-round games start to air. I don't know any results, except for the five from the day I was there. I watch every day, fascinated. Great players and friends fall almost daily.

Leszek is out. One mistake. Only one. One mistake at the end.

Mark Lowenthal, Chuck's co-author, whom I hope someday to thank properly, winds up with just one single dollar.

But my friends Fred and Jerome win easily. So does Grace. Mike Rooney gets through. And Dan Melia crushes his foes, both of whom finish with zeros.

Suddenly my one dollar against Dan looks pretty good.

Meanwhile, a full month passes at Jane's kitchen table. The second round is approaching. The time passes slowly, just textbooks and dictionaries, almanacs and readers. Cliffs Notes and Spark Notes and still more inch-thick notebooks, filled with sticky weird doodles burning into my brain.


Jane and I pop some champagne. This has nothing to do with my studies.

Jane and I don't care on what day we first met, but we have one date on the calendar we've watched now for years. And the anniversary has finally come.

No sign of cancer. Jane is now officially healthy. It's over. She's as well now as I am. More so, probably.

After all, I am studying for *Jeopardy!* again.

Back to the books. Another month in my own private green room. Practicing along with the televised games, I am soon scoring better than ever. In Final Jeopardy clues, even at this extra-hard tournament level, I'm getting well over 80 percent correct.

Again, I am given the first taping date available.

But this time, I'm more ready than ever before.

Just before taping, my sister's not doing so well. In the Snow Belt, Connie's having a fresh bout of Marvin, perhaps the most difficult yet.

She has been responding to treatment for Crohn's disease, even if the doctors were twenty years late ringing in.

But there's no cure for Crohn's. There's not even much study. They don't know the cause. They're not sure where to look.

I sit up and read. Perhaps it's bacteriological, caused by a widespread organism that only affects some people for genetic reasons. I could put ache in your ears with long Latin names and some fussing and pointing. But I don't know a damn thing. I just wish I did. And I'm surely just reading because I feel so damned helpless.

The doctors themselves aren't much further along. So Crohn's patients like Connie are given arthritis meds, some of which help some of the symptoms sometimes. There are side effects, of course. I'll spare you the details. You'd have a more pleasant chat with a coroner.

Connie now needs the rearrangement of bones. Some of her hip will become part of her neck, replacing a piece of her spine. Then, to recover, all she'll just need to do is lie perfectly still. While in agony.

For a month.

Or two.

Or quite possibly three.

She might need a nurse, just to get through the bother of still being alive. That's if Connie stays lucky. Her head, already heavy, could go *clunk* with bad luck.

It is possible to wear out galoshes entirely.

There has *got* to be something I can do about this.

The Sony parking garage feels like a block party. There's Eric Newhouse and India Cooper, whom I haven't seen since the Masters. There's Fred Ramen, and Mike Rooney, and Jerome Vered, and even our old friend Dan Melia.

Dan and I haven't been able to hang out in months. We start to catch up, meeting the other insatiably curious folks in our midst: Tom Walsh, the first seven-time winner. Shane Whitlock and Kyle Hale and Scott Gillispie, three college tournament champs. Steve Chernicoff and Steve Berman and Rick Knutsen and Bruce Borchardt, great champions all.

And—oh my—there's Michael Daunt, the reigning International Tournament champion on the day I made several lucky guesses and finally squeaked through the exam. I am long past awe. This is just really cool.

Michael's first-round game, taped several weeks ago, is scheduled to air that same night. A bunch of us decide we'll find a place to watch it together.

Those of us who win today will not be able to talk to other winners, of course. We all know this, and plan for it. There really is that kind of honor. Not to mention the bloodstained goatskin in fifth-century Latin, and the possibility of being subpoenaed by Sony lawyers across hypothetical space-time dimensions.

We settle into the bleachers, wondering who will play whom, and where we'll watch Michael that night.

"Dan Melia! Rick Knutsen! Kyle Hale!" for the first game.

Just before they begin, Rick turns to me backstage. He's a tall Nordic fellow with art in his haircut, part New York musician, part Viking marauder. Rick's an excellent player, with five runaway games to his name. But facing Dan, he's looking for help. He gestures at Dan (aka the Ameliarator, the Encyclomelia) and asks, half jokingly—but only half—"Any suggestions?"

I advise waiting for just the right moment, like a key Daily Double, and kicking Dan in the back of his right knee. It might disrupt his balance, and would probably be hidden from view by the podiums.

Rick nods and plays along with my deadpan expression. I almost expect him to kick Dan right now.

I sense, just as you do, that Rick has been beaten before the game even starts. Games really are lost in the green room.

Dan proceeds to dish out a near-historic nightmare, one of the most frightening displays I have seen. When Rick attempts a comeback, Dan picks up a city bus with one hand and crushes him with it.

Perhaps Ken will soon fight Dan, in the mountains above Tokyo.

I sit with Fred Ramen and Mike Rooney for a while in the bleachers. Fred still carries himself like he's Luxembourgian royalty. Then he opens his mouth and you have milk in your nose and you're catching your breath and you're trying to borrow a napkin. Mike's much the same, if more professorial. He takes eight extra words before your drink goes down funny or comes back again funnier. But at the end, you've learned something about Wittgenstein.

The day's second game is a close three-way fight. Steve Chernicoff overcomes Scott Gillispie and India Cooper. But all three have a great time. It is that kind of day.

We are all lucky, all of us, to have come this far, and we know it.

Game three is between my friends Mike Rooney and Fred Ramen and the seven-time champ, Tom Walsh. Tom is the first of the Nifties to play.

We debate in the bleachers: most of us think a bye is a real disadvantage. Everyone else has more recent experience. Tenths of seconds, after all, will determine the outcome. Sure enough, Tom doesn't survive.

"Michael Daunt! Bob Harris! Bruce Borchardt!"

On my right, Bruce is a five-timer, a doctor from Washington. In eight career games (including his ToC and this tournament), he has never once trailed entering Final. On my left stands Michael, destroyer of worlds, the guy who beat the whole planet when I was struggling to pass the *Jeopardy!* test.

"Quiet, please," John Lauderdale says.

I'm standing at the centermost of the three contestant podiums, which are wider and deeper than they look on TV. My feet are teetering on a wooden box, creating the illusion of height for the camera.

"Quiet . . . please," John Lauderdale says, stopping this book in this instant.

Not far away, on a hillside in Thailand, Yut feels a moment of inexplicable serenity.

CHAPTER

25

NOT QUITE
LETTING GO OF
OUTCOME

Also, A Massive
Explosion Caught Live
on Videotape

"Quiet . . . *please.*"

Though glowing with color from remote-controlled spotlights, the room is remarkably quiet and still.

The black plastic buzzer feels cold in my hand.

I look at the first round of categories, hoping there's a way to play ahead. The writers are not making the games easy.

HISTORIC QUOTATIONS *(Hmm . . . this could be anyone or anything.)*

PLAYING PRESIDENT *(This is probably movies and TV with actors playing the prez.)*

FISH, BIRD, OR MAMMAL *(OK. So no snakes, frogs, mushrooms, or viruses.)*

BRITISH SPELLING BEE *(Eek. Mike's Canadian. "Mike's spelling bee.")*

BEEN THERE . . . *(No idea what this is.)*

DONE THAT *(And this is also anyone doing anything.)*

The only think-ahead categories are BRITISH SPELLING BEE and PLAYING PRESIDENT. I choose the latter. Before the first clue, I've got Michael Douglas, Martin Sheen, and Harrison Ford in my head.

Bruce starts us off with the British spellings. Fine by me. Michael, being Canadian, will almost certainly know all of these, so let's get them out of the way, while we're warming up on the buzzer. But Bruce finds the timing first:

Bruce!

Bruce!

Bruce!

G-A-O-L, D-E-F-E-N-C-E, and M-E-T-R-E later, Bruce is running up a lead.

I'm behind on the buzzer. Then early. Then late again. The fraction of a second between Alex and the Go Lights seems faster than it was in the first round. I am struggling to find it.

On the fourth clue, my light comes on after a delay. I assume we have all rung in early, and my buzzer has simply come out of the lockout first. I'm in through pure luck.

Zero-for-four. My timing is badly off for some reason. The buzzer will be another opponent today.

If I don't figure out the rhythm, I'll go down the same way I did to Eric in the Masters. The same way I did to Kim and Dan, and Grace and Wes before the minor miracle. I will trail all game long, with only a Final mistake from someone else left to hope for. I'm a decent enough Jedi that I've rarely looked at the lights. But today I am dead if I don't change my plan.

Studying the timing right *now*, in this chaos, is my only hope of survival.

I will have to play Jedi, trying to feel the right millisecond, but while watching the Go Lights each time, to learn where this millisecond might be. Shaving and adding small fractions of time.

If this seems unlikely, I assure you—it is. I have never been able to navigate the Go Lights in midgame. I barely even know how to begin.

Late again. And again.

Michael beats me this time. Bruce loses the rhythm slightly, but Mike's homing in.

But then Mike blows a guess, and I pick up a rebound. OK.

BEEN THERE turns out to be about identifying the country by outline. Mike and I split that column, but I can hear his thumb clicking. I know what he knows, and he knows just exactly what I do. It is like I am wrestling my twin.

We both pass on Zambia—I did the same thing in Africa once, come to think of it—and I finally jump to the safety of Playing Presidents, hoping to coast on medium-strength clues while I focus more attention on the buzzer.

The first clue is mine, but there's no clicking from Mike. Only Bruce tries to buzz. Still, my timing was right. This is good.

The second clue is a video, so there's no timing to work on. (A video or audio clue just rolls, long after Alex stops speaking, and then at some point the Go Lights go on. You just plan a response and watch the Go Lights. Pure reflex. No timing at all.) I'm disappointed, since it breaks the rhythm I found only seconds ago.

CHARLTON HESTON IS SEEN HERE AS THIS PRICKLY CHARACTER BEFORE HE BECAME PRESIDENT

In the video, Heston slaps a man for insulting his wife Rachel. Andrew Jackson once killed a man after just such a scene.

Incidentally, Rachel died shortly before Jackson took office, supposedly due to the stress of the campaign, and Jackson held a grudge against his opponent for the rest of his life. Jackson's sworn enemy? John Quincy Adams.

I've never liked Andrew Jackson. But someday I must buy him a beer.

*Who is Andrew Jackson?* is correct. But the video means I still have no sense of rhythm.

On the next clue, the thirteenth, finally, I feel I'm finding the timing. There's a one-frame collision, the great *cliklikikkitylikkityclikit.* And my light comes on. At last.

But the commercial break stops us immediately.

I have an early lead—fairly large, the kind I once got routinely—but no rhythm quite yet. My feet are not on the ground. Three Daily Doubles await. And my opponents are strong.

In my chat with Alex, he asks about my travels, a silly detail that's good for a laugh. But in our previous visit during my struggle with Tom, we spoke of another departure, one that was still on my mind.

I'd just returned from a long trip through the sites of six of Pliny the Elder's ancient Seven Great Wonders. (As for the seventh, the Hanging Gardens of Babylon will have to wait until Babylon doesn't look so much like Iraq. This might be many lifetimes from now.) I told Alex a bit of what it thrilled me to learn:

In Halicarnassus (now Bodrum, a seaside resort where rich people buy cheap retirement condos), a cabbie, when asked for the great Mausoleum, will drive to a disco where young people dance. There are signs with the word "Mausoleum" outside. The club's pretty big, and it attracts kids with money. So these days that's what "Mausoleum" means here.

You have to walk off on your own in the sun up a hillside through neighborhoods filled with podiatrists' offices, satellite dishes, cars half on the curb, and a new laundromat. A kid rides a bike, singing along with his iPod.

By the side of a road, barely marked, is a kiosk. The tickets are gone, but the man doesn't care.

So you wander inside and it's like you imagined—which is to say old, and it's not a lot else. Few markers await you, and still fewer tourists. You might have the place to yourself.

In its time, on this spot stood the world's greatest temple, constructed by Mausolus's widow and sister. (These were the same girl, Artemisia of Caria. I guess when you're king, you're the king.) It was such a big deal that a lot of our own buildings emulate theories of how this thing looked. Grant's Tomb in New York is designed on what somebody figured King Mausolus liked. Two thousand years ago.

Which is weird, in this lot, in a small Turkish seaport, where people now come just to go somewhere else and to dance and get laid. There's nobody here, except me and some birds. I cough dust. The sound bounces across the far wall.

Next door is a house with a car up on blocks and a back porch that faces the relics. Two children in Turkey are now growing up thinking *everyone* has a vast tomb in their yard. *Mausolus? Yeah,* nonchalantly. *Who's yours? Say what? There's no Persian king at your house? Not even one dead guy, no satrap perhaps, no horny rich dude who was shtupping his sister? No kidding. I'll be. I thought everyone had one. Going without must be hard.*

There's not one thing in this place that the old king would recognize. Everything ends. Life goes on. I'll be gone. So will you. So hug people tightly. Take joy in their heartbeats and drink something cold and go play in the shade. That is all.

If that isn't youth, I don't know what youth is.

If wonder is ancient, I'm glad to grow old.

That's not quite what I said then, in chatting with Alex, because I was still thinking about Playing Presidents: Hopkins as Nixon, Hedaya as Nixon, Waterston's Lincoln, Devane's JFK. (Even more, I don't talk in that ponderous manner, much less venture into dactylic octameter. But Jane thinks it's sexy when words form that way.)

Besides, there's only, like, half a minute or so.

*Bweedwooo, Bweedwooo, Bweedwooo-dwoo-dwoo-dwah.*

I hit the game's first Daily Double.

> **WILLIAM PARRY WAS JAMES GARFIELD IN THE ORIGINAL PRODUCTION OF THIS SONDHEIM MUSICAL**

*James Garfield. Vice President: Chester A. Arthur. First Lady: Lucretia Rudolph. The guy by my mom's house. The smartest president ever, the ambidextrous Civil War general. What the hell about him overlaps with Sondheim? He wasn't in* Gypsy. Sweeney Todd? *He wasn't a demon barber, although he could have cut throats with both hands.* Sunday in the Park with George? *Into the Woods? Garfield wasn't shot by Bernadette Peters.*

Looking at the tape, Alex gives me fifteen full seconds. An eternity in *Jeopardy!* time.

*He had that metal bedframe that hid the bullet that Alexander Graham Bell went looking for with the metal detector. His house is called Lawnfield. It's on Mentor Avenue, just down from a big shopping mall . . .*

"Bob . . . ?" Alex prompts, waiting patiently.

*A shopping mall is a kind of forum. And* A Funny Thing Happened on the Way to the Forum. *But that was in Rome. Although Garfield spoke Latin. He could write it in one hand and write Greek in the other . . .*

Fifteen seconds, in TV time, is an entire cycle of Troy.

Alex has seen me pull obscure facts from every hole in my skin over the years, and I want to live up to his faith. But kindness goes unrewarded sometimes. I lamely guess *Merrily We Roll Along*, hoping perhaps to move backward in time as its characters do.

"What is *Assassins*?" Alex gently explains.

*Right. Garfield was* assassinated. *It's like his* one *act as president. Which is* why *his innards were probed by Alexander Graham Bell in the first place.* Amid all the noise, I did not see the obvious.

I miss the next clue, too, as always after Daily Doubles. Michael beats me on the buzzer. So my best category goes by, and I still can't find the timing.

Quotations zip by. Michael flies through the category. Clue after clue after clue. He is a millisecond ahead of me on the buzzer. I am late. I am late. I am late.

I can hang on just barely, and only because of my dad.


Dad loved words.

He wasn't a big reader, and he rarely wrote very much. His hands were so broken by his work that it took him a full hour to write a short note to his mom. But he loved long loopy lines of aleatory alliteration, he fastened to assonance, he savored the texture and rhythm of sounds.

My dad loved Edward Lear. Lewis Carroll. Ogden Nash. What a strange bird my dad were.

I do not imagine that a single month of my life passed—ever, during the thirty-two years, one month, eight days, six hours, and forty-five

minutes that my father and I shared this planet—that Dad didn't recite
Lewis Carroll's poem "Jabberwocky" to me, just for the sheer delight of
the apparently meaningless syllables. " ' 'Twas brillig, and the slithy
toves,' " he would begin. And then came this big loopy grin.

One other thing, completely unrelated, which he said many times,
for no reason: "You may fire when ready, Gridley." This was Dad's verbal ceremony when something was about to begin, whether it was a
driving lesson or a difficult personal talk. He never explained this. It was
just a fun phrase that he liked.

I was forty-one years old, and Dad had been gone for ten years,
when I saw those words again in a book while studying for a certain quiz
show. I was compelled to learn what they meant. In 1898, it was how a
great man in charge told another great man in charge it was time to
start killing other human beings in quantity. I think if Dad had known
this, he would have used another phrase.

> AT MANILA BAY, COMMODORE
> DEWEY SAID TO THIS CAPTAIN OF
> HIS FLAGSHIP, "YOU MAY FIRE
> WHEN YOU ARE READY . . ."

*Who is Gridley?*
Thanks, Dad.

Another clue. Michael outdoes me again.

Then I manage to get in, and respond incorrectly. He picks up the
rebound.

The three of us then split the few clues still remaining, but an odd
habit is starting to build. Michael has started lifting his hand as he
buzzes. This is easier to glimpse now, almost impossible not to feel. And
it reminds me, quite clearly, how often Mike's raising hand is winning.

Since the last commercial, Michael has outscored me $4800 to $200.

Double Jeopardy begins with more of the same:
Michael!
Michael!

He kills Bruce and me both on the buzzer, right away.
The categories are

EGYPTIAN LIFE *(Yes! I was just in Cairo.)*

1970S POP MUSIC *(I will save this if possible. My strongest category all game.)*

LABOR *(Dad was in the United Auto Workers. Yes!)*

YOUR NUMBER'S UP *(OK, this should be about average.)*

FILL IN THE TITLE *(Perfect for anyone who is memorizing, like me.)*

I'M JUST A "BILL" *(OK, wordplay. This one's fine, too.)*

Bruce gets the next clue. And he leads us to LABOR.

I get lucky on the timing, and pick up $800, although I still cannot make time behave. But then: *Bweedwooo, Bweedwooo, Bweedwooo-dwoo-dwoo-dwah.* I stumble into a Daily Double.

I consider my wager. I now trail by just $1600, one clue's worth of money. But Michael is death on the Weapon so far. If things proceed as they're going, I will trail entering the Final. That's very likely the end of my run.

If I don't make a move, I'll be done in five minutes. Besides, this clue is in LABOR—a strength, thanks to Dad—and it's in a relatively easy $1200 spot. You pick your shots. This is a good one to take.

*Let's make it a true Daily Double*, I say. If I miss it, it's over.

HIS ENTRY IN THE WORLD BOOK
LISTS BIRTH AND DEATH AS
(1913–1975?)

I was a paperboy when I was young. Every time a dog found a bone in the late 1970s, newspapers in the Snow Belt said this man had been found.

*Who was Jimmy Hoffa?* and I'm up $2800.

"Good one," Michael says. I can't see his face, but he means it, I'm sure. He's an excellent sport, probably much better than I am. I'm certainly too focused to respond right this second.

I get the next clue—the one after a Daily Double—which itself is surprising, enough that I'm late on the buzzer again. Mike blows through the next two.

Michael!

Michael!

This last clue is even more frustrating than usual. Sarah from the Clue Crew is on video, hinting at the Arabic word for a market. She does this while walking through the Khan al-Khalili, a souq (that's the word Sarah's hinting at) among the world's most historic. I've just come back from Cairo. I've just walked right by there.

Another kink in the Matrix? Maybe not. If you play well, the cards in the game *should* repeat on occasion. There's no end to Trebekistan, but the roads cross back and forth.

Michael's timing is better, by a smaller split-second. "What is a souq?"

I am late. I will have to shave time yet more finely again.

*Khan al-Khalili*, I should add, is also a novel by Nobel Prize winner Naguib Mahfouz. I've never read it, nor any of Mahfouz, not yet. But he's inside my notebooks, and easy to remember. It's a one-to-one: Egypt + novelist = Mahfouz.

Two clues later, I almost panic. It's more video from Egypt, focused on a picture of Mahfouz, and here's Jimmy from the Clue Crew:

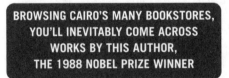

BROWSING CAIRO'S MANY BOOKSTORES, YOU'LL INEVITABLY COME ACROSS WORKS BY THIS AUTHOR, THE 1988 NOBEL PRIZE WINNER

*GAAAH! I MUST GET THIS!*

Michael's hand isn't moving yet. It must be nearly time to buzz in. I have to play Jedi, shaving off fractions of fractions. Aiming for the instant between the Go Lights and Mike's thumb starting to rise.

*Who is Mahfouz?* I say.

Alex takes a beat. I think he's checking my pronunciation, lest the tape need reviewing with air-puffing syringes. But this is correct. Maybe there's still a chance to gain some control over time.

But Bruce!

And Michael!

And Michael!

And Michael!

And Bruce!

Michael's now back in the lead. Ahead by as many dollars as milli-seconds.

FILL IN THE BLANK draws several blanks. We play some advanced Zombie Jeopardy. We're aiming our Weapons and firing carefully. The writers are pushing us hard. Ten clues remain.

Michael!

Michael!

I should be falling behind now, brain losing oxygen, starting to see a Great Jeopardy Light in the Sky. But both of Michael's responses are wrong.

Bruce and I split up the rebounds. And still:

Michael! again. He is murder.

Two clues later Michael calls for his next clue, and *Bweedwooo, Bweedwooo, Bweedwooo-dwoo-dwoo-dwah*. The last Daily Double.

I have a slim $200 lead. Michael bets for the win. He goes big. He goes courageous. He bets $3000 on himself. There will be only five clues left when he is done. The whole game may come down to Michael's response.

I stand to one side, helpless, watching my milliseconds running out.

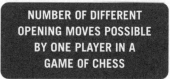

I know Michael will get this. Eight pawns can move one space or two. That's sixteen. Two knights can go forward and right or forward and left. That's four. $(8 \times 2) + (2 \times 2)$ equals Mike's gonna win.

"What is twenty?" he says.

And that's checkmate.

In the bleachers, I can feel the other players relaxing. The rest of the game will be killing time. We know how this ends. Michael has beaten me. He deserves to win. This game can fade now into blackness.

Besides, Mike has math on his side.

Five clues remain. All in 1970s POP MUSIC. This is good for me, but my opponents are old enough to have danced in those years.

In the last fifteen clues, I've given two correct responses. *Two.* I've won on the buzzer just once. I just came back from Cairo, and still I got passed over in Egypt. I've buzzed in first and been right only four times all round.

Not far away, on a hillside in Thailand, even Yut looks a little concerned.

Five clues remain for my *Jeopardy!* life. I will probably need at least four of the five.

I take a breath, preparing to fire when ready. I have been watching Michael's hand as it moves with each clue. Stealing glimpses, from my spot in the center, sensing rhythm, trying to feel my twin kick. I've been a hair late. Then half a hair. Then a quarter. Then an eighth. I need not to be late.

I need the right millisecond.

Right . . . *now.*

My light comes on. *What's "Weekend in New England"?*

Michael's lead is now $2400.

Right . . . *now.*

My light comes on. *What's "Rumours"?*

Michael's lead is just $1600. Distant commotion begins in the bleachers offstage.

Right . . . *now.*

My light comes on. *What's "the Captain"?*

$400 to go. Hushed whispers. In the audience, I feel bodies leaning forward.

Right . . . *now.*

My light comes on. *What's "Sir Duke"?*

And I am suddenly, improbably, back in the lead.

Adrenaline flows so intensely that I can feel my hand cooling from sweat on the buzzer's soft plastic. I'm up by $1200 with just one clue to go. If Michael still gets it, that whole run was just wasted. But if I am too eager and buzz in with a wrong guess, I'll take it away from myself. The last clue of the round:

> **"AND IF ONE NIGHT YOU HEAR CRYING FROM ABOVE, IT'S 'CAUSE" OF THIS, THE TITLE OF A 1976 HIT**

And I do *not* know the game's final $2000 clue.

I let go of the buzzer. I wait. I can only hope. I even gesture surrender.

And Michael and Bruce let the clue go, too.

It's the single best comeback I've ever made, a long march down the field with the clock running out. It's the best game I may ever play.

And I know it's still half luck. But so is my presence here in this game in the first place, a dozen ways over, not least being born.

That last clue, incidentally, refers to the song "Heaven Must Be Missing an Angel."

Last time I saw an angel disappear in this book, it was headed for the Taj Mahal. Maybe we should crank down the power on *Howard's End*.

I am breathing. My heart is beating. I know I have an 80 percent chance of winning. Just one more clue remaining, and I can go home.

The Final Jeopardy category—*p-TING!*

> **INVENTED WORDS**

> **IN WORKS BY LEWIS CARROLL, THIS WORD MEANS "FOUR IN THE AFTERNOON; THE TIME WHEN YOU BEGIN BROILING THINGS FOR DINNER"**

Merv's lullaby begins, ticking and tocking, measuring each passing moment as it slips into the past.

*OK . . . OK . . .*

Milliseconds pass.

*Where is there a cooking scene in Lewis Carroll? Does somebody cook Tweedledum and Tweedledee?*

I do not see the obvious.

*Broiling, OK, that's the clue. Broiling, cooking, roasting, broasting, poaching, peeling . . . But it's an invented word. For dinner. For cooking dinner.*

I do not relax and slow down.

The second chorus begins. From two other podiums, I hear the familiar *clackity-click-whap-clackity* of light pens on glass. Bruce and Michael have already finished. I still do not see the obvious.

*Four in the afternoon. That's about teatime. Which is British. But that's also not particularly invented. What am I missing here?*

Time ticks away. It goes in only one direction. The final notes finish. I write down *What is teatime?* as the tympani thumps its final *bum-BUM.*

In the thirty-two years, one month, eight days, six hours, and forty-five minutes that my father and I shared this planet, Dad must have recited the first lines of Lewis Carroll's poem "Jabberwocky" to me, just for the sound of the INVENTED WORDS, five or six hundred times, including three times in this book.

You already know the correct response. Even if, just like me, you don't see it quite yet.

The poem begins with this:

*'Twas brillig . . .*

"Brillig." Which sounds like "broiling." It's the second damn word.

When confirming Bruce's response, Alex begins to recite "Jabberwocky."

My spine comes unscrewed. My head is a torch. It's not about loss. Not *this* loss, anyway. I just miss my father with all of my heart.

Right . . . *now.*

It's actually funny to lose in this fashion. It's perfect, in fact. It's the ultimate Cleveland. After years of study, far-flung travel, and notebooks filled to the edges, I've somehow forgotten the poem that I heard from my crib to my dad's final bedside and all thirty-two years in between.

I'd have figured it out on the day when I first passed the test. I'd have thought it was easy, something every kid grew up with. "Doesn't your house have Lewis Carroll?"

When I first came on the show, I was afraid of a failure that in some sense might dishonor my family. This was mostly a joke, but that's exactly how this feels. I have forgotten my very own dad.

So the poem just erupts, a cathartic explosion.

I finish the rest of the stanza Alex starts, then skip ahead to another small morsel of Dad's favorite poem, which emerges with every emotion you've felt in this book, all at once:

> *And as in uffish thought he stood,*
> *The Jabberwock, with eyes of flame,*
> *Came whiffling through the tulgey wood,*
> *And burbled as it came!*

I'm trying to laugh. *What a magnificent coincidence. Perhaps the best one of all.* But I see Dad's broken smile, his laugh through bad teeth, a tired gray face with a child's soft joy in his eyes. So I spout glorious nonsense with grief in my voice and every inch of my body.

It is a slightly odd moment. Apparently, not many people recite whimsical poetry while grieving their fathers on game shows on national television.

Michael and Bruce are the pictures of sportsmanship. If I look a sore loser, they just let it slide.

Alex, whom you'll know by his "Oooh," looks concerned. There's no way to explain. We just smile and push on.

Center stage, credits roll, we wander off to the bleachers.

Dan Melia is standing there, waiting, the first face I see. The Ivy League Serial Killer hugs me at once.

Outside, on the pavement, rain assaults all of Sony. The sky is filling with my exact mood. It's cinematic as hell, the trip back to old Max in the Sony garage.

Max is waiting, just as always, in the same space as forever. The same one he was parked in when you opened this book.

But there's one major difference, in the years that have passed. I find it when I reach for my keys.

I have a coin in my pocket. From the Luxor. Jane's token. My favorite *Jeopardy!* memento.

I have already won after all. I now win every day.

It turns out, incidentally, that Dan Melia not only knew "brillig," but has in fact taught a college class in which Lewis Carroll's precise definitions for each word of the poem were specifically discussed.

This is just how things should be.

The eighteen who advanced from this round were amazing. About half were contestants I've played or know well.

Dan Melia and Michael Daunt both lost to Jerome Vered. Jerome then beat Frank Spangenberg (who had beaten Grace Veach) and a woman named Pam Mueller, who was terrific three games in a row. So Jerome made the Grand Final.

Brad Rutter, the Rutterminator, won out over Steve Chernicoff and Mike Rooney. He then defeated two folks I don't know but am impressed with, John Cuthbertson and Chris Miller, reaching the finals of his second straight mega-tournament.

Jerome, Brad, and Ken played at last for two million. Bradzilla won all three games. The Record Store Record Holder beat the Brigham Thumb in a blowout. Ken's last Final response also included: "Go Brad." I think this tells you more about Ken Jennings than do his seventy-four wins.

The Ultimate Tournament brought together more than a hundred old champions. Not just to play, but to play afterwards.

The tone was reflected by Alex himself, moments before the first game of the $2 million final. Jerome, Ken, and Brad had been breaking the tension by kidding about behind-podium nakedness. They didn't realize their mikes were live, or that ears might be listening.

The connections behind the walls remain unknowable, of course. It's not clear how the joke current flowed. But when Alex was introduced to begin the first game, he emerged with a straight face, his un-ruffled demeanor . . . and no pants.

Boxers, incidentally.

You can see this yourself on the *Jeopardy!* DVD. It is an Easter Egg, fun to find on your own, and it's pretty damn funny, although the shock the players felt can't be reproduced. It is only a shame that books can't include similar things. So for this moment, you'll have to enjoy the evidence of pants unseen, unseen.

The frat party was on, once the games finally aired. Now every old friendship among us could at last be renewed. New ones could finally begin. There are clusters of players around New York, L.A., and San Francisco, and other small scatterings in most other places. There are dinners and movies, as with any group of friends.

On the night that the public saw Brad win the $2 million, he and Jerome and Fred Ramen and Rick Knutsen got together in New York. A few hours later, when the shows aired in Los Angeles, Mike Rooney and Steve Berman and Jane and I were in a Santa Monica bar. The East Coast called the West Coast, and we passed the phone around.

It's all ad hoc and informal. I spend a few hours with the frat when I can. There have been several fine evenings out so far.

But the night of my last game is still the one I like best.

In the hotel in Culver City where traveling players usually stay, there's a place to sit down and relax. It is too bright to be a bar, but even so, we all know it's where we're going when we're done. It's big and it's empty and it's quiet like church. It's a fine place for a half-dozen tired players to sit together and share time at the end.

Dan buys the first round. His girlfriend Dara is here. She hugs me, a bit sad for my loss. Soon Eric Newhouse walks in. He has fallen, much as I have, and is in need of some cheer. So we trade tiny details and start to let our buzzer hands finally rest.

Fred Ramen comes by and drops himself at our table. The Luxem-bourgian prince has been hurled from a tower. We get some food, a bowl of nachos that taste a lot more like walnuts. There's a TV with nothing good on, playing silently in the background. Bruce Borchardt pulls up a chair. He's changed his shirt, and the new one looks cool.

322 PRISONER OF TREBEKISTAN

Michael Daunt, who can't talk to Dan because they're both still among the living, visits with me on the other side.

When it's time, we watch the TV, and see Michael win his first game, a match he played a lifetime ago. Soccer happens. We cheer.

By the bar, an old dog falls asleep.

Butter tea, everybody. Let me buy you this round.

My thoughts wander back to a small white house in the Snow Belt.

Last time I visited, Mom showed me a large red hat, which many women her age have begun to wear, inspired by a poem about growing old. She's doing well. Except her daughter has a tough time coming up.

Connie's surgery date is approaching. This will be the rearrangement of bits of her skeleton, after which she'll have to remain very still through months of a difficult recovery.

Even worse, Connie's old bed, too soft to navigate easily, will be a terrible hindrance, itself a likely cause of much pain.

At least there is one piece of good news.

It would help a great deal to have something fancy that rises, like hospitals have.

Fortunately, you can buy these. You can have them delivered.

And they cost only a little more than the consolation award for the game I've just played.

Jane will chip in, because that's how Jane is. But for once in my life, finally, I have used this small brain for Connie.

So at least that wasn't a total waste.

Empty glasses. Yawns and stretching. We've been here an eternity.

Oh, and Dara and Dan are engaged. Didn't they tell me?

*They didn't tell me.* We haven't been able to speak for months.

*Where and when?* It's fantastic.

They're still planning things now. But that's the thing. They don't know. But they do have a daydream idea.

They would like to marry on the *Jeopardy!* set.

No way, not a chance that the producers would say yes. But Dan and Dara will ask. Life's too short not to try. And sometimes daydreams come true.

Dara asks: So will *I* do it?

*Will I do what?*

Would I be willing to perform the ceremony, as their minister?

Dan throws back his head and applauds.

From Alex's podium, we will discover, you are much closer to the contestants than it might appear in the course of a game.

Perhaps you have to stand there to see what I mean.

CHAPTER

26

WHERE ALL
KNOWLEDGE
IS KEPT

Also, Eleven More
Sentences That Are
Actually True

These are the last six categories I will see on the *Jeopardy!* stage.

Dan and Dara are standing together at the center contestant podium.

Strangely, I'm the man standing on the host's mark, greeting a room full of family, old friends, and people I'm not allowed to consider old friends for security reasons. I have crossed briefly to the other side of the river-blue stage. It is quiet. It is calm. There are warm smiles as far as the lights let me see.

Alex is watching. From the audience. This is a very odd sight.

The impossible does happen in Trebekistan, it seems.

■ ■ ■

As you've gathered, the producers said yes to Dan and Dara.

And the state of California said yes to me being holy and all. For a strictly limited twenty-four-hour interval, required to use specific verbiage in several parts of the ceremony, and explicitly restricted to civil actions divested of all trace of the transcendent, I have the power to perform sacred rites.

It's the first marriage I've performed in my life.

This would have been strange enough. But the place, on this stage, pushes the day into reverie.

There is Dara, looking lovely in a silk Mandarin cheongsam. Dan is as dapper as always. They are signed in together with the electronic pen.

To Dan's right, at the champ's spot, is his brother John, the best man. On Dara's left, at the far podium, is the matron of honor, Dara's sister Carrie.

The two families are gathered at the edge of the stage. Jane's silently *GWEEEP*ing and perhaps slightly weeping with glee.

Besides Alex, the entire show is pitching in, showing Dan and Dara this kindness. The tech guys have rigged the game board with the vows. The soundman is up in the booth with the Think Music. Someone has even adorned the podium with fresh flowers.

It's the end of a long taping day. They are all staying late, with goofy smiles on their faces. There may be rationales—there *must* be, given the strictness of security and lawyers—so of course there's no friendship involved.

It's my role here, as vow-giver, to be a serene and comforting force. Consider what you've read, and see just how likely that seems.

But many years have gone by since I first took that one sharp breath in the green room. This is easy. It's a hillside. It's a temple. It's the Snow Belt. This is Ironwood. It's a cave in Malaysia. It's Trebekistan. I know my way here.

So as Dan and Dara have requested, the opening theme plays. I stride out in a suit and an old pair of shoes, which I will now choose to remember as my wedding shoes, and begin to relax. Welcome, everyone. It feels just like a chapel should feel.

I walk to Alex's podium and read a few simple wise words from the Book of Common Prayer. John reads a psalm. Carrie reads from Romans. Dan and Dara quote *Star Trek* and Francis Ford Coppola's version of

*Dracula*. They are happy and loving and a little bit loopy. And they mean every word to each other.

We begin the Ceremony Round. Dan has control of the board. He selects WEDDINGS for $200. The clue reads as follows:

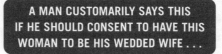

A MAN CUSTOMARILY SAYS THIS
IF HE SHOULD CONSENT TO HAVE THIS
WOMAN TO BE HIS WEDDED WIFE . . .

followed by the rest of the vow.

The Think Music plays. Dan buzzes in with a smile. It is softer than the one I first saw on this very spot. "What is 'I do,' Bob?" he responds, and Dan has $200 and a bride.

Dara takes her turn, choosing the $400 clue.

A WOMAN CUSTOMARILY SAYS THIS
IF SHE SHOULD CONSENT TO HAVE THIS
MAN TO BE HER WEDDED HUSBAND . . .

The Think Music plays again. Dara knows the correct response, as she has since the day she met Dan. "What is 'I do,' Bob?" and Dara has $400 and a husband. She also takes a $200 lead.

An exchange of rings later, that's how the scores end. So technically, Dara has won in a runaway. But we all call it even.

You can see some of the game as an extra on the *Jeopardy!* DVD. It's an excellent match between two very close equals. Dan and Dara are now husband and wife. A last win on *Jeopardy!* is the first thing they'll share.

It is exactly the wedding they wanted, and the happiest one I could hope to see. I stride over to shake Dan's hand, and then bring the marriage certificate. Alex signs this, as the wedding's official witness. Using his podium to write on, he looks completely delighted.

People often ask me what Alex is like.

I think now you know.

I notice, while he's writing, a small drawer on the podium. It's hidden from the camera and players. Few people realize it's there.

This is where *Jeopardy!* keeps all knowledge in the universe.

I am told, and you must believe, this is where they still keep the ancient coconuts handed down by the Merv. Not to mention everything learned since, through the ages.

It seems remarkably tiny, to hold so much information. But this is Sony, after all. They're pretty good with the small stuff.

For a moment, while everyone's taking pictures, I can peek if I want to. I can see how the rest turns out, and much time is left for us all in the round.

But no.

That would be getting ahead of the story.

So there's Susanne, now retired. It is so good to see her. And here's Maggie, the new head wrangler, and Glenn, Grant, and the rest. There are at least a dozen more folks whom I wish you could have met along with me. Harry, the man in charge. Rocky, a former player, now a senior producer. And Rebecca and June and Lisa and Kevin and Cole and Renee and Ayesha and Luci and a whole slew of people I will never admit the slightest affection for, out of respect for the show's security.

Jane and I stand to one side, near the giant game board. We are sharing a slow glass of champagne.

Center stage, Dan and Dara are dancing together, their first dance now as husband and wife.

This very stage, you should know, was used not long ago to film MGM musicals, before Sony and *Jeopardy!* moved in. Jane and I didn't know this when we sang in the car, but (in a Trebekistan turn we were both pleased to learn) Judy Garland herself once danced to a familiar old tune not far at all from this very same spot.

*Sing Hallelujah, come on, get happy, we're gonna chase all our cares away* . . .

Dan and Dara are dancing in a way Jane and I never quite have.

Perhaps someday soon we will dance this way, too.

So at last this is the end, the real end, of my *Jeopardy!* career, the part where Morgan Freeman begins to narrate, and you know it's time to get your coat.

I think it is, anyway. I assume. But I admit I don't know.

But I'm still, and will remain, gladly trapped in Trebekistan. I am eager to see more of its farthest fields.

Soon I will go off to find the wild pudu on a small Chilean island. I want to glimpse these tiny fragile deer with my own eyes. I would like to see Bhutan while I and it are both still here.

Jane might come with me. Or not. I hope and believe. But I admit I don't know.

I'll keep traveling, until the future comes, hoping to be a good passerby. With budget tickets, simple needs, and just one backpack to carry, it's amazing what it's possible to find. Leslie Shannon, now happily married in Finland, wants to meet next in Beijing. Chuck Forrest, now in Rome, tells me to not to miss Sarajevo. I've promised a full report when I see him next time. He'll choose the restaurant. I'll buy dinner. I'll let him choose the wine.

I have, in a way my father could have only dreamed for me, high hopes.

I don't remember what year it was the first time I failed the *Jeopardy!* test. I don't need to. They've given me much greater things to wonder.

Eleven more sentences, all true, and with deep appreciation to you for reading, as we stop twisting the timeline and at last slip back into the moment where I'm sitting right now:

I am not in a coffee shop, but at a bright blue kitchen table, where Trebekistan smells of fresh spices, wet paint, and a light ocean breeze.

In the spare bedroom, there remains a large mound of old boxes and plastic bags, my possessions still stacked in a quiet scared pile.

But the mountain is shrinking. The boxes are opening. Small items are gently climbing onto new shelves.

Jane is in the next room, rearranging books, merging collections, as I write this. She is singing, in fact, although I don't know the song.

This book itself has made me see connections I had not quite appreciated, subjects I should have learned long ago.

I realized at last it was time to unpack when I was writing the chapter where we scored the big touchdown. We are both finally home.

That's the real happy ending, so I'm telling you now.

**ACKNOWLEDGMENTS**

There are so many people to thank for their kindness that I could write an entire book for precisely that purpose. Fortunately, I just did, and you're reading it. However, above and beyond:

Shana Drehs, this book's editor, took a chance on me, embraced my habit of treating language like Tunisian crochet, and braved long hours as a result, while remaining so playful that I hope she'll continue to tell me I'm not making any sense yet many times in the years to come.

Marly Rusoff is the literary agent who realized that this book was more than just a possible magazine article. She took a chance on me, too, and then found Shana. This book wouldn't exist without her.

Arthur Phillips is a best-selling novelist and fellow *Jeopardy!* contestant whose modesty and encouragement made me imagine that maybe I could tell a decent story, too. He took a chance on me by introducing me to Marly.

Susanne Thurber, for many years the *Jeopardy!* contestant coordinator, was kind enough to laugh at my jokes and invite me to play in the first place. Without her, I never would have met Arthur.

Harry Friedman, the show's executive producer, and many other people behind the scenes have created a lighthearted world in which I have met many bright people I like very much. Without them, I never would have met Susanne, or anyone mentioned below. I would also mention Merv and a long chain of others, but you get the point. This could turn into the *Jeopardy!* credits themselves, which would not be completely mistaken.

Twenty of my fellow players (including Arthur, above) generously agreed to share their own memories, either in person, over the phone, or via e-mail. You've met most of them in the previous pages, but unfortunately not all, and none of them as much as I wish were possible. So thanks here to Alan Bailey, Robin Carroll, Josh Den Hartog, Eugene Finerman, Chuck Forrest, Leslie Frates, Matt Mann, Dan Melia, Eric Newhouse, Fred Ramen, Michael Rooney, Brad Rutter, Rachael Schwartz, Leslie Shannon, Ben Tritle, Jerome Vered, Grace Veach, Kate Waits, and Kim Worth. My affection and gratitude is such that I can only hope that someday all of us may again not be allowed to speak to each other.

Finally, special thanks to Alex Trebek, without whom the resulting book would have been called *Prisoner of Stan*.

## RECOMMENDED READING

Consider the following a basic starter kit for those who want to try this at home. Some players have other books they've found most useful. These are mine. A few are out of print, but you can probably find them online with diligence.

### Books by former players

Forrest, Chuck, and Mark Lowenthal. *Secrets of the Jeopardy Champions.* New York: Warner Books, 1992.
    Or, as it is known in my house, the Holy Scroll.

Dupee, Michael. *How to Get on Jeopardy and Win!* Secaucus, NJ: Citadel Press, 1998.
    A brief guide to game tactics and betting strategy, plus hundreds of things to study. Not mentioned in the story only because it came out after my first run through the show, and by then my apartment was pretty much a reference section anyway, so I didn't use it as much as you might.

Jennings, Ken. *Brainiac.* New York: Villard Books, 2006.
    No idea what's in it, actually, since it will be released about the same time this book is. But Ken's a bright guy—*this just in!*—and much funnier than a lot of folks may realize. I don't know if it's even about *Jeopardy!,* but I bet it's a good read.

### About *Jeopardy!* in general

Richmond, Ray. *This Is Jeopardy!* New York: Barnes & Noble, 2004.
More clues and history. Lots of neat color photos. The Final Jeopardy from my fifth game is on page 167.

*Jeopardy!* producers. *Jeopardy!* . . . *What Is Quiz Book 1?* Kansas City: Andrews and McMeel, 2000.
Along with volumes 2–4, a massive collection of actual show clues. The fastest way in print to get a handle on what categories come up most often.

Trebek, Alex, and Peter Barsocchini. *The Jeopardy! Book*. New York: Harper Perennial, 1990.
Show history, actual clues, and even sheet music for the *Jeopardy!* theme, which contains key signatures that will make your eyes cramp just looking at them. I believe the third chorus is in H-sharp.

### Other books good for long nights alone with your practice buzzer

Wright, John W., ed. *The New York Times Almanac*. New York: Penguin Reference, 2006.
Dry as your bones and almost as worth owning. Vast amounts of basic material, conveniently packed into one spectacularly dull volume, published annually.

Barraclough, Geoffery, ed. *Atlas of World History*. Ann Arbor, MI: Borders Press, 2001.
This at least has bright colors and lots of arrows zipping all over the maps. Don't go crazy, but this covers lots of history and geography in one neat lump. Good place for Hanseatic League stats, for you history rotisserie buffs.

Rubin, Louis D., ed. *A Writer's Companion*. New York: Harper Perennial, 1995.
A fantastic source of raw material for making insane notebooks filled with lots and lots of cartoons you can never show anyone. More exciting than porn. OK, that was a complete lie. But still.

Gombrich, E. H. *The Story of Art*. London: Phaidon Press, 2004.
An unbelievable value. Incredible photos of significant stuff, and lots of them. Heavy enough to break a horse.

Jones, Judy, and William Wilson. *An Incomplete Education*. New York: Ballantine, 1995.
Whatever your worst subject is, there's probably a chapter or two in here that will help. You'll laugh, too. Fabulous.

Petras, Kathryn and Ross. *World Access*. New York: Fireside Books, 1996.
A good companion to the previous book. Some overlap.

Murray, Chris, ed. *Dictionary of the Arts*. New York: Gramercy Press, 1994.

If you don't know Dickens, there's a complete list of his works on page 149, next to Diaghilev, *The Dial,* the diatonic scale, and the goddess Diana.

Tuleja, Tad. *The New York Public Library Book of Popular Americana*. New York: Macmillan, 1994.

More focused on the U.S.A. John Singer Sargent, William Saroyan, and Sasquatch, all in the same place—under *S,* not under THINGS THAT REALLY NEED A SHAVE.

Moore, Bob and Maxine. *Dictionary of Latin and Greek Origins*. New York: Barnes & Noble, 1997.

A good start on your derma. Not quite enough sclera. But you could do worse.

Baggaley, Anna, ed. *Human Body*. London: Dorling Kindersley, 2001.

Lots of anatomical and medical stuff. Also, the drawings will occasionally make you feel a little oogy. So that's fun.

Murphy, Bruce, ed. *Benet's Reader's Encyclopedia*. New York: HarperCollins, 1996.

The mother ship. More here than you will ever need or read in your lifetime. Best to skim the 1,144 pages, just looking for half-familiar stuff you want to know. That said, I've seen both the first and last entries (Aaron and Zwingli) come up on the show. This is a good time to recoil in terror.

Smith, Nila Banton. *Speed Reading Made Easy*. New York: Warner Books, 1983.

This paperback edition is the right heft for tacks, finishing nails, and other small jobs. For masonry, cold chiseling, or any metalwork, you'll need the bigger and heavier 1987 edition.

# INDEX

*A Clockwork Orange*, 137
Adams, Abigail, combustibility of, 174
Adrenaline, 22, 44, 120, 164, 188, 276, 316
Allen, Woody, 46
Anchoring, 121–22, 124
Asia Minor, 133, 281, 309–310

Baboons, wild, chased by, 196, 273, 276–77
Badgers, ravenous, 124, 128
Bailey, Alan, 291–92
Barker, Craig, 148
Bate, Jeremy 244, 266, 267, 272
*Batman*, 35
Bauhaus, 183
Beals, Jennifer, 184
Bell, Alexander Graham, unaware of bed construction, 206, 311
Berkeley, University of California at, 5, 21, 107, 147, 178, 237, 239
Berman, Steve, 303, 321
Bhutan, 4, 240–241, 272, 284, 286, 328
Bioluminescence, 116, 141, 264
Boleyn, Anne, self-portraits of, 39–40
Bones, rearranged surgically, 73, 302, 322
Bonobo chimpanzees, best form of hello ever, 197
Book of Common Prayer, 201, 325
Boone, Daniel, 68
*Boong*, not *buzz* or *ring*, 20

Borchardt, Bruce, 303–04, 307–08, 313–15, 317–19, 321
Borg, the, 118, 162
Brain-freeze, 24
Burnett, Carol, 218
Butterworth, Mrs., 118, 198, 203, 273

Camaros, "his & hers," 127, 129, 132, 142, 197–98, 291
Cameron, Burns, 14
Carroll, Lewis, 67, 102–03, 311–12, 317–20
Carroll, Robin, 16, 236, 245, 264–65, 273, 288
Cement, connected to chickens, 59
Cher, 226
Chernicoff, Steve, 303–04, 320
Chickasaw Indians, link to Elvis Presley's sex life, 96
Cholinesterase inhibitors, 62, 64
Chumash Indians, 215
Cleveland sports teams, futility of, 9, 173–74, 190–92, 228
Clue Crew, living in van and fighting crime, 16
Coconuts, lovely bunch of, 12, 17, 327
Codpiece, armored, 6
Cognitive dissonance, 83
*Concordance of the Bible*, 69, 103, 136, 201
Coppola, Francis Ford, 325
Cooper, India, 244, 266, 289, 303–04

Corpses, dancing in cheese, 183
Costner, Kevin, on his knees, 110
Cover Girl, in a blowhole, 25
Cubbage, Tom, 289, 292–301, 309
Cuthbertson, John, 320

Damnation, eternal, 68
Daunt, Michael, 6, 16, 289, 303–04,
    307–08, 311–20, 322
Day, Doris, blown to bits, 103
Dead guy, body of, used to signal the
    cops, 20
*Dead Man Walking*, 39, 149
DeGeneres, Ellen, 108
Den Hartog, Josh, 148
Depp, Johnny, 184
De Vere, Edward, seventeenth Earl of
    Oxford, 16, 60, 102–103, 269–70,
    300
*Die Hard*, 20
*Dotto*, 12
Douglas, Michael, 307
*Dracula*, 326
Drug lords, Colombian, 75
Dwarf, kickboxing, used to memorize
    U.N. Secretaries-General, 97

Ebola, 159
Ecuador, place to flee to, 39, 76
Eightfold Path to Enlightened Jeopardy,
    25, 28, 29, 38–39, 48–49, 60, 84,
    109, 113, 124–25, 145, 151,
    155–56, 171, 185, 239, 246,
    293–94, 298
Einstein, Albert, 50, 136
Ephesians, disappointing relationship
    with, 55
Epstein, Frank, 293–95, 297–300
Erythema nodosum, 185–86, 254
Ethic of reciprocity, 200
Ettinger, Bob, 246

Fairy penguins, 284–86, 295
Farrell, Will, 15
*Fight Club* 80, 195
Fillmore, Millard goddam, 23, 24,
    28–29, 95, 192, 235
Flanders, Ned, cuckolded, 34
Fleming, Art, 13, 14
*Flowers for Algernon*, basis for film *Charly*,
    215
Forearm, correct amount of, 75, 275
Ford, Harrison, 278, 307

Forrest, Chuck, 6, 73–74, 85–87,
    99–100, 103, 110–111, 116, 118,
    123, 207, 236–37, 244, 264–67, 272,
    288, 291, 301, 328
"Forrest Bounce," 6, 73, 85, 87, 149,
    187
Forster, E. M., 89, 92
Fosse, Bob, 233
Frates, Leslie, 244, 264–66, 273, 289,
    291–92
Freeman, Morgan, voice of, 5, 327
Friedman, Harry, 247, 248, 327
Fuel, discharged from shuttlecraft, 20

Game Show Congress, 220–21, 290
Gandhi, Mohandis K., 136, 157, 200
Gangs, dancing, in New York, 122, 271
Garfield, James, 205–06, 310–11
Garland, Judy, 168, 327
Gilbert, J.H. Company of Willoughby,
    Ohio, 56, 60–61, 63, 66, 70, 71, 74,
    209
Gilbert, Johnny, 7, 14, 31, 152, 198, 234,
    250, 292
*Gilligan's Island*, 70
Gillispie, Scott, 303–04
Glucocorticoids, stress response, 120,
    254, 270
Goatskin, bloodstained, 80, 290, 303
Gödel, Kurt, 135, 150
"Go Lights," 35, 40, 50, 157, 161,
    179–82, 245, 268, 269, 272, 307–08,
    314
Graham, Heather, 214
Grant's Tomb, 309
Grape jelly, your brain becoming, 48
*Greed*, 218–19, 221
Griffin, Julann 11–12, 17
Griffin, Merv, 11–14, 16–18, 155, 158,
    317; owns one-third of earth's crust,
    17; reincarnated, 114; keeper of
    ancient wisdom 114, 327
Gropius, Walter, 183
Gutowski, Paul, 148

Hagia Sophia, 281
HAL computer, 244
Hale, Kyle, 303
Halicarnassus (Bodrum), 309–10
Harvard University, 5, 50, 147
Hats, red, various, 69, 241, 285, 322
Havel, Vaclav, 283
Hellman, Dara, 239, 321–23, 324–27

Heston, Charlton, 308
Hiawatha, eight-ton, fifty-foot-tall statue
    of, 11–13, 17, 145
*High Rollers*, 72
*Hindenburg*, the, 39
Hoffa, Jimmy, 313
Hopkins, Anthony, 115, 141, 193, 269,
    310
Houdini, Harry, 43, 169
*Howards End*, 90–92; re-imagined as
    thirty-foot buttocks, 91–93, 317;
    actual end of a real guy named
    Howard, 219–20

"Incunabula," meaningless syllables, 189
Internal Revenue Service, 180
Ironwood, Michigan, 11, 14, 18, 325
Isolation booths, 12

Jackson, Andrew, owed a beer, 308
Jaws of Life, 18
Jell-O shooters, 137
Jennings, Ken, 6, 9, 16, 94, 287–89, 295,
    304; not giving a spongebath, 94; as
    Japanese monster movie, 287;
    penmanship of, 287–88; possible
    explosion of, 288
Jesus, 200, 281, 295
Jeopardy Mansion, lush, 152
Jeopardy Weapon, 21, 48, 112, 202, 257,
    268, 293–94, 315
Jiu-jitsu, 107
Johnson, Kim "Howard," 219–20, 285
Jones, Inigo, 183

Kagan, Glenn, 45, 109, 118, 119, 127,
    128, 158, 176, 246, 327
Kampala, Uganda, confused with Kigali,
    Rwanda, 259
Kazakhstan, many sheep of, 48
Keisters, various sizes, 11, 133, 219
Keller, Helen, 136
Kennedy, George, lack of bad breath,
    115
Kenobi, Obi-Wan, 245
Kent, Clark, 22, 47
Kevlar, use by public school teachers,
    81
*Khan al-Khalili*, both the novel and the
    souq, 314
King World Productions, 14
Knesset, different from Althing, 139,
    265

Knickers, rubber, 57
Knutsen, Rick, 303–04, 321
Kung Fu Grip, realistic, 21

"Lake effect" snow, 11, 61
Lauderdale, John, 29, 250, 305
Library of Alexandria, 69
Lincoln, Abraham, 19, 23, 137, 178, 190,
    192
Lint rollers, 88
Lohan, Lindsay, 214
*Lord of the Flies*, 70, 128
Loud, Grant, 45, 109, 119, 128, 158,
    176, 246, 327
Lowenthal, Mark, 85, 301
Luminiferous ether, 135
Luxor casino, as trans-millennial Dada
    masterpiece, 245

Mackenzie, Bob and Doug, 182
Mahfouz, Naguib, 314
"Manamana" song, applied to linguistic
    morphology, 225
Mandela, Nelson, 283
Mann, Matt, 22–23, 30, 43, 47, 56, 105,
    107, 115, 150
Market research, completely useless, 13,
    14, 15
*Matrix, The*, 300, 314
McCullers, Carson, 184
McGuire, Jimmy, 314
McKellen, Ian, 270, 300
Melia, Dan, 68, 147, 157, 160, 162, 176,
    177–79, 181–85, 187–90, 193,
    201–02, 206, 210, 212, 215–16,
    234–35, 237, 239, 247, 248, 268,
    273, 288, 290, 301, 303–04, 307,
    319–20, 321–23, 324–27
*Miami Vice*, 75
Miller, Arthur, 136
Miller, Chris, 320
Monkeywrenchfish, 189
Moo, 159
Mosquitoes, size of lawn darts, 18; bird-
    eating, 61; fighting with bare hands,
    62; unlike any I remembered, 208
Mouse deer, 277
Mueller, Pam, 320
*Muppets, The*, 225

Neutron, Jimmy, 56
Newhouse, Eric, 244, 264–65, 267–72,
    288, 289, 303, 307, 321

Norwegians, cruel, 83
Nugent, Ted, 186

"One-to-ones," 238, 299, 314
Oooh, the, 114, 152–53, 155, 156, 157, 193, 212, 217, 319
One-True-Eternal-Soulmates™, 37, 39, 55, 76, 221, 229
*Oxford English Dictionary*, 23

Pacino, Al, 294
Paine, Lyn, 148, 159–60, 164–66, 169–75, 178
Pandas, arthritic, 233
Pandolfo, Tony, 234, 246
Pardo, Don, 13, 14
Patinkin, Mandy, 214
Pavlov, Ivan, 8, 138, 290
Pawlowicz, Leszek, 221, 290, 301
Penis, fifteen-foot statue, 75–76, 233
Perk, Ralph, mayor of Cleveland, on fire, 228
Perry, Claudia, 146, 244, 266
Phillips, Arthur, 56, 147, 289, 291–93, 301
Pong, 6, 33, 71
Potent Potables, 68, 152, 179, 239–40, 290; literary variety, 179
Pitt, Brad, in a leather skirt, 134, 299
Pork bellies, 261
"Portcullis," meaningless, possible nonsense word, 151
*Price is Right, The*, 14
*p-TING!*, two F notes an octave apart, 15
Pudu, 244, 249, 252, 257–58, 269, 328

Radio City Music Hall, 9, 13, 18, 74, 234, 242, 246, 249, 256, 261, 262, 266–68, 271, 300
Ramen, Fred, 148, 156–57, 289, 301, 303–04, 321
Renal organs, 170
*Rollerball*, 106
Roast turkey, molested, 115, 117, 198
*Robinson Crusoe on Mars*, 35
Rooney, Michael, 289–90, 303–04, 320, 321
Rugby players, plane-crashed in the Andes, 9
Rutter, Bradford, 6, 9–10, 16, 236, 245, 265, 272–73, 288, 292, 320, 321
Ryan, Sean, 287, 288

Saarinen, Eero, almost confused with Salonen, Esa-Pekka, 183
*Saving Private Ryan*, live version with penguins, 285
Schmidt, Rocky, 327
Schwartz, Rachael, 236, 245, 248–50, 253–59, 261–67, 272, 289, 291–92
Scissors, giant, and *Little Women*, 111
Scott, Peter, 148, 164–66, 169–72, 175
Secretaries-General of the United Nations, 90, 96–98, 99; connected via a kickboxing dwarf, 97
*Secrets of the Jeopardy! Champions*, 85–87
Seven Wonders of the Ancient World, 4, 309
Sewage, former secretary of state William H., 298
Shannon, Leslie, 244, 266, 267–69, 271, 328
Shatner, William, singing a Beatles song, 169
Sheen, Martin, 307
Sibelius, Jean, 238–39, 283
Signaling Device, 20–21, 35, 80
Singing Revolution, 239, 283
Skinner box, 142
Simpson, Homer, 27, 122
*Smush*, 216–18
Solitary confinement cells, 12
Sondhein, Stephen, 310–11
Space aliens, naked, on rollercoaster, 28
Spangenberg, Frank, 6, 73–74, 118, 234, 236, 244, 248–50, 252, 254–65, 288, 320
Speak, Maggie, 45, 246, 327
*Speed Reading Made Easy*, 6, 33, 56, 98
Sporks, plastic party, 65
Srinivasan, Babu, 244, 264, 266, 289, 291–93
Stamos, John, 224
*Star Trek*, 325
State-dependent retrieval, 37–38, 50, 79, 126, 137, 165
Stein, Ben, 221
Stewardess, Ukrainian, 45
Stewart, Patrick, 214
Strindberg, August, 184
Sutherland, Kiefer, 184
Switchblades, 44

Tarantino, Quentin, 27
Tasers, 6

Tattoos, inexplicable, 56
Tennyson, Alfred Lord, 299
"Think Music," 13,16, 17, 154, 155, 174, 175, 262–63, 325–26
Thor, 166
Three Stooges, 91
Thurber, Susanne, 9, 22, 52, 148, 158, 162, 164, 234–35, 246, 248, 267, 327
Thurman, Uma, 27, 60
Timanus, Eddie, 245, 264, 266, 289
*Tonight Show, The*, 12
Torvalds, Linus, 285
Toutant, Ed, 221
Trebek, Alex, 7, 9, 14–17, 20, 24, 29, 31–32, 46, 72, 79, 108, 109, 117, 123, 139, 150, 158, 164–66, 169, 174, 185, 186, 190, 193, 212–13, 245, 247–49, 251–52, 256, 262–63, 271, 272, 297, 299, 307, 309–10, 314, 318–21, 323, 324, 326; without a physical body, 2; rebooted, 6; guest announcer, *Wrestlemania*, 15; worshipped on tropical islands, 17; rarely talks about your nose, 24; dressed as Statue of Liberty, 31–32; disappearing into mist, 52; devising tournament format, 144; and the role of the "Oooh," 152–53; hitting players in head with clues, 180; forming as the result of quantum fluctuation, 193; his pity not needed, 211; helping the poor, 280; without pants, 320–21; witness to holy event, 326
Trebekistan, 134–36, 139, 154, 155, 173, 195, 204, 206, 210, 215, 216, 263, 266, 269–70, 273, 275–76, 278, 281, 283–84, 314, 324–25, 327, 328
Triple-stumpers, 112
Trivial Pursuit, 14
Triangle Shirtwaist Fire, 39
Troy, ancient, 134, 281–82
Turner, Ted, throwing up, 111
Twain, Mark, 118, 135–36, 157
*Twenty-One*, 12

Ulm, Wes, 148–53, 157–60, 235, 247, 307

Vaseline, 63
Veach, Grace, 148–53, 157, 160, 177–78, 206, 234, 237, 247, 289, 301, 307, 320
Vered, Jerome, 221, 290, 301, 303, 320, 321
Verini, Bob, 244, 266, 272, 288
Vieira, Meredith, 220

Waits, Kate, 244, 264, 266
Waldorf-Astoria hotel, 234, 244, 266
Walsh, Tom, 287, 303–04
Warhol, Andy, 223
Weenieness, advanced, 185–87, 190
Weikle, Brian, 288
West, Adam, 35
*Wheel of Fortune*, 14
Whitcomb, Sarah, 314
Whitlock, Shane, 303
*Who Wants to Be a Millionaire*, 9, 219–20, 285
Winfrey, Oprah, 200
Wisconsin, unknown location, 163–64, 250, 299
*Wizard of Oz, The*, 289
Woolery, Chuck, 218
Worth, Kim, 148, 162–63, 177–79, 181–82, 184–85, 187–88, 193, 199, 202, 210, 212–13, 215–16, 234, 237, 247, 268, 299, 307
*Wrestlemania*, 15, 241

*X-Files, The*, 15

Yak meat, 241, 286
YMCA, 74
Yoda, 245
You, 4, 5, 6, 10, 18, 20, 25–29, 37–39, 43, 45, 51, 56–57, 59–60, 82–83, 88, 90–101, 113–14, 118–21, 131, 163, 167–68, 193, 227, 228, 319, 328
Yut, 280, 294, 300, 304, 316

Zombie Jeopardy, 112, 315

Bob Harris has written for media ranging from the TV show *CSI: Crime Scene Investigation* to *National Lampoon* magazine. In between, he has been a nationally syndicated radio humorist, an online columnist for *Mother Jones*, and a playful debunker of urban legends on the TLC reality series *Almost True Stories*.

The *Hollywood Reporter* once described his work as "goofy and well-informed." This seems about right.

He lives in Los Angeles.

For more of Bob's work, visit BobHarris.com.

To spend more time in Trebekistan, visit PrisonerOfTrebekistan.com.